Red Flags of LOVE FRAUD

Best wishes

Donna Anderson

Red Flags *of* LOVE FRAUD

10 SIGNS YOU'RE DATING A SOCIOPATH

DONNA ANDERSEN

Anderly Publishing
Egg Harbor Township, New Jersey

Back cover photograph by Bill Horin

Anderly Publishing
3121-D Fire Road, #304
Egg Harbor Township, NJ 08234 USA
www.anderlypublishing.com

Library of Congress Control Number: 2012900536
ISBN: 978-0-9827057-1-1

First softcover edition June 2012

CONTENTS

With gratitude to all Lovefraud.com readers,
who generously shared their experiences so that others
can learn to avoid the social predators who live among us.

Introduction

"It felt like magic to me," says a woman whom we'll call "Charlotte" about the dreamy beginning of her relationship with "Anthony." "It happened very quickly … and I let it. He met all of my needs; it was like a fairy tale."

Charlotte and Anthony met at the gym in an exclusive country club. Anthony told Charlotte that he had multiple university degrees, and had also worked as an underwater welding engineer. He struck Charlotte as strong and protective.

Charlotte, a single mother, was making it on her own — but all she ever wanted was a complete family. Anthony seemed like the man who could make it happen. He was charming. They shared the same values. Judging by all the calls, texts and emails she received, Anthony adored her, and the sex was extraordinary. He swept Charlotte off her feet.

They married, but after a year, the bubble burst. Everything Anthony had told Charlotte was a lie. He didn't have all those university degrees — he hadn't even graduated from high school. He was never a welding engineer, and he certainly didn't almost die on a welding job, as he claimed. "He exaggerated stories to get his way; he abused and killed animals; he was a thief," Charlotte said. Anthony cheated on her and threatened her life.

Charlotte kicked him out. The marriage cost her more than $50,000, and a massive amount of heartache.

"Allen" and "Jocelyn"

"Allen" and "Jocelyn" met on a popular Internet dating site. "Everything was fast, exciting and she made me feel as if I were the most important thing in her life," Allen remembered. He liked Jocelyn's spontaneity, charm, intelligence, sex appeal and caring nature. Allen was going through hard times — a separation and divorce, while caring for a sick parent. Jocelyn supported him as he dealt with his problems, and assured him of a new beginning with her.

Jocelyn asked Allen about his hopes and dreams, and promised to make them come true. She was in constant communication through phone, text and email, although she was evasive when questioned about her past. Allen had a gut feeling that something was amiss, but ignored it, chalking up his apprehensions to stress from all his other worries. He also ignored the misgivings of his family and friends, and didn't even listen to Jocelyn's family and friends, who thought she was phony and uncaring.

Allen and Jocelyn were together for a few years, but the honeymoon period was over after four months. By the time Allen got out of the relationship, he had lost his job and his home, he had been physically abused, and the stress had made him ill. He estimated that the relationship with Jocelyn cost him well over $100,000 — in fact, she stole money right out of his bank account.

"Barbara" and "Luis"

After her husband of 23 years passed away, "Barbara" met "Luis." "It was wonderful," she said. "I thought he was my forever. He was respectable, caring and loving, showing more love for me than anyone ever had. He said faith had brought us together, and we were meant to be forever."

As with Charlotte and Allen, Barbara's romance was a whirlwind. Luis shared her beliefs and interests, and lavished attention upon her. She, too, though, felt something wasn't quite right. "I let it go," she said. "I thought it was just me being paranoid." Even when Luis admitted legal problems, he blamed them on others and claimed that he got the raw end of the deal. Barbara accepted his explanations.

Barbara and Luis married, but it didn't last very long. Luis picked fights and left for weekends, or even weeks at a time. Then he called and begged Barbara to take him back. At first, she did. Later, however, she figured out that Luis started the arguments purposely so he could leave. He went to parties and stayed with other women — or men. Barbara caught a sexually transmitted disease from her husband. She became anxious and depressed, and thought about suicide. Luis, too, threatened suicide — although he also, Barbara said, "offered to kill a girl I caught him with if I would take him back."

My marriage to a sociopath

The three cases that you just read are true. I have learned that they are typical of what I call love fraud.

Love fraud is the intentional exploitation of an individual through manipulating emotions in a personal relationship. The exploitative relationship is frequently romantic, but can also be between family members, friends and associates. The relationship can take place in real life, or exist only through communications media — phone calls, email, text messages, even snail mail. The people who engage in love fraud are sociopaths.

Like Charlotte and Barbara, I married a sociopath. His name was James Alwyn Montgomery, and although I met him not far from my home in the United States, he was originally from Sydney, Australia.

What I remember most about the beginning of my relationship with Montgomery is how he pursued me.

He'd posted an ad in the America Online romance section — this was back in 1996, when AOL ruled the Internet. He sounded much more intriguing than most men — a former Green Beret; a background in advertising, TV and movies; now negotiating with local movers and shakers for his next big business venture. The reason for the ad? His wife had died, and his "grieving was complete."

Reading Montgomery's claims now, one could wonder why anyone — specifically me — would believe them. But this was before we all knew that online profiles can be full of lies. It was before I knew that sociopaths did not necessarily look like Charles Manson, with long scraggly hair and a swastika etched into his forehead. And it was before I knew that someone who proclaimed he was so head-over-heels in love with me could be lying.

When I met Montgomery, I was 40 years old, never married. As a single girl, I'd dated a lot of men, but I'd never experienced anything like the attention this particular man lavished on me. He called many times a day. He proposed marriage within a week of meeting me in person.

Why wasn't this a huge red flag? Since childhood, I'd heard all those fairy tales about love at first sight. In fact, I knew people who had fallen in love right away and, decades later, were still married. I'd been waiting for my chance at true romance for years. I thought my time had come.

Montgomery frequently told me how much he respected my talent, and how I would be such an asset to his business plans. We were a formidable team, he said, and he wanted me to benefit from the success that his ventures were sure to become. So, not long after he proposed, he also recommended that I invest in his businesses — he wanted to make sure that I personally profited from our efforts. An investment of $5,000 would buy me a few percentage points of ownership.

So began the money drain.

Montgomery never asked for money for himself. All requests were presented as investments in our future, needed to secure a business deal. Usually there was a crisis that had to be resolved immediately — with my cash. What I didn't know was that he created the crises so I wouldn't have time to think about his requests. And I also didn't know, until after I left my husband, that much of my money was spent entertaining other women.

A year and a half after we married, I knew Montgomery was cheating on me. But by that time, my husband had ravaged my savings and maxed out my credit cards. I was in desperate financial straits, and one of his business ventures, a Titanic exhibition, looked like it was actually going to work. I decided to ignore his infidelity until I got my money back.

Introduction

Unfortunately, the Titanic sank again, and all my money — $227,000 — was gone. Then I learned that Montgomery was not only cheating on me, but had a child with another woman during our marriage. Then I found out that there were multiple other women, and Montgomery took money from all of them. Then I found out that Montgomery married the mother of the child 10 days after I left him, which was the second time he committed bigamy.

My head was spinning. "What kind of person does this?" I asked my therapist.

"It sounds like he might be a sociopath," she said.

What is a sociopath?

In this book, the word "sociopath" is used not as a formal diagnosis, but as a generic description for a social predator, someone who lives his or her life by exploiting others. In fact, "sociopath" is no longer used as an official diagnostic term. Related clinical terms are psychopath, narcissist, antisocial personality disorder, dyssocial personality disorder and borderline personality disorder. People with these personality disorders have one big trait in common: They routinely disregard the rights and needs of the people around them.

Sociopaths are detrimental to our physical, financial, emotional, psychological and spiritual health. The best way to deal with sociopaths is to keep them out of our lives. But this is difficult, because millions of sociopaths live freely among us. Most of them are not locked up in jail or mental institutions. They are not crazy nutcases. Rather, they often appear to be charming and charismatic, cool and confident.

In order to protect ourselves from sociopaths, we must explode three common cultural myths that frequently influence how we view others.

Myth #1 – All sociopaths (psychopaths) are deranged serial killers

Hollywood has learned that sociopaths make great villains, so horror movies, thrillers and crime shows often feature, with varying degrees of accuracy, characters who have this personality disorder.

The classic is Alfred Hitchcock's *Psycho*. In this 1960 film, the antagonist, named Norman Bates, viciously kills two people, and had previously killed four others. This movie forever united the term "psycho" with the behavior of deranged multiple murders. Audiences tend to think that the *"Psycho"* title is short for "psychopath," but Bates was actually psychotic, meaning he had lost touch with reality. Psychopathy is a totally different disorder. Psychopaths are not delusional; they know exactly what they are doing.

This is portrayed in the 1991 film, *The Silence of the Lambs*. The villain, Dr. Hannibal Lecter, is a brilliant psychiatrist and cannibalistic serial killer. Early in the movie, the prison doctor describes him: "Oh, he's a monster. A pure psychopath. So rare to capture one alive."[1] Hannibal Lecter is highly intelligent, sophisticated, charming when he wants to be, calm, calculating and utterly ruthless. These traits have come to be associated with diabolical killers in the movies, and the traits often *do* describe the psychopathic personality. In the real world, most serial killers probably *are* cold-blooded psychopaths, and sometimes delusional as well.

The problem is that because of this heavily reinforced image in pop culture, people think *all* psychopaths/sociopaths are serial killers. In the news media, the terms "psychopath" and "sociopath," if they are used at all, are applied mostly to people who commit murder.

The truth is, most psychopaths never kill anyone.[2] And even among those who kill, the number that are serial killers is miniscule.

But it's almost impossible to overcome the ubiquitous influence of Hollywood. Today, many of us have the preconceived idea that "psychopath" and "sociopath" equal "serial killer." So when we see exploitative behavior from our partners, it's difficult for us to recognize that they may be sociopaths. After all, they haven't murdered anyone. The Hollywood image prevents us from realizing that our husbands, wives or dating partners may have serious personality disorders.

Myth #2 – There's good in everyone

In the United States, from the time we are small children, we are bombarded with messages about fairness, equal opportunity, giving people a chance, and tolerance. In school, we learn about the Declaration of Independence and its most famous line, "We hold these truths to be self-evident, that all men are created equal" (with the understanding that "men" now includes "women"). In church, we're told that "we're all God's children."

Most of us have been taught to believe that there's good in everyone, and advice abounds on how to find it: When people do things that hurt us, don't react right away, but consider the reasons for their actions. Remember that everyone can have a bad day. Sometimes people aren't wrong, they're just different.

All of this is true, correct and appropriate — except when we're dealing with sociopaths.

It's difficult for most of us to comprehend just how different these serial exploiters are from the rest of humanity. In fact, sociopaths are literally missing the qualities and abilities that make us truly human. They do not feel empathy for others — not their fellow citizens, not their family members, not even their own children. Sociopaths have no conscience. They usually know, on an intellectual level, the difference between right and wrong, but they have no emotional investment in doing what is right, and weak to nonexistent internal prohibitions against doing what is wrong.

When we see bad behavior in someone, especially a romantic partner, we look for reasons that we can comprehend—perhaps the person had a difficult childhood or an abusive first marriage. Because we want to uphold our own values of fairness and charity, we are blind to the truth: Sociopaths exploit us because they want to.

If you go looking for good in a sociopath, you won't find it. Underneath a charming, caring, attentive façade, these people are thoroughly rotten.

Myth #3 – Everyone wants to be loved

Ever since human beings invented poetry, storytelling, music and art, the favorite subject of our creativity has been love: The joy of finding love. The frustration of loving from afar. The unbearable pain of losing love. People long for love. Love completes us; love makes life worth living. We know this instinctively, but researchers have evidence that, as social beings, love is vitally important to us. For example, when psychologist Abraham Maslow developed his famous hierarchy of needs, it included the need for belonging, love and affection.

Maslow's *Theory of Human Motivation* suggests that people move through stages of growth — as basic needs are met, we move up to more intangible needs. The concept is often explained using the visual aid of a pyramid. At the base of the pyramid are physiological needs, such as air, water, food and shelter. The next step up is the need for safety and security. The third level is the need for love and belonging, including friendship, intimacy and family. At the top of the pyramid are esteem and self-actualization. According to Maslow, love is right in the middle of human motivation.[3]

Plenty of other scientific research has documented the importance of love to human health. Love helps us cope with stress. Happily married people have lower blood pressure and recover from injuries faster.[4] Being in love even helps us resist the common cold.[5]

Since love is so good for us, everyone must want love. Right? Wrong. Sociopaths do not care about love, which Maslow stated in his paper. "The so-called 'psychopathic personality' is another example of permanent loss of the love needs," he wrote.[6] In fact, the core of this personality disorder is an inability to love.

This makes sense, of course. Sociopaths do not feel empathy and do not form emotional bonds with other people. How can they possibly feel love?

They don't, although they are excellent actors and can convincingly pretend to be loving, if it suits their purpose. They understand the cause-and-effect relationship — if sociopaths say, "I love you," people who hear those words give them what they want. It may be sex, money, a place to live, business opportunities, entertainment — whatever. For sociopaths, the expression of love is nothing more than a tool, a means to an end.

Sociopaths, you see, have their own hierarchy of needs. They want power, control and sex, and they'll do anything to get what they want.[7]

Lovefraud.com: teaching people to recognize and recover from sociopaths

My ex-husband told me that he loved me soon after we met, and throughout our relationship. He was convincing, and he got what he wanted — access to my money, credit and business connections.

It didn't take me long to figure out that James Montgomery's big plans weren't working, and my finances were rapidly deteriorating. When I complained and demanded changes, Montgomery promised that the problems were temporary. He begged me to believe in him. He cried at the thought of losing me.

It was all manipulation so he could continue to bleed me.

When I left him, and learned that he had a diagnosable personality disorder, I was astounded. I was a college graduate with degrees in journalism and psychology, yet I was clueless! If I didn't know what a sociopath was, I reasoned, other people didn't know either. The public needed to know that human predators lived among us. So I created a website, Lovefraud.com, to teach people how to recognize and recover from sociopaths.

Lovefraud launched in July 2005. Six years later, we were attracting over 50,000 unique visitors a month, and more than 2,800 people had contacted me to tell me of their own betrayals by sociopaths. In their anguished stories, I kept hearing the same patterns of behavior, over and over. It seemed that sociopaths — both male and female — operated out of the same playbook.

I realized that people needed to know the warning signs of sociopathic behavior.

Although I had plenty of anecdotal information about how sociopaths targeted romantic partners, I also wanted standardized, formal data. To gather it, Lovefraud conducted two Internet surveys of our readers.

The first took place from February 12 through March 3, 2010.

It was inspired by the American Psychiatric Association's request for public comment on its new *Diagnostic and Statistical Manual of Mental Disorders* — the bible that mental health professionals use in diagnosing and treating patients. In the draft of the fifth edition posted on the Internet, the description of antisocial personality disorder had changed significantly from previous editions of the manual.[8] Some of the changes matched the experiences of Lovefraud readers, and some didn't.

Working with my Lovefraud colleague, Dr. Liane Leedom, a psychiatrist who was also conned into marriage by a sociopath, I developed a survey, called the Lovefraud DSM-5 Survey, to ask our readers about the sociopaths in their lives. We received a total of 1,378 responses from all over the world, with 1,188 completing the entire survey. Eighty percent were filled out by people who had been married to, or in romantic relationships with, individuals who they came to believe were sociopaths. The rest of the surveys were completed by parents, children, and other relatives or associates of sociopaths.

The second survey, called the Lovefraud Romantic Partner Survey, was designed specifically to gather more information on how sociopaths behaved in romantic situations. It was available on the Internet from February 15 through April 18, 2011. A total of 1,352 people responded from around the globe, with 1,053 of them completing the entire survey. Data quoted in this book are from all the surveys, both complete and incomplete.

Dr. Leedom had also collected data in 2007 for her contributions to a book about women in relationships with psychopaths. For this effort, the women described their experiences and also agreed to participate in personality evaluations. Dr. Leedom made her research available to me to use in this book.

Red Flags of Love Fraud is a compendium of all this information. I summarize the data from the Lovefraud surveys — they show clear patterns of manipulation exhibited by people who are probably sociopaths. I include verbatim quotes from survey respondents — the comments are chilling. I also summarize the experiences of some survey respondents. When I tell their stories, I give the survey respondents, and their romantic partners, fictitious

Introduction

first names, which appear in quotation marks. Although the stories are real, I don't know who provided them, because all survey data were collected anonymously.

In the Epilogue, I also reprint one of the thousands of emails that I have received, in which Lovefraud readers tell their stories in their own words. This letter paints a clear and scary picture of how sociopaths draw people into romantic relationships, and then exploit them.

My goal is to show you how sociopaths behave in the real world, when they're targeting real victims. Read this information. Think about your involvements. If you ever see these behavior patterns in someone who claims to be your "soul mate," run as fast as you can.

CHAPTER I

The Red Flags of Love Fraud

*I*t *was like I was living a dream. We had the best time together and it felt wonderful to be so loved by one person.*

It was heaven. It was a fairy tale. Everything I dreamed love could be.

I'd met the one I'd been waiting for all my life. The intensity of his attention was extremely flattering. He told me a psychic had predicted me.

From fairy tales to Shakespeare to romance novels, we've all heard stories of falling head-over-heels in love. Poetry and songs describe attraction so powerful that nothing in this world is more important than the beloved. Perhaps we doubted the possibility of such strong emotion — assuming that it was nothing but wishful thinking. Then, suddenly, magically, thrillingly, dramatic love finds us.

The beginning of a love fraud relationship can be absolutely exhilarating. Like the three women quoted above, many respondents to the Lovefraud Romantic Partner Survey reported that in the beginning of their relationships with people who turned out to be sociopaths, they felt loved, admired and pursued as never before. Other survey respondents were at first not interested in the individual or hesitant about the relationship, but through charm and persistence, the sociopaths drew them in. So how can you tell if it's love — or predation? The *Red Flags of Love Fraud* are 10 warning signs of sociopathic behavior that you may see early in a relationship. Unfortunately, some of the warning signs are also characteristics of a dream date — who wouldn't want to go out with a man or woman who is charming, sexy and attentive? Therefore, keep in mind that if people exhibit one or two of the traits, it does not necessarily mean that they are sociopaths — good news if you feel amazing sexual chemistry with your new romantic interest. But if you see most or all of these warning signs — the entire pattern of behavior — be careful.

The problem is that sociopaths have also heard those fairy tales and Shakespearean sonnets, and read the romance novels, or at least watched romantic comedies on television. And they are incredible actors. So they've observed what romance is supposed to look like, and they pretend to offer it to you.

The three women introduced above learned the hard way.

The first woman married her "dream," but after four months, the relationship started going downhill. "He became verbally and physically abusive," she said. "He called me horrible names; he would 'snap' and throw household items at me. He pinned my arms behind my back so I couldn't do anything and he held them there for what seemed like forever, which left bruises."

The second woman also married the man she described, but at one point left him. "I walked away with two young children but he starved me back into his clutches," she said. She was stuck in the marriage for more than 10 years.

After three months, despite the initial intensity, the last woman's relationship fell apart. She said, "Once he knew I was completely in love with him, he broke up with me, saying I wasn't what he really wanted after all."

At some point in their relationships, these women saw all or most of the warning signs that follow. But, not knowing what the signs meant, the women stayed longer than they otherwise would have — much to their regret.

Here are the *Red Flags of Love Fraud*. If they are waving in your face, pay attention.

Red Flag #1: Charisma and charm

Because the word "sociopath" is often used to describe criminals and murderers, you may expect these people to have angry, foul temperaments, and they often do. But that comes later, after they have their hooks in you. When you first meet them, many sociopaths have an attractive, appealing energy about them. They demonstrate their interest in you through lavish attention, flattery and kindness.

The Lovefraud Romantic Partner Survey included a preliminary list of the "10 signs you're dating a sociopath." An objective of the survey was to validate the list. One item on it was "charisma and charm" — and fully 91.5 percent of respondents agreed that their partners, who turned out to be sociopaths, exhibited charisma and charm.

These attributes, of course, are not necessarily bad. Charisma is often a characteristic of a strong, inspiring leader, and synonyms for charming include delightful, lovable, amiable, engaging and 40 additional positive adjectives.

The problem with charisma and charm in sociopaths is the hidden agenda. These people use their magnetic personalities to deceive, manipulate and exploit. This is readily apparent in the Lovefraud survey, as people described the appeal of sociopaths in the beginning of their relationships, and how the relationships ended:

THE APPEAL: His charm and what seemed like total honesty. Instant chemistry on meeting.

THE END: He was a manipulative, controlling monster, who portrayed himself to be a God-fearing, loving Christian.

THE APPEAL: Her charisma and confidence. Every-

thing was charming; she was sweet, always overly attentive to my needs.
THE END: She will be so mean and abusive toward me that all I could do was to leave. Then she'll come back and say I was too sensitive, I had no sense of humor, that I was bad tempered. She was blaming me for everything. I felt guilty and came back. It was like that until I became aware of her madness.

Charisma describes personal magnetism — sociopaths exude a mixture of enthusiasm and self-confidence that is often irresistible.

Take, for example, the case of a survey respondent whom we'll call "Tanya." When she was a student, Tanya rode a bus back and forth to school. "Larry" was the bus driver. Larry came right out and told Tanya that he was interested in her.

"Although Larry was not what I was usually physically attracted to, as he was much older than me and was not really my type, he was very funny, charismatic and intelligent," Tanya said. "He was the type of person that when he walked in the room, everyone knew he was there, because he was such a prankster, and would just make everyone laugh and change the whole energy in the room. He had a light around him that I found interesting, since I have a completely different personality, as I am rather quiet and not really outgoing. I thought he was exciting.

"I guess he just won me over with his charm, personality and intellect," Tanya continued. "He made it seem as though he really cared about me, as he always wanted us to be together. He also made me feel beautiful and sexy."

Larry turned out to be extremely controlling. He kept tabs on Tanya, would not allow her to speak to men, and attempted to draw her away from her family. The two were together for a couple of years, although they frequently fought, broke up and made up. In the end, Tanya became depressed and was physically abused.

Sociopaths like Larry are seductive, and not only in a sexual way. With their flair, finesse and glibness, sociopaths convince their targets — that would be you — to accept their ideas and plans. You may find yourself doing what the sociopath wants, and pushing way outside of your comfort zone in the process.

How do they do it? How do sociopaths convince you to go along with their agendas, even to your own detriment?

They command it. This is a function of their charisma — because they command unflinchingly, with complete self-confidence, they get results. Now, this doesn't mean sociopaths are always barking orders. Often the commands are delivered on cushions of sweetness, or camouflaged as appeals for sympathy. But in their minds, whatever sociopaths want, they are totally entitled to have. Therefore, when they make their desires known, they show no doubt, only certainty. Compliance is demanded, and targets respond.

Related to the sociopathic charisma is an overabundance of ego. In fact, "egocentric and grandiose"[1] is a key symptom of the disorder identified by Dr. Robert Hare, a Canadian psychology researcher who is a preeminent expert in the field. In the Lovefraud survey, 68 percent of respondents said their romantic partners had enormous egos.

Sociopaths consider themselves to be several notches above the rest of us. They see themselves as smarter, more attractive, sexier and more likely to succeed than anyone around them. And they're not shy about telling you just how wonderful they are.

A big ego doesn't necessarily mean that someone is a sociopath — plenty of people in the world are highly accomplished and their egocentricity is justified. The key difference with sociopaths is that they hold inflated views of themselves whether they deserve it or not. If their actual life accomplishments are thin, sociopaths simply pad their resumes with lies.

But they tell the lies so charmingly. Charm is how sociopaths soften you up, paving the way for using you. Sociopaths work their charm through their extraordinary verbal skills. Usually they are smooth talkers — always have an answer; never miss a beat. Witty, clever, articulate — they can talk you into giving them what they want, and they know it.

"He was so great with words," one survey respondent wrote. "He knew what to say and he knew how to say it. He totally swept me off my feet."

These people walk into a room and they're "on" — especially if the room is full of potential targets. Sociopaths thoroughly understand that appearing friendly, helpful, interested and solicitous helps them ingratiate themselves with others. If they're looking to use anyone or anything, these people pour on the sweetness and concern — at least in the beginning.

For example, "Lauren" was a professional in her 40s when she met "Tom." "I thought he was lovely, very capable, a different lifestyle, all this wrapped up with charm and intelligence," Lauren said. "His life was so different from my corporate world. He charmed his way into my life, through words. He knew instinctively what I needed to hear. Constant late night calls, wanted to know, seeming to care. I had been single for quite some time, and he filled the gap beautifully, always willing to please."

Lauren and Tom married. Although they were together for more than five years, the honeymoon didn't last long. Tom lied all the time, blamed others continually, had many extramarital affairs and became abusive.

"He tried to destroy my yacht, not caring about the people on board," Lauren wrote. "Then when we arrived at the marina, he had his former partners come aboard. We did not reunite for seven months, and this was only because I was sick, and he declared his undying love. Eighteen months later he tried to murder me ... tried to gas me in a confined space on the yacht."

In Lauren's case, what began with intelligence and charm ended with attempted murder.

Red Flag #2: Sudden soul mates

When sociopaths target you for romantic exploitation, it seems that their favorite term of endearment is "soul mate." They gush about finding the man or woman of their dreams, the person they've wanted all their lives. They liberally talk about destiny, how the relationship was meant to be. If you, the target, are religious, sociopaths smoothly proclaim that God has brought you together.

Asked to describe the sociopaths in their lives, 64 percent of

Lovefraud survey respondents agreed with the statement, "The individual said we were 'soul mates;' I was the person he/she was waiting for." But the words were said only for seduction, and the targets eventually learned the hard truth.

"Diane" was in her 30s, with four children, and going through a difficult divorce when she met "Steve" on the Internet. He had held his job for 25 years and had custody of his two children. Therefore, Diane felt he was reliable and dependable.

Steve poured on the devotion. "He homed in on our 'likenesses,' insisting we were 'soul mates' and were destined to be together," Diane said. "He acted as though he was a 'stand-up' guy and that 'our' love would conquer all, as though I would never have anything to worry about, ever."

They married, but eventually Diane learned that Steve was secretly into pornography and was cheating on her. "The relationship changed for the worse when I took a step back and realized what he was all about," she said. "He realized that I stopped believing in him and our relationship. Once he knew I was onto him, saw through him, it was over. His true identity kicked in and he was out to destroy me completely."

Diane discovered that Steve was committing massive fraud and turned the information over to authorities. She, herself, lost more than $50,000, incurred debt, and had a lawsuit filed against her.

So why do sociopaths like Steve seem, in the beginning, to be your soul mate? Because they are chameleons. When they target you for seduction, they figure out what you are looking for and then make themselves into that person. It often works. In the Lovefraud survey, 79 percent of respondents agreed with the statement, "In the beginning, the individual seemed to have so much in common with me." Also, 83 percent agreed that "in the beginning, the individual seemed to share my values."

"He became everything I wanted," said "Shelly," describing her relationship with "Mark." "He and I enjoyed the same activities. We shared similar stories and feelings. We seemed to have the same perspectives on life and love."

They married, but the sense of togetherness was gone after the first year. "He lied about everything to make situations appear as he wanted them to," Shelly said. "He was verbally, emotionally and physically abusive. He punched holes in walls and broke anything meaningful to me."

Shelly endured abuse and threats to her life. After many loud, screaming fights with a man who once seemed to be her perfect mate, Shelly made the final break, losing her home and more than $100,000.

How did Mark know what Shelly wanted? How does any sociopath figure out what we want? It's quite simple. They ask us, and listen carefully to our responses. Most of us interpret the acute attentiveness to mean that our new romantic partners are totally fascinated with us. Believing we are building a lasting connection, we willingly share our deepest desires.

In the Lovefraud Romantic Partner Survey, 56 percent of respondents agreed that "the individual asked about my hopes and dreams, then promised to make them come true." What sociopaths are really doing is interrogating us to discover our vulnerabilities, and using the information as ammunition to bring down our defenses.

Sometimes sociopaths actually engage in subterfuge to find out what their targets want. This is what happened to "Larissa" when she met "Jesse" at her aikido class.

"He was an amazing listener, and seemed to care about what I had to say," Larissa related. "Obviously, his listening skills were all part of figuring out my weaknesses and learning the easiest ways to manipulate me. I later found out that he set his sights on me, that he told his friend he would 'have me.' He read my journal when I wasn't home, and created a Prince Charming personality based on what I had written in my journal. He embodied every requirement I laid out in my journal, from being a vegetarian to loving the ocean and dolphins. Every single thing he said he was, he fabricated."

Within six months of meeting, Larissa and Jesse married. Jesse immediately moved Larissa out of state, to a mobile home on nine acres of land. But life wasn't as Larissa anticipated.

"About three weeks into the beginning of our life together, the

FBI came to our back door with guns drawn (five or six agents) and hauled him off to prison," Larissa recounted. "Jesse told me he had been framed for his crime (armed carjacking), and I stood by him for a year. I got pregnant just before his seven-year sentence. When I was eight months pregnant, he sent me a confession letter, stating that everything he ever told me was a lie, from the crazy Special Forces stories, to the traumatizing deaths of (imaginary) friends. I divorced him while he was in prison."

Jesse was such a good manipulator that, before his confession letter, he had Larissa believing he had just made a mistake. She finally realized the truth about her husband. "The intricacy of his lies is astounding, and the number of lies he can catalog in his head — who he told what to — is mind-boggling," Larissa said. "All of his behaviors are antisocial. He is constantly, always, every minute of every day, scheming ways to control the people in his life, to hurt the people who have pissed him off. He doesn't ever stop playing to win. What winning means changes with each circumstance and all of its particular variables."

Sometimes we make it easy for sociopaths to fashion themselves as our soul mates by building fantasy relationships in our own minds. This is what happened to "Robert" when he met, or actually, re-met, "Sophie." The two had crushes on each other in high school, but never dated then. Eighteen years later, they reconnected via the Internet.

Sophie told Robert that she was leaving her abusive, live-in boyfriend. "Her story was so terrible I just had to help her; she was one of my best friends in school," Robert said. "She actually is a very poor liar, but there is something about her that makes you turn a blind eye to it ... Now I think that has a lot to do with my own imagination of the romantic story of reuniting with 'the one that got away.'"

Sophie told Robert that she wanted her next relationship — with him — to last forever. "She wanted rescuing and I wanted to rescue her," Robert said. "She wanted another child, and I wanted a child of my own ... She just used my own desire for the fantasy romance and kind of molded herself to be that person."

They married, and Sophie quickly got pregnant. As soon as

she did, the fantasy relationship was over. She actually moved out of Robert's home, but wanted him to keep paying her bills, although she declined to tell him what they were — she preferred for him to just send money. Then Robert found out that the man she'd been living with previously wasn't her boyfriend, but her husband, and in marrying Robert, Sophie had committed bigamy. Apparently, her plan was to hook Robert with a child so that he would have to financially support her for the next 20 years.

Red Flag #3: Sexual magnetism

Great sex. Many people who have slept with a sociopath say it was the best sex they ever had. Comments in the Lovefraud Romantic Partner Survey describe the sex as intense, wonderful, exciting, amazing and plentiful.

Wild and uninhibited sex.

Sex sex sex and more sex.

Had intense sex 3 times per day. No kidding. In our forties.

In the survey, 78 percent of respondents said "sexual magnetism" was characteristic of the relationship. Why is this?

First of all, sociopaths are hard-wired for sex. Secondly, sociopaths are frequently good lovers. There's much more to say about sociopaths and sex, so Chapter 6 is devoted to the topic.

Red Flag #4: Love bombing

He came in like the gangbuster of love and romance. He was so attentive, caring, affectionate, sexy, exciting, interesting, and willing to go to any lengths to be with me.

He called me from one of the islands in the southern Caribbean, it cost him $20 just to make the call, he breathed in really deep and said he felt like he was *drowning and I was his air. He was constantly saying things like that, always into ME. No one had ever paid so much attention to me.*

I hadn't been romantically involved w/ anyone in a very long time and I had never met anyone who was so enthralled w/ me, who I was, or even what I had to say. I suppose the attention she poured upon me was enough for her to secure me as her next victim.

If you are targeted as a sociopath's new romantic interest, it's quite possible that you will be showered with more attention, adoration, and maybe even gifts than you've ever experienced. You may feel giddy with excitement. You may feel that you have been placed on a pedestal so high that the air around you is thin and you can hardly breathe.

When they're in full seduction mode, sociopaths want to be with you all the time, and if they're not physically with you, they want to be in constant communication with you. They proclaim their love — quickly, frequently and persistently. Most of us interpret this ceaseless devotion as an indication that our new partner is truly smitten. But it's not love — it's love bombing.

Unlike true love, love bombing is insincere. It is not an expression of your new partner's deepest feelings; it is a strategy to achieve an objective. The objective is winning you over, so that you will give the sociopath what he or she wants.

The cases quoted above are examples of sociopathic love bombing. So how did these relationships turn out?

The "gangbuster of love" lasted less than a year. When the woman met his children, they told her that their father "was not always this nice." His six-year-old son announced, "My dad is a cheater." Then she found out that the man also solicited prostitutes. "After I finally cut him off, he stalked me," she said. "I had to take legal action. I was mentally and psychologically anguished by the relationship for another two years."

The deep breather was married, although he claimed it wasn't for long. But the relationship was officially an affair for three years. Eventually, he divorced and did marry the Lovefraud survey respondent. Then the woman found out that her husband was an exploiter. She lost money, lost her home, incurred debt and considered suicide.

In the third case, the sociopathic woman was indeed looking for a victim. Here's what the man wrote about his experience:

> *She was very charming & attentive. She would stare at me w/ what I misunderstood to be amazement. She quickly moved the relationship to the bedroom. She told me she didn't think she could get pregnant & I foolishly had unprotected sex w/ her. She was soon pregnant w/ twins & we were married just 2+ months after we met.*

The term "love bombing" is believed to have originated with the Unification Church. The founder, Sun Myung Moon, used the term in a speech back in 1978, describing how church members were always smiling because they were so full of love.[2]

Critics of cults, however, say that love bombing is a recruitment technique, a deliberate use of intense attention and affection in an effort to draw new people into the organization. Dr. Margaret Thaler Singer, an expert on brainwashing and coercive persuasion, said that love bombing was more effective than the brainwashing techniques used by North Koreans on prisoners of war.[3] Here is how she described it in her book, *Cults in Our Midst:*

> Love bombing is a coordinated effort, usually under the direction of leadership, that involves long-term members' flooding recruits and newer members with flattery, verbal seduction, affectionate but usually nonsexual touching, and lots of attention to their every remark. Love bombing — or the offer of instant companionship — is a deceptive ploy accounting for many successful recruitment drives.[4]

Many cult leaders are sociopaths. They are charismatic, charming, egocentric, manipulative, and meet other criteria that will be discussed in Chapter 2. I doubt that most run-of-the-mill sociopaths have spent time as cult members, yet they all seem to know the love bombing technique. Therefore, I believe that feigning love and affection in order to achieve an objective is instinctive sociopathic behavior. Cult leaders simply take what they do naturally and apply it to hundreds or thousands of recruits, pouring on the charm, or directing subordinates to pour on the charm, until the recruits became followers.

Love bombing is highly conditional. As long as cult members are mesmerized and unquestioning, they are showered with affection. But people who have left cults found that the affection they previously received vanished — instead, they were shunned and even vilified. This also happens when a romantic partner realizes that he or she is being used, and is no longer willing to be a member of a sociopath's personal cult. Sociopaths often turn on them with stunning ferocity.

But that's later in the relationship. In the Lovefraud Romantic Partner Survey, 75 percent of respondents described the sociopaths in their lives as "overly attentive." Early in the relationships, the attention was usually perceived to be flattering, but in some cases it became suffocating, even unwelcome. Here is how two respondents described their experiences:

He basically began to monopolize all of my time. When I would protest that we were too far apart in age, lifestyle, likes/dislikes, he seemed to glom on even more.

Overly attentive, which was flattering at first, but became creepy within two months.

Sociopaths practice their attentiveness not only in person, but via communications media as well. In the Lovefraud survey, 75 percent of respondents reported that the sociopath called them frequently, 41 percent said the sociopath sent a lot of text messages, and 38 percent said the sociopath sent frequent emails.

This is what you need to understand about sociopathic over-communication: Multitudes of phone calls, texts and emails are not about keeping in touch. They're about keeping in control.

Many Lovefraud readers reported dozens of contacts daily, and this is not an exaggeration. In the beginning, the sociopath may say things like, "I just want to hear your voice." Later on, as sociopaths escalate control, they demand to know where you are and with whom. Should you fail to answer a call or respond to a text, you may be subject to punishment, ranging from an outburst of rage to the cold, heartless silent treatment — a dramatic change from over-the-top love bombing.

Red Flag #5: Blames others for everything

Nothing is ever a sociopath's fault. When sociopaths have any problems, or are in any kind of trouble, it's always because someone else lied, screwed up, didn't honor agreements, is out to get them, or is jealous of them. Whatever drama is going on in their lives, sociopaths cast themselves as the victims.

So what do sociopathic excuses sound like? Here are a few recounted by respondents to the Lovefraud Romantic Partner Survey:

Convicted of federal crime, spent 5 years in prison, on parole for 3 years and still owed the government 14 million dollars, but it wasn't his fault.

Her husband had stolen all her money with a good lawyer and the money that she did have was gone due to her cancer issues and treatment.

It was the other person's fault that he had sex with a 14-year-old girl. He said that the way she acted around him he couldn't say no.

Blaming others is a critically important red flag indicating that you might be in a dangerous relationship.

First of all, it's something that almost all sociopaths do. In the Lovefraud Romantic Partner Survey, 82 percent of respondents said that the sociopaths in their lives blamed others for their problems.

Secondly, it's a warning sign that doesn't masquerade as something you'd want in a dream date. Unlike "charisma and charm" and "finding your soul mate," hearing your lover blame others for his or her troubles is not romantic. The excuses may be just the cold dose of reality that you need, amid the magic of attraction, to see what is really going on.

The key is paying attention to the hard facts, rather than the explanations. Having just been released from prison, a sociopath will complain about "legal injustices" with a voice full of outrage. With no income after being fired, a sociopath will rail against the "idiot boss." Owing thousands of dollars in back child support, a sociopath will blame the ex for frivolous court orders. As they do this, sociopaths are very convincing. But, rather than being swept up by their justifications, focus on the facts: This individual was in prison, has no job, and isn't paying child support.

As sociopaths are tossing blame around, their favorite targets are the exes — ex-wives, ex-husbands, ex-girlfriends and ex-boyfriends. According to comments in the Lovefraud Romantic Partner Survey, this is especially true when it comes to explaining their legal and financial problems:

> *He had been paying child support but his ex was 'psycho' and wouldn't admit he had been paying his debts. He then said his mother threw away all his money order receipts to 'screw him.' That they all were out to get him.*

> *His crazy borderline personality + bipolar ex girlfriend had filed a false rape charge against him in retaliation for him dumping her.*

Not only do sociopaths frequently blame their exes for their problems, but they tend to trash the lovers who came before you in general. In the survey, 63 percent of respondents said that the sociopaths disparaged previous spouses and love interests. Sociopaths accuse their exes of cheating and using drugs. They say the exes are money-grubbers and gold-diggers. Perhaps the most persistent claims are that the exes are jealous, mentally unbalanced, psycho stalkers. These descriptions, many Lovefraud readers later learn, usually apply to the sociopath, rather than the ex.

Sociopaths generally will not accept any responsibility for the demise of previous relationships. As with all of their problems, it's always the other person's fault.

Red Flag #6: Lies and gaps in the story

Sociopaths lie. They tell small lies. They tell enormous lies. They lie when telling the truth would serve their purposes better. They lie for the fun of it. When their lies are discovered, they lie to cover up their lies.

All sociopaths lie to the extreme. If someone isn't lying, he or she is not a sociopath. In the Lovefraud Romantic Partner Survey, 95 percent of respondents said that the sociopaths they knew were extremely or moderately deceitful.

Sociopaths are particularly prone to distorting or misrepresenting their personal histories. The goal, of course, is making themselves seem more accomplished and more romantically appealing. So they fabricate impressive resumes — 65 percent of survey respondents said the sociopaths told elaborate, detailed stories about their past. Or, they conveniently fail to mention actual exploits — like marriages, kids and prison terms. Fifty-six percent of survey respondents said the sociopaths were evasive when questioned about their past.

The Lovefraud survey asked this question: "When you first met, or early in your involvement, did the individual make claims, which you later learned to be false?" Here are some of the narrative answers:

1. Pilot and Instructor with Instrument License and Navigation License. 2. A Lawyer 3. Black Belt in Karate 4. Owner of 5 homes - Investment Homes - Homes all with Equity, and rented out! Showed me all the addresses and Equity in them. Had these addresses memorized, so he could refer to them at his leisure when he was with me without the list. 5. College Graduate - Law with Bachelor of Finance from a Florida University - all the above were lies. He also said he was married once, later found out he has been married as many as 6 times at the age of 40, which he now is.

I met her online. She claimed to be a business owner pursuing paralegal certification in order to save legal costs for the business; a former model (included pictures of an obscure Dutch model) who used her modeling money to go to Harvard. Claimed to be divorced. Unsure of her actual marital status, sexual orientation or occupation, but she did fake a fall at a Walmart in order to sue.

Claimed to work undercover for a Computer company to uncover inside theft, but he actually worked as a line inspector. Claimed to have a Real Estate business, but license had expired and wasn't actively selling real estate. Claimed he worked at one company for 2 yrs during our relationship. He provided names of staff, would describe the job and daily functions, spoke of promotions and special presentations he was asked to give because of his expertise. Found out he never even worked there!!

Stockbroker for Goldman Sachs — used that to con money for investing. I called to verify employment, then he said he had only sold his client list to them and kept 12 of his most personal ones. Claimed his father was CIA Special Operative in Iran where he was caught and beheaded. He claimed he was also CIA affiliated and used his knowledge to break down countries' economies by trading money. I could go on and on of things he said he did and knew, but it would be just that — "Things he said."

Two categories of lies that sociopaths tell deserve special attention. Many sociopaths claim heroic military records. And, many sociopaths falsely claim to be religious, born again, spiritual or even ordained clergy.

Ten percent of Lovefraud survey respondents said that the sociopaths they knew lied about serving in the military or Special Forces, and an additional 4 percent falsely claimed to be law enforcement, CIA or a spy.

False claims of military heroism are epidemic in the United States. Wannabes particularly like to claim that they served as elite commandos, like the Navy SEALs. In 2010, one authentic SEAL veteran who worked to expose fakers estimated that there were 300 impostors for every real SEAL.[5] After Osama bin Laden was killed by American commandos on May 1, 2011, watchdog organizations reported that the number of wannabe claims skyrocketed.[6]

I don't want to say that every person who fudges his or her military service record is a sociopath — sometimes the claims are just idle boasting, or stories that get started and are difficult to stop. But when people use false military claims to manipulate others, or to acquire benefits that they do not deserve, I'm willing to bet that these individuals are high in sociopathic traits.

When sociopaths make these claims, called "stolen valor" by military fraud busters, they have an agenda. They're trying to convince a target to give them what they want — money, sex, a place to live. They need to be believable. They deliberately cloak themselves in the honor and respect earned by men and women who truly serve in the military so that they can pull off the con.

Claiming to be a veteran can work, but posing as a SEAL or a Special Forces soldier is even better. Then sociopaths, when asked for proof, can say their work is covert, their service is classified, or records have been destroyed. The average victim, unfamiliar with the military, would have no idea how to investigate such statements.

Pretending to be in the Central Intelligence Agency, Drug Enforcement Agency, or Federal Bureau of Investigation works as well. Sociopaths get to be perceived as the "good guys." They can disappear for extended periods of time without explaining where they are going. They have plausible explanations for excess cash, weapons and secretive phone calls. Sociopaths like the government agent story — it's the perfect cover for a double life.

For example, when "Samantha" was on vacation in Spain, she met "Gary," another American, at a bar. "He was sexy and charming and interested in what I had to say," Samantha said. "We stayed up all night walking the streets of Spain — it was like a movie. I was 'done,' as they say. He didn't kiss me until six in the morning and I went home. It was the most romantic night of my life. After this, and meeting the next day for lunch, I thought I had found the person I wanted to marry."

At some point, Gary revealed why he was in Spain: He was a CIA agent.

Gary called Samantha continuously and sent nonstop texts and emails. He convinced her to change her travel plans to stay with him. Samantha was infatuated. "He was mysterious," she said. "Sexy. Worldly — so it seemed. Smart. He was SO into me and seemed to 'get me.' He cared about the things I cared about — family, career, love, though I later realized he didn't, but he was great at observing and mimicking me. He was 100 percent focused on nothing but me — I felt like a princess."

Samantha returned to the United States, but the involvement continued for almost two years. Twice, Gary was supposed to move to live with her, and twice, at the last minute, he cancelled his plans. The third time he actually showed up. But within two weeks Samantha found out the truth — Gary wasn't in the CIA, but he was married, cheating on his wife with her, and cheating with yet another woman, too. Samantha kicked Gary out of her apartment.

Looking back, Samantha said she probably did have a gut feeling that Gary's whole story was fabricated. "But I silenced it because I so desperately wanted this amazing romantic story to be true," she said. "A sexy man in the CIA I met in Spain loves ME! How could you not want that to be true? I guess over time, my gut feelings were building, and I responded by ASKING him time and time again questions — but he either deflected them, answered them with what I later found to be a lie, or made me feel like a bitch for asking."

Another favorite fabrication for sociopaths is the religious lie. Nineteen percent of respondents to the Lovefraud Romantic Partner Survey reported that the sociopaths they dated or married falsely claimed to be religious or born again. An additional 1 percent claimed to be clergy. Nineteen survey respondents said they met the sociopath in church.

Churches and religious dating sites are often happy hunting grounds for sociopaths looking for targets. An important function of religion is to provide guidance for moral living. Simply by identifying with a religion, sociopaths imply that they have the same morals as other church members, when the truth is, they have no morals at all.

"I believed that when someone said they are Christian, they are trustworthy," wrote a woman whom we'll call "Andrea." She learned that people who make these claims may instead be frauds and cons.

Andrea met "Tom" on a religious dating site and married him. "I believed he was a real man of God," she wrote. "I found out he is a psychopath. He is still actively being investigated for unsolved cold cases."

The marriage lasted less than a year, but it was enough time for Andrea to lose her job, lose more than $10,000, incur debt and be physically abused. "Tom was extremely violent," she wrote. "He uttered threats and sent death threats. Injured animals ... one died suspiciously. He has been seen in the company of some very hardcore criminals."

In another case, "Sharon" met "Brad" when he was living in a halfway house after spending two years in prison for embezzlement.

"Brad had become a Christian in prison, so he appealed to my faith," Sharon wrote. "We went to church every Sunday. The fact that he was asking for a second chance ... I have always been a sucker for the underdog. He wanted to pay back the money he embezzled so he could have a normal life with me."

The relationship caused controversy in Sharon's family. One brother warned her against Brad, and her ex-husband had a file on him two inches thick. But Sharon had another brother who was a missionary, and devout parents. "Brad played to their Christian values," she said. "They supported the relationship."

Red Flags *of* Love Fraud

Sharon dated Brad for less than four years. During that time, she discovered that Brad cheated on her and was secretly into pornography. She lost more than $50,000, lost her home and incurred debt.

This sociopath, Brad, took advantage of a belief that's at the core of Christianity — redemption. If people repent, Christians believe, their sins will be forgiven. So sociopaths repent. They claim that they have found religion, and God will help them turn their lives around. People who are authentically religious believe them, and forgive them. This is exactly what the sociopaths want — to be forgiven, so they can continue their scams.

Sociopaths don't limit themselves to exploiting Christianity — any religious or spiritual beliefs are fair game for abuse. Lovefraud survey respondents reported con artists who claimed to be Buddhists, yogis, shamans and ministers of nondenominational churches.

Unfortunately, sociopaths have natural talents for presenting themselves as spiritual leaders, which enables them to become gurus and cult leaders. They are charismatic. They always know the right thing to say. Through love bombing, they establish powerful connections with followers or potential followers.

Society usually holds spiritual leaders in high regard and deems them to be trustworthy. When sociopaths convince people that they are connected to a higher power, they gain carte blanche to do anything they want. This is, perhaps, the worst kind of lie.

Sociopaths use lies to hook their targets, and then continue to lie throughout romantic involvements. People who completed the Lovefraud Romantic Partner Survey described constant lying, pathological lying, lying on matters from critical to inconsequential.

If his mouth was open, he was lying.

He was an incredibly convincing liar, and would lie even when telling the truth would have served him better.

Lied even when he didn't have to just to stay in practice.

Sociopaths use every imaginable technique of deception. They tell falsehoods. They lie by omission — conveniently neglecting to divulge something that you should know about, like a sexually transmitted disease. They mix lies with truth, so that the story sounds plausible. And they tell totally outrageous lies, fictions that a normal person, even one prone to exaggeration, would never think of making.

You may ask, "Do they believe their own lies? Are they delusional?"

Generally the answer is no. In some cases, sociopaths are also psychotic, meaning they've lost their grip on reality, and they may actually believe their own stories. But this is unusual. Most sociopaths know they are not telling the truth; they just don't care.

Sociopaths lie to get what they want. They also lie for the thrill of it — sociopaths have admitted to feeling an adrenalin rush at deceiving people. Dr. Paul Eckman, who studies lying and teaches people how to detect it, calls this "duping delight." He explains it as "the exhilaration, pleasure, glee, or satisfaction a person may experience during the process of deception."[7] As one survey respondent noted about her ex-husband, "He liked to lie and get away with lies."

Red Flag #7: Intense eye contact

A Lovefraud survey respondent met the sociopath she married, who was her mother's physician, when she accompanied her mother to a doctor's appointment. Here is how she described the encounter: "When my mother was in the exam room he walked in. It was the most intense eye contact that I ever experienced. So much so that it was all I could describe years later when I recalled 'how we met' ... His eyes burned into my soul even though they were brown, and I didn't like brown eyes!"

Sociopaths are male, female, old, young, well groomed, disheveled. They come in all shapes and sizes. There is nothing to physically distinguish sociopaths from non-disordered individuals — except possibly the eyes.

Sociopaths frequently engage in intense eye contact. In fact, it's called the predatory stare — a direct, unflinching gaze, like that of a lion stalking its prey. If you get the feeling that someone is sizing you up for his or her next meal (in a metaphorical sense), you may be correct.

Some people instinctively recoil from the stare. Others, however, override any sense of apprehension and interpret intense eye contact as a sign of attraction. "I remember his intense eye contact from the first moment I saw him, which made me a bit uncomfortable but made me believe he was strongly interested in me," one survey respondent wrote.

The sociopath *is* interested in you — but not for the reasons that you think. He or she will not, however, reveal the true agenda, at least, not right away. If you ask, "Why are you staring at me?" the answer will be along the lines of, "You're so beautiful," or "I can't believe how lucky I am to have you in my life."

Sometimes, however, the sociopath's eyes tell a totally different story — they seem dead and lifeless, like the black eyes of a shark. If the "eyes are the windows of the soul," looking into the eyes of a sociopath, you may doubt that there is a soul. Lovefraud readers have observed that sociopaths smile with their mouths, but not with their eyes. You won't see any empathy, any compassion, any sense of human connection.

But sociopaths are good at distracting us from their emptiness, so early in an involvement, you may see the lifeless eyes only fleetingly. In fact, this characteristic is often easier to notice in a photograph of the individual, rather than in person.

Neither the intense eye contact nor lifeless eyes are universal traits among sociopaths. In the Lovefraud Romantic Partner Survey, 59 percent of respondents said that they experienced intense eye contact, and 60 percent agreed that "sometimes, the individual's eyes seemed to be lifeless." Still, these are important clues, the only potential physical symptoms of the disorder.

If you notice something odd about your new love interest's eyes, in conjunction with the other *Red Flags of Lovefraud*, be careful.

"I did not realize it until years later, but she had a strange look in her eyes when we met," one survey respondent wrote. "I now know how the gazelle feels when the lioness is about to attack and devour it. There was a cunning lifelessness in her eyes that was belied by a nice smile. I should have paid attention to the message the eyes were conveying."

Red Flag #8: Moves fast to hook up

"Jean" and "Greg" worked together in the medical field. She was in her 30s, he was in his 40s, and both were divorced. "Greg asked me to move in with him after one date," said Jean. "He totally consumed me and my time."

Greg apparently had been looking for an opportunity to make a move on Jean. "He invited himself to the movies when he heard I was going," Jean related. "Greg was to meet me there, then asked if he could give me a ride there since he had to pass my house anyway, then called me and asked if he could take me to dinner first since it was near dinner time. Then I realized this had become a date. After the movies, he asked if we could go to his house to watch a basketball game before he took me home. He is a doctor and his house was amazing. I spent the night."

It was a whirlwind romance. "Greg was spontaneous, exciting, sexual, did crazy, unexpected things, like take me to Vegas for the weekend without notice," Jean said. "I had been a single parent for several years, did not have a lot of extra money for expensive things, trips, etc. I didn't want to be alone anymore and wanted someone to take care of me."

The romance was hot and heavy — for a month. Then Greg broke up with Jean and got engaged to his ex-girlfriend. A month after that, Greg told Jean he'd made a mistake and wanted her back. Three months later they married.

Jean was with Greg for more than 10 years. Eventually, she became aware of his antisocial behavior: "Prescription drug abuse, wanting to swing, slept with people at work, resulting in him losing more than one job as an M.D. Has been fired from several hospitals, but it was always the fault of someone else. Pathological liar, steals things, though he could more than afford to buy them."

Because of her husband's cheating, Jean was infected with an STD. She lost more than $50,000 in the marriage. Lawsuits and criminal charges were filed against her. She became anxious, depressed, and suffered from post-traumatic stress disorder. Her life was threatened, and she considered suicide — all due to a man who wanted her to move in after their first date.

Sociopaths typically rush to hook up. In the Lovefraud Romantic Partner Survey, 77 percent of respondents said that the individual "moved fast — quickly proclaimed love, quickly wanted to be exclusive."

There are two reasons for this. First of all, sociopaths tend to hyperfocus. This means they focus intently on something that interests them in the moment, often disregarding everything else. (This tendency is associated with ADHD — attention deficit hyperactivity disorder. In fact, sociopathy and ADHD are genetically related.) If you're the new interest, the sociopath will hyperfocus on you — wanting to be with you all the time, showering you with attention, pushing to become a couple.

Secondly, sociopaths want to get their hooks into you before you escape. Sociopaths are well aware of the fact that they manipulate and use people. If you have something that they want — money, sex, a place to live — they will do everything they can so that you'll give it to them quickly.

So they swoon about how wonderful you are. They proclaim that God or the universe brought you together. They push you to commit, pleading, "We're in love. Why should we wait?" It all seems so heartfelt.

It's not. For sociopaths, claiming instant love is just a means to an end.

"Paul" learned this the hard way. Paul, a professional in his 40s, knew "Cindy" from the past. Cindy, also in her 40s, was beautiful and bright. In fact, she was a lawyer.

"She came on very strong and was very attentive and proclaimed love within three days," Paul said. "She pushed sex very fast and was extremely sexual. We had a tremendous sexual chemistry. She was quick to introduce me to kids and family."

Paul wanted to be married and have kids. Plus, a favorite aunt had just passed away. Paul was feeling emotionally drained, and Cindy seemed like a breath of fresh air. She pushed the relationship hard, and Paul did not resist.

Eventually Paul discovered the reason for the rush — Cindy was a bundle of financial and legal trouble. For their wedding, Cindy's grandmother gave them a card that said, "My gift to you on your wedding day is to forgive all the money I have loaned to Cindy, so you can buy a house instead of repay me."

It turned out that Cindy had declared bankruptcy three times by the age of 42. She had been let go by a law firm for fraud, and had committed fraud in her own legal practice. Paul broke up with her.

He described what happened next: "She pushed to reconcile many times and I finally gave in. I then found out she had been spending a lot of time with her ex-husband before me — the current husband. I told her there was no way for reconciliation. She then got into my house and faked a suicide. The first responders told me it was fake. I told her to never contact me again. She did anyway and let me know that the weekend after her suicide attempt, she went away to the mountains with her ex-boyfriend — the one she left her first husband for."

Red Flag #9: Pity play

Sociopaths have no empathy. However, they thoroughly understand that non-disordered people — their "marks" — have empathy, and they gleefully manipulate those feelings to get what they want.

It's called the "pity play." Sociopaths make you feel sorry for them, and then take advantage of your sympathy.

Dr. Martha Stout identified this phenomenon in her book, *The Sociopath Next Door*. She wrote, "The most reliable sign, the most universal behavior of unscrupulous people is not directed, as one might imagine, at our fearfulness. It is, perversely, an appeal to our sympathy."[8]

In the Lovefraud Romantic Partner Survey, the "pity play" was not the dominant characteristic of the sociopathic relationship — that honor went to "charisma and charm." Still, when asked if the individuals they were involved with "tried to make you feel sorry for him/her," 75 percent of respondents said yes.

Sociopaths can twist any events of their lives into sob stories, or if the tales aren't compelling enough, they completely invent tragedies. For example, several men stated in the survey that the women they dated falsely claimed to suffer from cancer:

> *Her children were being orphaned because of her fake terminal cancer ... used her position as a fake police officer dying of cancer to invoke trust-like "loans" that would be secured with fake securities.*

> *Within the first month she told me she had just been diagnosed with cancer and asked me if I would care for her daughter while she went for chemo treatments once a week. I later found out she used this lie as a way to see other men while I was home with the daughter.*

Financial problems, unemployment, terrible childhoods — all of these, in the skilled mouths of sociopaths, are exaggerated into appeals for sympathy. Sociopaths especially like to lament the abuse they suffered in previous relationships, blaming ex-partners for their heartbreak. The truth, should it come out, can be shocking.

"Alicia," a woman in her 50s, was working and going to school when she met "Frank" through business. Alicia told Frank that she did not have time to devote to a relationship. "He pushed his way into my life with statements that we were meant to be, that I was the one, that we met for a reason," she said.

Frank also used the pity play. "He 'acted' shy, and as though he was very wounded from his divorce," Alicia remembered. "He tearfully claimed he missed sharing every day with his children. The father of my own children never took interest in family life or our children. This man appeared to love and care for his children."

Alicia and Frank were together for more than five years, but eventually they were breaking up and making up in 90-day cycles. Frank swore that there weren't any other women, but Alicia investigated and found that he was engaged in rotating relationships. And that's not all she learned:

"I found a website where he was soliciting sex from underage girls," she said. "One of his daughters suffered anorexia/bulimia and was hospitalized; the other daughter was in a lock down program as the victim of sexual abuse. He claimed their teenage boyfriends did these things to his daughters. I no longer believe that."

Sociopathic men easily turn on the tears, like Frank did. Sociopathic women are particularly good at the "damsel in distress" routine, and some men see themselves as the knights in shining armor who are riding to the rescue. In fact, some men are so committed to making things right for these needy women that they ignore blatant warnings to stop.

"Stuart" was a single professional man in his 30s when he met a younger woman, "Rebecca," who seemed like a lost puppy dog. "She manipulated me to feel sorry for her and want to rescue her," Stuart said. "She was way far from home and appealed to my desire to be a protector. Then she set the hook with sex."

Stuart married Rebecca, even though plenty of people warned him not to. "Her mom, step dad and sister all told me they gave up on her many years earlier, as she has no conscience and no honor," Stuart said. "Her own mother warned me to get the hell away from her if I wanted to survive. I attempted to explain, believed I could rescue her, save her, etc., and didn't listen."

He should have. Rebecca filed false police reports against Stuart that cost him nearly $1 million and the best job of his life. She turned his friends, family and only son against him. Rebecca also attempted to have Stuart killed.

Red Flag #10: Jekyll and Hyde personality

The beginning of a relationship with a sociopath is all charm and romance. He or she proclaims that the two of you are soul mates. You are love bombed. The sociopath quickly wants your relationship to become exclusive, and may talk about marriage on the first date. Perhaps even before the first date.

This is the behavior you see as the sociopath is seducing you. Then the loving behavior may disappear, either suddenly or gradually, and be replaced by disinterest, criticism or rage. Instead of the attentive romantic partner who first swept into your life, you're faced with someone so cold and callous that you don't know who it is. And then the solicitous lover may return, again showering you with affection.

The sociopath can exhibit a total personality change, very much like the classic story of Dr. Jekyll and Mr. Hyde. He or she is sweet and caring — and then, instantly, a monster. In the Lovefraud Romantic Partner Survey, 64 percent of respondents said the people they were involved with exhibited a Jekyll and Hyde personality.

What does this look like? Here's how one respondent described it in the Lovefraud DSM-5 Survey:

> *When close contact was established, he passionately expressed feelings verbally and physically, such as, "never felt this way before," "you are my high school fantasy come true," "the universe has brought us together," "loved you the moment we met," "we are soul mates," was gentle, caring and passionate, possessive and obsessive about me. Sudden change while driving cross-country ... phone call ... voice would change, personality would change, intense anger, sarcasm, projected his problems as mine. Showed up at front door without warning, stayed for two weeks, presented extreme Jekyll/Hyde behavior, loving/hateful, emotionally abusive.*

Sociopaths can turn loving behavior on and off like flipping a switch. In the Lovefraud Romantic Partners Survey, 57 percent of respondents said that their partners switched love on and off.

It's really quite shocking — and confusing — to be on the receiving end of such treatment. Here's how one woman described the man that she lived with for more than five years:

> *He could tell me he loved me and hated me right in the same sentence. Or tell me he was going to do something horrible to me (destroy me or bring me down or whatever), then turn right around 5 minutes later and say how much he loved me and would do anything in the world for me, then 5 minutes later something else*

*horrible he was going to do, or he would on impulse say
something nasty and leave to go do something else, then
show up an hour later with words of love and not understand why I didn't think he loved me or why I would be
upset, because didn't he just tell me he loved me?*

If you're the target in a situation like this, you never know
which person you'll be dealing with — the romantic or the raging
maniac. You feel totally off-balance and afraid to say or do anything that may set your partner off — a phenomenon described as
"walking on eggshells."

This is how cycles of abuse begin. You are built up with words
and actions of love, then battered down with words and actions of
contempt. You don't understand what is going on, and do everything you can to make the loving suitor come back — slowly losing
yourself in the process.

Early in your relationship with a sociopath, you may get just
a glimpse of coldness — a reaction or an outburst that seems stun-
ningly out of character. The sociopath may quickly apologize or
make an excuse — it was just frustration or stress, nothing to
worry about. Then the sociopath resumes love bombing.

If you see this, you are witnessing the mask of normalcy slip-
ping. The sociopath has been acting as a caring lover, and tem-
porarily breaks character. He or she then works to convince you
that what you just saw was an aberration, never to be repeated.

Some sociopaths can keep the charade of love going for a long
time — at least until they are sure you are hooked. So it is possible
that you won't notice any overt change in a sociopath's loving behavior until you are totally committed to the relationship —
moved in, married or pregnant. Several Lovefraud survey respondents experienced this:

*Initially (he expressed love) with dates, flowers, gifts
and little thoughtfulness's. After I married him, he said,
on the honeymoon, "I can stop acting now." I thought that
he was joking. I later learned he did not do jokes.*

From very loving to cold indifference ... started right after we were married ... The change was startling ... cold, distant, indifferent, condescending, mean spirited, accusatory ... self righteous, irresponsible.

In the beginning of the relationship (before marriage) he was loving, caring, could not do enough for me. Called me his soul mate, his true companion in life. This contin- ued until the day I married him, within hours after the wedding ceremony his personality shifted. It was as if I had dated and fell in love with one person, but married someone I was completely unfamiliar with. He was a stranger to me in all ways.

If you're uneasy, look for the Red Flags of Love Fraud

Sociopaths convincingly proclaim their undying love. When we hear those words, of course we want to believe them — espe- cially if we've been alone for awhile, hoping love will find us.

We know that nobody's perfect and real love means accepting the entire person, flaws and all. So, mesmerized by charisma, charm and love bombing, we may overlook the facts that the so- ciopaths' stories don't add up, they blame others for all their prob- lems, and they want us to feel sorry for them. We cut them some slack. After all, they love us.

Generally, however, if you're involved with a predator, you'll have a sense of trouble. The Lovefraud Romantic Partner Survey asked, "In the beginning of the involvement, did you have a gut feeling or intuition that something wasn't right about the person or the relationship?" A total of 71 percent of respondents answered yes. Unfortunately, most of them did not listen to their instincts, and proceeded with the relationships. I believe that they saw the warning signs but did not know what they meant, so they ignored their apprehensions. I'll tell you more about this in Chapter 9.

If you feel a sense of uneasiness, do not brush your concerns away. Again, one or two signs do not mean that your new romantic interest is a sociopath. But if you see most or all of the *Red Flags of Love Fraud*, get out of the relationship immediately.

You may think, "It will never happen to me. I'm smart; I'm confident; I know the score." Well, plenty of people thought that way and got snared — you'll read their stories in this book. Sociopaths are very, very good at what they do, and what they do, in essence, is mess with your mind. That's why it is so important to pay attention to the early warning signs. The longer you're involved with a sociopath, the harder it is to escape.

Recap

The *Red Flags of Love Fraud*
1. Charisma and charm
2. Sudden soul mates
3. Sexual magnetism
4. Love bombing
5. Blames others for everything
6. Lies and gaps in the story
7. Intense eye contact
8. Moves fast to hook up
9. Pity play
10. Jekyll and Hyde personality

CHAPTER 2

What is a sociopath?

A sociopath is a social predator. Sociopaths are woefully lacking in empathy and conscience. They live their lives by exploiting others.

The degree to which sociopaths are fundamentally different from the rest of humanity is extremely difficult to grasp. Imagine someone who:

- Does not feel love towards any other person — not a spouse, not a friend, not his or her own child.
- Knows the difference between right and wrong, but feels no moral obligation to do what's right.
- Doesn't really care about the welfare of others, but pretends to when it furthers his or her agenda.
- Is only interested in winning, whatever winning may mean at the moment.
- Acts as if the world is made up of predators and prey — he or she is the predator, and everyone else is prey.

Now imagine that when you meet the person described above, he or she appears to be outgoing, friendly, charming, helpful, fun and caring. You see absolutely no indication of the emptiness inside. Because sociopaths are wonderful actors, and have learned to cover up their hollow cores, you are fooled.

What is a sociopath?

What are they really like? Here is how respondents to the Lovefraud Romantic Partner Survey described the sociopaths in their lives:

> *No conscience or empathy whatsoever. Enjoyed exploiting people and would find their weaknesses amusing. Not financially, just emotionally. Thought they were "suckers."*

> *Her lies turned our 5 children (4 adult), my sisters, community, church, etc. against me. Her favorite expression, "I love my bitterness toward you, I wouldn't trade it for anything. I want to make your life as miserable as possible." She has!*

> *He often told me how easy it was to kill someone, and made bombs. He didn't really like anyone it seemed, just pretended to be friendly to use people.*

Although the man described in the last quote talked about killing people, he didn't actually do it. Some sociopaths commit serious crimes or kill, but usually they "only" abuse their partners, neglect their children, defraud credit card companies, indulge in drugs and alcohol, bilk customers, steal from employers, bully co-workers and find more ways to disregard and violate the rights of others.

Sociopaths are the most destructive people of the human race, yet few of us know they exist.

Summary of sociopathic traits

Before explaining what a sociopath is, I want you to be clear on what a sociopath is NOT.

A sociopath is NOT delusional. Sociopaths know exactly what they are doing. When their actions harm others, they know that, too. They just don't care. (The only exception is if sociopaths also have another disorder, such as schizophrenia, in which case they can be delusional — and especially dangerous.)

A sociopath is NOT ALWAYS a serial killer, or, for that matter, any kind of killer. Yes, some sociopaths kill, and they can do it with a coldblooded detachment that shocks the humanity in the rest of us. Famous sociopathic killers include Ted Bundy, who murdered as many as 40 young women,[1] and John Wayne Gacy, who raped, tortured and murdered 33 young men.[2] But the overwhelming majority of sociopaths never kill anyone.

A sociopath is NOT ALWAYS a convicted criminal. Many sociopaths break the law, get caught and go to jail. But many more sociopaths break the law and don't get caught, or commit acts that are unethical but not illegal.

So what exactly are the traits that make up this disorder? Actually, it depends on whom you ask. Mental health professionals — from doctors to therapists to psychology researchers — do not totally agree on the characteristics that define social predators, or even what these people should be called. Several different sets of diagnostic criteria are in use. Below, therefore, I have compiled summaries of the main categories of traits exhibited by sociopaths, based upon the definitions used in the mental health field, along with the observations of thousands of Lovefraud readers and contributors.

You will notice overlap between the traits described below and the *Red Flags of Love Fraud*. That's because what sociopaths are determines what they do.

Lying

All sociopaths lie. With sociopaths, lying is more than a distasteful behavior tipping you off that the person should be avoided. Lying is central to the sociopathic personality.

We all lie sometimes, perhaps to avoid an argument or spare someone's feelings. Sociopaths lie to the extreme, and they enjoy it. They misrepresent themselves by piling one lie on top of another, until they've created a completely alternate reality. Again, they are not delusional, so they know they are lying. But they act like they believe what they are saying, and are so convincing that we believe them, too. Then, when we find out that everything they told us was, at best, exaggeration, and at worst, complete fabrication, we are shocked.

"If you are astounded by another person's capacity to lie and misrepresent reality, you can be sure you have encountered a sociopath," said my colleague, Dr. Liane Leedom, in one of her articles for the Lovefraud Blog.[3] If she had to choose only one criterion to identify the sociopathic personality disorder, Dr. Leedom said it would be lying.[4]

Sociopaths are successful liars because they experience no distress while lying. Many, if not most, sociopaths are naturally glib. They have the gift of gab and are never at a loss for words. But even those sociopaths who aren't incredibly smooth talkers can make up stories, excuses and reasons on the spot. Because we see no hesitation, we assume that they must be answering our questions or conveying information truthfully. In fact, sometimes there *are* grains of truth in their statements — which makes it that much more difficult to discern the lies.

According to common wisdom, you can spot liars through body language or fleeting facial expressions. Liars supposedly avoid eye contact, touch their faces or throats, fidget and raise the pitch of their voices. Normal people may exhibit these signs as they lie because they are uncomfortable with what they are saying or want to conceal their true feelings, but these tips do not necessarily work with sociopaths. Sociopaths can easily look you directly in the eye, with totally natural expressions on their faces, and tell you complete lies. They don't get nervous; they don't sweat. This is why they can pass lie detector tests.

Unfortunately, humans are lousy lie detectors. Psychological research has found that generally, people can distinguish truth from lies only 53 percent of the time — not much better than flipping a coin.[5] Odds are even worse in romantic relationships. When our romantic partners are saying all the right words, especially, "I love you," we want to believe them.

Exploitation

Sociopaths enter into a romantic relationship, or any relationship, for one reason only: Exploitation.

They are not capable of the give and take of a healthy relationship. When you're involved with sociopaths, it's you give and they take. In their eyes, you are nothing but a source of supply — in one way or another, you are supplying what they want. If sociopaths appear to be giving, it's only a ruse to set you up so that later, they can take much more.

Usually the exploitation is obvious. Once you're hooked, sociopaths start asking for, or demanding, money, sex, business connections, a place to live, a place to party — whatever you have that they want. In the Lovefraud Romantic Partner Survey, 47 percent of respondents said they were manipulated to pay for dates, 60 percent said they incurred debt due to the sociopaths, and 76 percent said they lost money.

Sometimes, however, what sociopaths want is a façade of normalcy. They want to present a certain image to the world. You are part of that image, so they may treat you exactly as you would expect, pretending to be the doting husband, wife or partner. Behind your back, however, the sociopath may live a completely double life, which could involve cheating, prostitutes, drugs, crime and perhaps even murder.

Other times, all they want is entertainment. I've heard of many cases in which sociopaths got nothing from a relationship but the thrill of duping the victim. These sociopaths wanted to convince their targets to fall in love with them, and then break their hearts, just for the fun of it.

So how do sociopaths accomplish their goals of exploiting you? Through manipulation. In the Lovefraud Romantic Partner Survey, 97 percent of respondents said that the individuals they were involved with were moderately or extremely manipulative. In the Lovefraud DSM-5 Survey, the figure was 98 percent.

Sociopaths use deception, pretense and subterfuge to influence and control you. They employ whatever techniques work — flattery, seduction, charm, love bombing, building your trust, ingratiation, lies, blaming others, the pity play. A favorite ploy is time pressure — if you don't act RIGHT NOW, some terrible disaster will occur.

Then, when you are no longer useful, it's over.

This is called "devalue and discard." Perhaps the sociopath has taken all your money — you're in debt, even bankrupt, with nothing left to bleed. Perhaps the sociopath has decided to trade you in for a younger model. Perhaps the sociopath has found someone with more money, a bigger house or better business connections. For whatever reason, you are no longer a juicy target. You're thrown into the Dumpster, and the sociopath moves on to exploit a new victim.

Entitlement

Sociopaths view themselves as the center of the universe, and that's how they expect to be treated. They are amazingly egocentric, and have an even more amazing sense of entitlement.

With breathtaking grandiosity, sociopaths claim to be the smartest, best-looking, most successful people around. My ex-husband came out and stated, quite seriously, that he knew everything. Many sociopaths are intelligent, and many do have legitimate skills and accomplishments. Even so, their egocentrism is extraordinary — especially when you find out that everything the sociopaths say they are, own or have accomplished is highly exaggerated, or an outright lie.

Sociopaths feel entitled to lie. In fact, sociopaths feel entitled to say or do absolutely anything as they pursue gratification of their desires. They seem to believe that the world owes them whatever they want, just because they want it. And if they don't get what they want, someone will pay the consequences.

This mind-set often leads to abuse. Here's how Lovefraud contributor Steve Becker, LCSW, explains it:

> As in all narcissistic/sociopathic disturbances, an inflated self-entitlement informs, indeed *drives*, the abusive mentality. Not only do abusers feel entitled to *what* they want, but also *how* they want it, and *when* and *where* they want it.
>
> Merely by virtue of their wanting it, abusive individuals will feel *automatically entitled* to your cooperation, undivided attention, compassion, tolerance, respect, compliance, admiration, you name it. And because they feel enti-

tled to these things, they feel they *don't have to earn any of them.*

This, of course, is the very nature of entitlement. Theirs are *unearned privileges,* yet their unearned status in no way diminishes the abusers' perceived right to them.[6]

Sociopaths only care about getting what they want. It doesn't matter if, in the process, they violate social guidelines or ethics. They have no internal moral standards, and feel that the rules do not apply to them. They live for their one objective: Satisfying themselves.

Shallow emotions

According to Dr. Liane Leedom, at the core of sociopathic personalities is an inability to love. People who have this set of disorders do not feel any emotion that entails truly caring about the well-being of another human being.

Sociopaths do not feel empathy. They cannot put themselves in another person's shoes and comprehend what that person is feeling or experiencing. They have no concern about the needs or suffering of others.

Sociopaths do not feel remorse. When they hurt or mistreat another person, they experience no sense of guilt or regret. Often they don't even acknowledge that they did anything wrong. In the Lovefraud Romantic Partner Survey, 74 percent of respondents agreed that after hurtful words or actions, the sociopathic individuals acted like the incidents never happened.

Because the range of emotions sociopaths experience is so limited, they are frequently puzzled by the emotions of others. Oh, they understand anger, rage and hatred. But they do not understand tenderness, compassion or even fear. So when they're around someone who is displaying these emotions, sociopaths have to figure out how to interpret what they see. In a seminar that I attended, Dr. Robert Hare, the well-known expert, suggested that for these people, understanding emotions is like trying to understand a foreign language. "It's like they have to translate it," he said.[7]

Many sociopaths realize that even though they don't feel caring emotions, they have to act like they do in order to fit into society and make themselves appealing to their targets. So they observe people — and perhaps movie characters — to learn how to emulate the emotions of others. Sometimes they don't quite pull it off, and even though sociopaths can teach themselves to cry on demand, you get the impression that they are playacting. Or, their reactions to emotional situations are delayed, because they must first look around to see how other people are reacting in order to know what to do.

Other times, sociopaths don't even try to fake it, and their responses to emotional situations are totally inappropriate. Many Lovefraud readers have tearfully informed their sociopathic partners of the death of a parent, favorite relative or pet, only to be greeted by a statement like, "He's gone. Get over it."

Such a response is shockingly callous. It is also highly indicative of the sociopath's true internal state — shallow, barren, cold and unemotional.

Dominance

We all have a social dominance drive — that's what makes us want to be first in line, own a stylish car, win at sports, or lead our organizations. In most of us, the dominance drive is tempered by a love motivation — yes, we want to win, but we're not going to break the rules or intentionally harm others to do it.

Sociopaths are different. According to Dr. Liane Leedom, they only want three things: power, control and sex — in other words, domination. Because they do not feel love and caring for other people, they have no internal prohibitions to slow their pursuit of domination.

In fact, Dr. Leedom believes that an out-of-control dominance motivation, unmitigated by love, is the key feature of the sociopathic personality disorder. "An excessive drive for social dominance is at the root of the destructive behavior of sociopaths," she said. "The most sociopathic people also have the most insatiable drives for social dominance."[8]

Many sociopaths seek social dominance through hostility and aggression. They are rude, nasty, irritable, hot-tempered, cruel and belligerent. They humiliate and demean others. They respond to insults and slights, whether real or imagined, with anger and vengeance. Sometimes sociopaths engage in violence. In the Love-fraud Romantic Partner Survey, 36 percent of respondents reported that they were physically abused or injured by their sociopathic partners, and 34 percent said their lives were threatened.

Sociopaths who are not physically violent still assert domination through intimidation, coercion and controlling behavior. In a workplace or neighborhood setting, you'll see a bully. If you're in a romantic or family relationship, you may experience emotional, psychological, sexual and/or financial abuse. Dr. Leedom explains:

> All a sociopath cares about is gaining interpersonal power over those he or she is with for the moment. Sociopaths may not care that they are low in status in comparison to the whole of society, so long as they have a few people they can control.
>
> Usually, the people they control are family, but it can be any group, from a corporation, to an organization, to a criminal gang, to a religious cult. Sociopaths live in the moment and want to have power in the here and now. For this reason, they focus on dominating those closest to them — immediate family, friends and co-workers. They often seem charming and amicable to outsiders, while those closest to them come to know otherwise.[9]

Irresponsibility

Most sociopaths can't be bothered fulfilling their obligations. They don't pay their bills, and have the horrific credit histories to prove it. Still, they like credit cards, but no longer able to get their own, they want to use yours. This, they discover, is a great deal — they run up the charges and you're stuck with the bills.

Sociopaths are equal-opportunity deadbeats — most are happy to ignore any financial obligation. They are unreliable about paying the mortgage, child support, legal and hospital bills, electric bills or phone bills. Yet they seem to have money for entertainment, travel, fancy clothes — oh yeah, that's your money. Or the money of some other poor target who has been conned. Money isn't the only irresponsible area of their lives. They fail to show up at work, or fail to complete their assignments. They may not show up for visitation with their children. They may not show up for a date with you, and then have a long, involved explanation for why you were left waiting at a restaurant.

And promises? Well, a promise is not a commitment. It's a statement of what a sociopath might do if the action will further his or her objective. If keeping a promise will groom you for further exploitation, then the sociopath may come through. But if keeping the promise provides no immediate benefit to the sociopath, then he or she may deny that the promise was ever made.

Sociopaths do not take responsibility for their obligations. In fact, they do not take responsibility for their own lives. When bad things happen — a common occurrence with this personality disorder — according to the sociopath, the fault always lies with someone else. With an attitude like this, of course, they never learn from their mistakes.

Need for excitement

Sociopaths crave stimulation. They want excitement, change, variety and thrills. They get bored easily, and some of them don't sleep much. They're always looking for the next rush, such as:

• **Drugs and alcohol.** Many sociopaths like getting high. They drink or use drugs whenever they want, and end up with substance abuse problems. In fact, sociopathy and addiction are genetically related.

• **Sex.** Nothing is more stimulating than sex, so sociopaths want it. They start young, indulge frequently, and are not necessarily fussy about the gender, marital status or sexual orientation of their partners.

• **Crime.** Some sociopaths break the law to take what they want; others commit crimes for the thrill of it. If they get caught, they assume they'll be able to talk their way out of trouble. They frequently succeed.

Many people have a "need for speed" — like fighter pilots and race car drivers — but they are not sociopaths. What do successful speedsters have that sociopaths lack? Usually, it's impulse control — the ability to work for, and wait for, something that they want. This is called delayed gratification, and most of us start learning it as toddlers.

Sociopaths, on the other hand, are impulsive. There is no filter between idea and action. Because of their low impulse control, they act on the spur of the moment to achieve immediate satisfaction or pleasure, without considering possible consequences. This approach to life can mushroom into recklessness. Many sociopaths take unnecessary risks, ignoring danger to themselves and others.

So what does craving excitement combined with poor impulse control mean for romantic relationships? Sociopaths cheat. In fact, they frequently cheat with multiple partners simultaneously, assuring each individual that their relationship is exclusive. Some sociopaths brazenly manipulate events so that their partners almost meet each other. Why? It adds to the thrill of the game.

Antisocial behavior

The culmination of these personality traits, drives and attitudes is antisocial behavior — acts that violate the rights of others, societal norms or the law.

Sociopaths engage in all kinds of negative behaviors — everything from cheating on a spouse to committing mass murder. It's important to note that sociopaths are not all the same, and the actions of some are definitely worse than the actions of others. What's striking, however, is that these individuals exhibit their soullessness and lack of conscience in all areas of their lives. Sociopaths don't just cheat on their spouses with multiple affairs. The same sociopaths also steal from their employers, abuse drugs or alcohol and refuse to pay child support.

Here is how some respondents to the Lovefraud Romantic Partner Survey described the antisocial behavior that they witnessed:

Threatened to burn the house down with me and the kids in it. Made death threats towards others. If we had friends over he would make something awful happen so they'd leave. He discharged guns and kept weapons. He made loans (worked for banks) and altered paperwork. Did property appraisals & altered paperwork. He also bilked older people out of $$, booze & vehicles and a boat. He stole things from me and sold or pawned them. He stole money from my little business; he also set fires.

Animal cruelty. Assaults/threats against other persons. He was very dodgy in his real estate dealings. From what I can gather he stole a motorbike at one job and he continually drove whilst drunk. He now pretends to be a police officer when he is not. He has assaulted me whilst I was pregnant, kicking me in my face and punching me numerous times, breaking my nose. He has threatened to kill me and burn down my house. He has broken numerous items of mine.

She stole drugs, classified as "controlled substances," from her workplace, she carried on a secret affair with a married man for 5+ months, prior to meeting me, she had unprotected sex with a "stranger" and got pregnant.

To make matters even worse, sociopaths frequently engage in antisocial behavior without any real reason or provocation. Afterwards, if confronted, or arrested for criminal acts, they concoct plausible-sounding excuses. But probably the real reason they violated the rights of others was simply because the impulse struck, and they felt entitled to do what they wanted.

Female sociopaths

Women can be sociopaths. Statistically and biologically, there are more male sociopaths than female sociopaths — mental health professionals generally estimate that in the United States, sociopaths are three times more likely to be men than women.[10]

However, Dr. Liane Leedom says that if women who live like parasites and control others through emotional blackmail were included in the tally, there may be just as many female social predators as there are male. And as anyone who has dealt with a female sociopath will tell you, the women are just as nasty as the men — deceitful, controlling and manipulative.

The Lovefraud DSM-5 Survey asked respondents to describe how their partners expressed love in the beginning of the relationship, and how it changed over time. Here are some of the comments about women:

> *She was the most expressive of love of any person I have known. I felt like I lived in a dream world to be with such a perfect woman for me. But in the end I saw how it was all an act to get what she really wanted, her own home. She used our relationship for financial gain. There was no love at all once I found out what she was doing, and what our relationship was really about.*

> *Praised my talents continually, spoke of her luck in knowing me and then turned on me like a Rottweiler on crack!! Belittling, degrading, extremely rude and projected severe rejection toward me.*

> *Was initially flattering and generous with gifts and sex. Prepared meals and made drinks. Offered to help wherever possible. All of these were gradually withdrawn and replaced with theft, gaslighting, manipulation and bullying.*

Two main differences separate sociopathic men and women: The women are less likely to be criminal and are generally not as physically violent towards others.

Within intimate relationships, however, women are almost as violent as men. Multiple research studies have shown that women assault their intimate partners at about the same rate that men do.[11] These findings were validated by the Lovefraud Romantic

Partner Survey — 36 percent of males and 29 percent of females were described by the respondents as physically abusive.

Sociopathic women are often abusive towards their children — if not physically abusive, then certainly emotionally and psychologically abusive. Many people find this hard to believe — after all, in order for the human race to survive, Nature programmed females to be empathetic caregivers. But this trait is exactly what is missing from sociopathic women. Dr. Liane Leedom says, "One of the best indicators of sociopathy in women is seen when the woman fails to care for her own child."[12]

Take the case of a survey respondent whom we'll call "Luke," who was married to "Belinda." Belinda was extremely affectionate, attended to Luke's every want, and was friendly to his family and widowed mother — until they married, when everything changed.

Luke and Belinda had a daughter, and when the child was two, Belinda's nephew was convicted of molesting the child and three other little girls. Yet Belinda continued to allow the nephew to be around the child. Luke strenuously objected, so Belinda filed for divorce, claiming that Luke was controlling and was refusing to let her see any of her family. "She testified in the divorce that it was 'humorous' and 'appropriate' that our child and three other little girls were molested by her nephew," Luke said.

Obviously, a woman who can display such shocking disregard for her child's safety lacks empathy, just like male sociopaths. But there are subtle differences in how the disorder manifests between the sexes — women are less angry, less impulsive, and not as emotionally shallow. As a result, it's more difficult to spot female sociopaths than male sociopaths.

Nature and nurture contribute to sociopathy

What makes a sociopath? Both genetic and environmental factors play parts. Multiple research studies indicate that genetics account for more than half of the variation in the features of the disorder.[13] The rest is due to the environment, including the parenting that an individual receives as a child.

Because the condition is highly genetic, when sociopaths reproduce, their children have a good chance of inheriting a predisposition to the disorder. Plus, as self-centered as they are, sociopaths make terrible parents. Their children, therefore, get a double whammy — the genes for a personality disorder, and a dysfunctional, even abusive, home environment.[14]

This is scary stuff — especially considering how sociopaths like to reproduce. If you've had a child with a sociopath, you need to be concerned and take action. It may be possible to prevent the disorder from developing through parenting techniques that focus on love and positive attention, rather than punishment. I strongly recommend that you read *Just Like His Father?,* by Dr. Liane Leedom.[15] With her thorough understanding of the sociopathic personality disorder and child development, she explains what you can do to try to prevent or mitigate the disorder in your child.

The sooner you start working with your child, the better. Once a sociopath is an adult, there is no known treatment for the disorder. Therapy doesn't help. In fact, research has shown that therapy makes sociopaths worse.[16] Why? Because they learn new psychological buzzwords and techniques, which they then use for further manipulation.

Sociopaths are often so slick that they frequently fool therapists. I've heard of many cases in which sociopaths in marriage counseling convinced the therapists that they were fine, but their partners, who were suffering from nothing but exposure to the sociopaths, needed help. Some of the non-disordered partners ended up on medication.

Multiple descriptions of the disorder

Back in 2005, when I launched Lovefraud.com to educate the public about these disordered individuals, my first problem was deciding how to refer to them. Why? Because psychology researchers, psychiatrists and other mental health professionals disagree on what social predators should be called, and how they should be diagnosed.

Although some professionals would argue with me, I believe that all of the following terms describe pretty much the same disorder: psychopath, sociopath, antisocial and dyssocial. Related conditions include narcissism and borderline personality disorder.

What is a sociopath?

Let's take a look at how these terms are presented in the scientific literature.

Psychopath

Research psychologists tend to use the term "psychopath." This was the word used by Hervey M. Cleckley, M.D., a psychiatrist who wrote *The Mask of Sanity*. Originally published in 1941, this book was the first comprehensive description of the disorder. Based on his clinical interviews with incarcerated men, Cleckley identified 16 characteristics of psychopaths:

Psychopathy traits identified by Cleckley
1. Superficial charm and good intelligence
2. Absence of delusions and other signs of irrational thinking
3. Absence of nervousness or psychoneurotic manifestations
4. Unreliability
5. Untruthfulness and insincerity
6. Lack of remorse and shame
7. Inadequately motivated antisocial behavior
8. Poor judgment and failure to learn by experience
9. Pathologic egocentricity and incapacity for love
10. General poverty in major affective reactions
11. Specific loss of insight
12. Unresponsiveness in general interpersonal relations
13. Fantastic and uninviting behavior with drink and sometimes without
14. Suicide threats rarely carried out
15. Sex life impersonal, trivial, and poorly integrated
16. Failure to follow any life plan[17]

Drawing upon the work of Cleckley, Dr. Robert Hare, the Canadian psychology researcher, developed a method of evaluating an individual's degree of psychopathy. It is called the Psychopathy Checklist Revised (PCL-R), and was published in 1991.
Hare started his career in the Canadian prison system, and the

original purpose of the PCL-R was to help determine which prisoners, if released, were likely to offend again. Since then, the PCL-R has been used and validated in hundreds of scientific studies, and is considered the gold standard in diagnosing psychopathy.

When the PCL-R is administered, individuals are assessed on each of the following traits, which Hare defined as indicative of psychopathy:

Hare Psychopathy Checklist Revised
1. Glibness/superficial charm
2. Grandiose sense of self-worth
3. Need for stimulation/proneness to boredom
4. Pathological lying
5. Conning/manipulative
6. Lack of remorse or guilt
7. Shallow affect (emotions)
8. Callous/lack of empathy
9. Parasitic lifestyle
10. Poor behavior controls
11. Promiscuous sexual behavior
12. Early behavior problems
13. Lack of realistic, long-term goals
14. Impulsivity
15. Irresponsibility
16. Failure to accept responsibility for actions
17. Many short-term marital relationships
18. Juvenile delinquency
19. Revocation of conditional release
20. Criminal versatility[18]

Note that neither Cleckley nor Hare mentions anything about a person being a serial killer. The association between the words "psychopath" and "serial killer" was made primarily by the entertainment industry.

Sociopath, antisocial personality disorder, dyssocial

The American Psychiatric Association (APA) publishes a book called the *Diagnostic and Statistical Manual of Mental Disorders* (DSM). This is the psychiatrist's bible; it describes and defines all mental disorders.

The DSM never included "psychopathy" as an official diagnosis. The first edition, published in 1952, used the terms "sociopath" and "sociopathic personality disturbance." The second edition of the manual, published in 1968, dropped "sociopath" and introduced the term "antisocial personality disorder." After that, psychiatrists and clinicians tended to use "antisocial personality disorder" when describing the condition, and "sociopath" as a shorthand way of referring to a person who had the condition.

In 2010, the APA was in the process of producing the fifth edition of the manual, the DSM-5. On February 10, 2010, the association posted a draft of the revised manual on the Internet. The description for antisocial personality disorder had changed significantly from previous versions of the manual, and included the following list of traits.

Antisocial Personality Disorder traits in DSM-5 (draft version)

- Callousness
- Aggression
- Manipulativeness
- Hostility
- Deceitfulness
- Narcissism
- Irresponsibility
- Recklessness
- Impulsivity[19]

The DSM-5 committee invited public feedback on the first draft of the manual. Dr. Liane Leedom and I decided to not only express our opinions, but back them up with data. That's why we developed the Lovefraud DSM-5 Survey. Lovefraud readers were asked to complete it in reference to a particular individual whom they knew — a spouse, romantic partner, family member or associate.

Our first objective was to establish whether or not survey respondents were, in fact, involved with sociopaths. Readers were asked to rate the individuals using the criteria published in the DSM-5 draft. For each of the traits, respondents could describe the individuals as, "little or not at all like that," "mildly like that," "moderately like that" or "extremely like that." The evidence of pathological traits was so overwhelming that I am confident in saying yes, our survey respondents did tangle with sociopaths.

A year later, we conducted the Lovefraud Romantic Partner Survey. Again, respondents were asked to rate the individuals they were involved with according to these nine traits. The results were almost identical:

Lovefraud surveys based on first draft of DSM-5
Percentages indicate the number of respondents who selected "moderately like that" or "extremely like that" to describe individuals they were involved with. N = number of surveys.

Trait	DSM-5 N = 1,378	Romantic Partner N = 1,352
Callousness	96%	92%
Aggression	82%	81%
Manipulativeness	98%	97%
Hostility	82%	79%
Deceitfulness	98%	95%
Narcissism	92%	90%
Irresponsibility	85%	84%
Recklessness	79%	77%
Impulsivity	83%	81%

Since the Lovefraud surveys were completed, the descriptions of all personality disorders in the DSM-5, including antisocial personality disorder, were revised further. A new assessment approach was introduced that added descriptions of impairments in personality and interpersonal functioning. The list of antisocial personality traits was changed — "aggression" and "narcissism" were removed, and "recklessness" became "risk taking." The revision also included another name for the disorder — dyssocial personality disorder, which is similar to the term used in the World Health Organization's *International Statistical Classification of Diseases and Related Health Problems,* 10th edition (ICD-10).

Narcissism and borderline personality disorder

Everyone with antisocial personality disorder is also a narcissist, but not all narcissists have antisocial personality disorder.

Antisocials and narcissists both have highly inflated opinions of themselves, consider themselves entitled to have everything they want, and view others merely as objects to serve their needs. The key difference between the two disorders is the degree of inherent malice. Those with antisocial personality disorder are predatory — their objective is to exploit people, and if their targets get hurt, well, that's just part of the game. Narcissists, on the other hand, also hurt people, but usually it's because they are simply clueless about how their actions affect others. Narcissists are so focused on gaining recognition and validation for themselves that they don't notice the feelings and needs of the people around them.

Borderline personality disorder is a sister condition to psychopathy and antisocial personality disorder. Like the antisocials and narcissists, people who have this disorder have difficulty recognizing the feelings and needs of others. They also tend to have unstable emotions, on-and-off mood changes, and emotional reactions that are out of proportion to whatever events triggered them. So what is different? Unlike antisocial personality disorder or psychopathy, a central feature of borderline personality disorder is anxiety.

Researchers estimate that 1 percent to 2 percent of the population has borderline personality disorder.[20] However, according to the DSM-4, about 75 percent of those diagnosed with borderline personality disorder are women.[21] It is possible that many of these women are actually antisocial. "There is a gender bias in diagnosis such that women are often labeled 'borderline,'" wrote Dr. Liane Leedom in a Lovefraud Blog article. "These women can also be sociopaths who leave a trail of victimized friends, lovers and children in their wakes."[22]

Diagnosing personality disorders is not an exact science. Research has found that people who were diagnosed with a personality disorder — antisocial, narcissistic or borderline — also had high scores on the PCL-R.[23] This means the disorders frequently overlap, and it is quite possible for someone diagnosed as narcissistic or borderline to also have antisocial traits.

Disagreement among mental health professionals

So psychology researchers call the people who are the topic of this book "psychopaths," and the psychiatrists and clinicians refer to "sociopaths," "antisocial personality disorder," and now, "dyssocial personality disorder." In addition to disagreeing about the terms, experts also argue about what the terms mean.

- Some consider a "psychopath" to be an extreme form of "sociopath."
- Some say "psychopath" describes personality traits and "sociopath" describes behavior.
- Some see this as a nature vs. nurture issue — "psychopaths" are born, "sociopaths" are the result of bad parenting and deprivation.
- Some people use the terms depending on how a person is diagnosed. If psychiatric standards are used, the person is a "sociopath." If the PCL-R is used, the person is a "psychopath."
- Some think of a sociopath as someone who is socialized into an antisocial subculture, such as a gang.

Mental health professionals, searching for possible causes and treatment, engage in nuanced debates with each other about definitions and diagnostic criteria. For example, are antisocial personality, narcissism and psychopathy distinct disorders, or are they different points on the same continuum of abusive behavior? In practice, the behaviors and traits exhibited by individuals diagnosed with psychopathy, sociopathy, narcissism and even borderline personality disorder overlap, so it's hard to tell where one ends and another begins.

All of these disorders are harmful, although not necessarily to the people who have them. People diagnosed with psychopathy or antisocial personality disorder rarely experience distress because of their conditions. It's the people around them who suffer — the people who are deceived, exploited and brutalized. In fact, it's the victims who end up in therapy, trying to rebuild their shattered selves after encounters with these predators.

From the perspective of people who have tangled with one of these individuals, the clinical diagnosis doesn't matter. Our lives were turned upside-down. We lost money, our homes, our children. We suffered post-traumatic stress disorder or other maladies. The point is that we were involved with a disordered person, and we were damaged.

The sad thing is that much victimization could be avoided if people knew sociopaths existed, and learned the warning signs of sociopathic behavior. The mental health profession could really help people protect themselves from these predators by agreeing on a name and definition for this personality disorder.

Public confusion about psychopaths and sociopaths

How bad is the problem? I wanted to gather data to find out. In the Lovefraud DSM-5 Survey, I specifically asked about the name of the disorder. Here are the questions and the results:

Before your involvement with this disordered individual, what did you understand the term "sociopath" to mean?
- Criminal — 19 percent
- Serial killer — 19 percent
- Someone who was delusional — 6 percent
- Person without empathy or a conscience — 20 percent
- I didn't know what it meant — 35 percent

Before your involvement with this disordered individual, what did you understand the term "psychopath" to mean?
- Criminal — 15 percent
- Serial killer — 51 percent
- Someone who was delusional — 13 percent
- Person without empathy or a conscience — 9 percent
- I didn't know what it meant — 12 percent

The correct definition of both of these terms is "a person without empathy or a conscience." This was selected by 20 percent of the respondents in reference to "sociopath," and only 9 percent in reference to "psychopath." On the other hand, half of the respondents thought "psychopath" meant serial killer, and the largest number of responses for "sociopath" was "I didn't know what it meant."

These results clearly indicate that the general public does not understand what the words "sociopath" and "psychopath" mean. If we don't know what they are, how can we avoid them?

Solving the problem: A proposal for a name

The purpose of this book, *Red Flags of Love Fraud*, is to help you avoid exploitative personalities. Keeping these people out of your life is not a diagnostic issue, but an education and communications issue.

Some Lovefraud readers suggested sidestepping the sociopath/psychopath naming debate by referring to these predatory individuals as "abusers" or "toxic." This is not a viable solution. These individuals have a medical disorder. They are not merely making a lifestyle choice.

I am calling all of these exploiters "sociopaths." I am fully aware that "sociopathy," at this time, is not an official clinical diagnosis, and that's fine. In fact, I propose to solve the naming problem by using "sociopathy" as a generic, layman's term, similar to "heart disease." I suggest using the word "sociopathy" as a general description of a personality disorder in which the people who have the disorder exploit others.

Let's compare the term to "heart disease." There are various types of heart disease, like a heart attack, or, clinically speaking, a myocardial infarction. Related conditions are cardiovascular disease, coronary artery disease, and so on. The American Heart Association tells us to keep our heart healthy by not smoking, avoiding fatty foods, and getting regular exercise. The association doesn't tell us to avoid heart attacks by doing this, or avoid strokes by doing that. They provide information that helps us protect our hearts from all dangerous ailments.

With my suggestion, under the umbrella of "sociopathy," the professionals can determine the criteria that define each disorder and craft the actual clinical diagnoses. In the meantime, Lovefraud can continue to educate people about these social predators.

I've talked to and corresponded with hundreds of people who have tangled with these exploiters. Time after time I've heard, "I never knew that people like this existed." This is the problem that needs to be solved — alerting the public that social predators exist. To do this effectively, one agreed-upon term is critical.

"Sociopath" has the advantage of already being in the lexicon, without the serial-killer cultural baggage of "psychopath." People are generally aware that the word has something to do with bad behavior towards others. But, as our survey pointed out, most people don't really know what "sociopath" means. This provides an opportunity for education.

Settling on a clear name for this disorder, or range of disorders, is a public health imperative. Through education, people have learned how to protect themselves from heart disease. Sociopaths cause physical, emotional and psychological injury, illness and trauma. We need to learn how to protect ourselves from them.

If we know that sociopaths exist, and know the warning signs of exploitative behavior, we may be able to escape them before too much damage is done.

Recap

Traits of a sociopath

1. Lying
2. Exploitation
3. Entitlement
4. Shallow emotions
5. Dominance
6. Irresponsibility
7. Need for excitement
8. Antisocial behavior

CHAPTER 3

Sociopaths are everywhere

The number of sociopaths in society is truly staggering. Experts estimate that 1 percent to 4 percent of the population have psychopathy or antisocial personality disorder. That means there are 3 million to 12 million of them in the United States. If the percentages hold true for a world population of 7 billion, then there are 70 million to 280 million of these predators on the planet.

In Chapter 2, I explained the views of various experts regarding identifying and diagnosing social predators. These differing opinions also account for the range of estimates in their numbers.

Researchers who focus on the psychopathy construct use the Psychopathy Checklist Revised (PCL-R) to measure the disorder, which is more stringent than other diagnostic tools. In October 2004, I attended a workshop presented by Dr. Robert Hare on administering the PCL-R. He estimated that 1 percent of the general population would meet his definition of a psychopath as scored by the PCL-R.

In 2008, Hare and Dr. Craig S. Neumann published the results of a study in which 514 people who lived in a particular community were selected at random and evaluated using the screening version of the PCL-R. The study group included European American and African American males and females, all between the ages of 18 and 40. The researchers found that 1 percent to 2 percent of the participants achieved scores that indicated potential psychopathy.[1]

The *Diagnostic and Statistical Manual of Mental Disorders,* DSM 4-TR, published by the American Psychiatric Association, states that 3 percent of males and 1 percent of females meet the criteria for antisocial personality disorder, defined as a pervasive pattern of disregard for, and violation of, the rights of others.[2]

Another estimate appears in *The Sociopath Next Door,* by Dr. Martha Stout. She wrote, "Many mental health professionals refer to the condition of little or no conscience as 'antisocial personality disorder,' a noncorrectable disfigurement of character that is now thought to be present in about 4 percent of the population — that is to say, one in 25 people."[3]

So, depending on the source, 1 percent to 2 percent of the population, or 1 percent of females and 3 percent of males, or 4 percent of the population, have psychopathy or antisocial personality disorder. Then there are the people with narcissistic personality disorder — estimates range from 1 percent[4] to 6 percent[5] of the population. Plus, 1 percent to 2 percent of people are believed to have borderline personality disorder. So using the word "sociopaths" as an umbrella term for people who exploit others, it could include 3 percent to 12 percent of human beings. All in all, millions of social predators live among us — and I mean literally among us.

The United States has the largest incarcerated population in the world — nearly 2.3 million people are in federal, state and local prisons.[6] A scientific review of prisons in western countries found that 47 percent of male and 21 percent of female prisoners had antisocial personality disorder.[7] Applying those percentages to the number of people in U.S. prisons, we can estimate that just over a million sociopaths are locked up. The rest — 2 million to 11 million predators — are on the loose in our communities.

That sounds bad, but actually, the problem is even worse. The prevalence rates quoted above indicate the number of people who would meet the diagnostic criteria for the disorders. *The estimates do not include people who have partial disorders.* Believe me, you do not want someone who is even partially sociopathic as a relationship partner. So in addition to the millions of diagnosable sociopaths, you need to be on the lookout for millions more people who have some traits but not all of them.

Syndrome and continuum

The clinical disorders included in sociopathy — such as psychopathy, antisocial personality disorder and narcissism — are syndromes. That means in order for individuals to have the disorders, they must exhibit all or most of the diagnostic criteria. People who have only one or two traits do not qualify. Each disorder is also a continuum, meaning individuals can have the relevant traits to greater or lesser degrees. This was apparent in the Lovefraud Romantic Partner Survey, where, for example, 85 percent of respondents rated their partners as extremely manipulative, but only 53 percent rated them as extremely reckless.

With each disorder being a syndrome and a continuum, it is possible for people to have some traits but not the full disorder. These individuals are generally abusive in some way. They may be correctly termed jerks or creeps, but their nasty behavior may not rise to the level where they would be professionally diagnosed as personality disordered.

People with sociopathic tendencies, even if they would not be diagnosed with a clinical disorder, make lousy relationship partners. But because their antisocial tendencies are not as predominant, they are more difficult to recognize. They may even have other issues that you can identify and sympathize with, such as addiction. So because they seem to have more human qualities, you may feel like you've encountered a lost soul who, with enough love and understanding, will blossom into a happy, wholesome, caring partner. You may endure a lot of heartache waiting for this person to change, and it may never happen.

Sociopaths inhabit all demographic groups

Here's another reality check: Sociopaths can be found in all demographic groups. They are male, female, old, young, rich, poor, all races, all nationalities, all religions, all sexual orientations, all professions and all education levels. No segment of society is free of sociopaths.

This is demonstrated in the Lovefraud surveys. Basic demographic questions were included in both of them. Our respondents turned out to be mostly heterosexual Caucasian women, and the individuals they described were mostly heterosexual Caucasian men. However, this does not mean sociopaths and victims are primarily Caucasian; the lopsidedness is a result of sampling bias in the research. The surveys were promoted only on Lovefraud.com, and most Lovefraud readers are heterosexual Caucasian women. If a more diverse population were surveyed, I'm sure the results would have been more diverse.

Still, as can be seen in the following statements from the Lovefraud Romantic Partner Survey, all demographic groups were represented in both respondents and exploiters, and all the usual exploitative behaviors were described.

African female about an African male:

THE APPEAL: The beginning was so unreal ... I believed I finally met my Prince Charming ... he swept me off my feet ...

THE END: I found out about all the women, the drug use and all the lies ... I tried to leave several times and could not do it because I craved this man ... we were together for 3 yrs ... that last yr was the worst ... he wasn't paying his bills and I was giving him money to help pay his bills, plus he had a job ... he was spending it all on drugs.

Caucasian female about a mixed-race female:

THE APPEAL: She was 'everything' I 'thought' I wanted, she was ultra charming, ultra caring, ultra protective, ultra kind, ultra thoughtful, name it and she 'acted' that way ...

THE END: I got accused of doing things that I never did. She broke into my email account, read all my emails in the very beginning ... I still don't know the truth about *her other than she is a true evil thing from hell ... she stole over $224,000 of my LIFE SAVINGS ...*

Hispanic female about a Middle Eastern male:
THE APPEAL: It was "love at first sight." He swept me off my feet.
THE END: After physical abuse, I would leave and he would beg me to come back.

African male about a Hispanic female:
THE APPEAL: It was almost as if she picked me and ran with it. I just went for the ride.
THE END: She would "steal" money from me and lie about it. She made all of her missteps my fault. She would expose our kids to danger in attempts to get my attention. She never let anyone get close to her.

Caucasian male about a Caucasian male:
THE APPEAL: Charming and charismatic, sexual, friendly, attentive, fun, affectionate, warm, appeared mature for age, intelligent.
THE END: I became so lost and started to have thoughts of harming myself. It was my lowest point in life. We reunited after a year breakup, I caught him in a lie 3 months after that and ended it for good a few months later.

Asian female about an Asian male:
THE APPEAL: He seemed to be so genuine, and incessantly intellectual. He'd ask simple questions in informal chats and I'd give short simplistic answers but he really wanted to dig deeper. He seemed to be a confident person, which I thought was lovely.
THE END: I know he used his voluntary position at the Catholic Church to steal money. I know he used his position at work to steal people's credit card information. I know he stole an object from work — that's plainly theft. I will still try to prosecute him for rape.

Caucasian male about a Hispanic female:
THE APPEAL: Flew to Chile to meet her. Sex the first
night. Then she immediately professed unrelenting love
for me.
THE END: I slipped away in the night and ran to hide
in Argentina. But she caught up to me on an island off the
coast of Brazil ... and got pregnant as she planned. That
day was the end of my life as I knew it. It is now an end-
less battle until I die to protect my son.

As these anecdotes indicate, sociopathic behavior can be seen
in people of all races and sexual orientations. Respondents in the
Lovefraud surveys also described sociopathic behavior in people
of all age groups.

Youthful start to predatory behavior

Sociopaths start exhibiting predatory behavior while young —
the age of onset for the disorder ranges from small children to
early 20s. Usually, by the time an individual goes through puberty,
sociopathic tendencies are apparent.

Fifty-six respondents to the Lovefraud Romantic Partner Survey stated that they met the sociopath who became a love interest
while they were young — in grade school, high school or college.
Here are two of their comments:

High school sweethearts. After 2 weeks of dating,
aged 15, he told me we would be married. He was
sexually inappropriate but I was naïve and didn't under-
stand.

He was the first guy who made my knees go weak.
He took me back to my dorm after meeting me out one
night, and kissed me good night and that's all she wrote.
Our first real date was a school dance — and he didn't
have enough money to pay for tickets — so I did (the be-
ginning of me paying for nearly everything).

Getting involved with a sociopath at a young age is particularly damaging, especially for those who stay in the relationships. If you're a young person reading this book, pay close attention. You need to know the early warning signs of an exploitative personality, so you can get out of a problem situation as soon as possible. The longer you stay, the harder it is to leave.

Take, for example, the case of "Rosemary." At age 17, she was kicked out of her home and became involved with "Marshall," who was a few years older. "He was handsome and I was young and naïve," Rosemary said. "I mistook lust for love."

Rosemary got pregnant, so she and Marshall married. It was awful.

"I don't think we ever had a relationship," Rosemary said. "Marshall wouldn't even acknowledge my presence in public, even though nights were spent together ... I ended up having three children in three years, all before I was 21. I was with him for 26 years of pure hell. Not allowed any friends, physically abused, mentally abused.

"When my children were 1, 2 and 3, I tried to leave him," Rosemary continued. "He immediately quit his job so he wouldn't have to pay child support. In the early '80s, child support wasn't enforced. I worked two and three jobs for a year trying to handle everything. After a year, failing, I went back to him, reasoning that at least my children would have a roof over their heads and food in their bellies. This decision is my major regret in life. The effect it had on my three children was horrible. One daughter is a sociopath. My son is like his father in the emotional abuse. Because of my decision, my kids think what they witnessed was 'normal.'"

"Natalie" and "Chris"

"Chris" was the new kid in school, and "Natalie" was a shy bookworm. She thought Chris was also shy. Years later, she realized that his bashfulness was an act that he used to lure her. "I fell in love with him at 15 because he claimed to be my best friend," Natalie said. "He told me he would marry me if I waited for him until he was done dating other girls."

So from age 15 to 22, as Chris dated other women, slept with other women, and even married another woman, Natalie was his best friend/confidante/whatever he wanted her to be. Other people told her to dump him. "I listened to them and tried to convince myself that he wasn't right for me," Natalie said. "Other times I flat out ignored them, because he said we were soul mates."

Finally, at age 22, Natalie moved in with Chris.

She was abused. She was raped. She caught a sexually transmitted disease. She became anxious, depressed and suffered from post-traumatic stress disorder. While Chris cheated, Natalie thought about suicide.

"He secretly videotaped his date raping me, losing my virginity," Natalie said. "God only knows how many other times he videotaped me, and other girls too. He had an 'untouchable bag,' a duffel, FILLED TO THE BRIM with blank black video tapes. I never dared to touch them. I know what they are now."

A week after taking her virginity, Natalie found Chris in their bed with his ex-wife. Natalie was heartbroken, but Chris' mother told her, "Don't you DARE shed another tear over my son; he is NOT WORTH IT."

Still, Natalie didn't give up on Chris. Then, one day, she failed to wash the dishes before leaving for work. Later, Natalie walked into the kitchen and found all her knives sticking point down in the linoleum floor. That's when she left.

"The last time we spoke," Natalie related, "Chris told me he had painted his room red with the blood of the 'hooker whose throat I just slit.'"

At 15, Natalie fell in love with the fantasy of Chris. She kept the fantasy alive for seven years, and when she finally moved in with him, discovered the truth: Chris was a monster.

Sociopaths during the marriage years

As you would expect, most of the hookups described in the Lovefraud Romantic Partner Survey took place during the prime dating and marriage years, from ages 20 through 49. Respondents reported the age of the sociopaths at the beginning of their involvements:

- 26 percent were in their 20s.
- 29 percent were in their 30s.
- 25 percent were in their 40s.

In the United States, the average age of first marriages is 25 for women and 26 for men.[8] Sociopaths and their targets fit right in with this typical social pattern. Half of the people who completed the Lovefraud Romantic Partner Survey married the sociopaths. Of this group, 37 percent of survey respondents married sociopaths who were in their 20s.

Unfortunately, getting involved with sociopaths at a young age often means that the relationships drag on for many years. Twenty-eight percent of survey respondents who married the sociopaths in their 20s stayed in the relationship for 20 years or more, compared with 7 percent of respondents who met sociopaths in their 30s and 3 percent who met sociopaths in their 40s.

And, relationships that start when both the sociopaths and the targets are young tend to be more dangerous. According to the Lovefraud survey results, targets who became involved with 20-something sociopaths were more likely to be physically abused, injured and have their lives threatened. And, this group of sociopaths was more likely to threaten or commit suicide.

"Gail," for example, certainly saw violence in her marriage with "Pete," but not right away. Pete was in his 20s, and Gail was younger, when they met at church. Pete, who already had legal problems, played up to Gail's belief that everyone deserved forgiveness. He was also charismatic, physically attractive and extremely focused on Gail.

"I didn't see it at the time," Gail said, "but when I would say we would have to wait to see if things worked out before we could be together, he would completely ignore it and go into fits of rage if I wouldn't give him a date when we were getting married."

So they married — even though Gail had misgivings and her family and friends were petrified. With good reason. Gail filed for divorce after the first choking incident, but Pete promised he would never do it again, and convinced her that it wasn't as bad as she thought. Gail stopped the divorce.

Pete's behavior got worse. "On many occasions he locked me in the house, taking all forms of communication, started the process of killing me, choked me, hit me, spit on me, made me watch him kill an animal with his hands," Gail said. "He was later charged with kidnapping, attempted murder, malicious assault and robbery on me, and child endangerment resulting in risk of serious bodily injury of our 2 1/2-month-old son."

Gail's experience was just one of hundreds of horrific descriptions of marriage to sociopaths that respondents to the Lovefraud Romantic Partner Survey related. Following are more of their stories.

"Emily" and "Chen"

"Emily" was in her 20s and divorced when she met "Chen," who was in his 30s. At first, Emily felt they were too different — Chen was outgoing, confident and fun, while she was quiet and reserved. She worried about being burned, as she had been by her first husband. Emily didn't want to date Chen, but he showered her with attention until she agreed to give him a chance.

"He spoke like a Hallmark card," Emily remembered. "I was so impressed by his what seemed like openness and way with words. I thought he fell for me very fast. He was almost addicted to me. With me all the time. Moved in with me fast. Showed me that money and expensive gifts were not an issue. Promised to take me places and do things I had never done."

Chen made Emily believe that she had found love again. They married, but by the end of the first year, the honeymoon was over. Eventually Emily discovered that her husband lived a double life.

"I believe I was a cover he used to make people think he was normal," she said. "He also used me to manipulate his mother, who wanted him to get married and have kids. I thought he was my husband and father of our son. He had a decent job and worked hard for us. Meanwhile, he had another life with a very full social calendar. He participated regularly at swingers parties, sexual internet websites and multiple dating profiles, pornography, and parties with prostitutes."

After six years, Emily divorced him.

"Wilson" and "Marjorie"

"Wilson" and "Marjorie" where both in their 40s and divorced when they were introduced. Wilson had two young children who lived with him 50 percent of the time, and he paid child support. He wanted a relationship, but not with someone whom he had to support financially. Marjorie was attractive and seemed to be self-sufficient. And, unlike his first wife, she didn't drink.

About six months into the relationship, Marjorie called Wilson — the mortgage company was about to foreclose on her home, could he help her out? Wilson gave her $8,000 and thought the issue was resolved. He didn't know that financial problems were a pattern with Marjorie.

Not long after that, Wilson was at work and thought Marjorie was at home, looking for a job. He was wrong.

"On this Monday, she packed up her stuff and much of mine and moved out," Wilson wrote. "She went to London. I HAD NO IDEA THIS WAS GOING TO HAPPEN. This is where I should have let her go, but unfortunately, I didn't. Eventually, we reunited, got married, and the wrath of hell exploded from there. The marriage lasted eight months and was one chaotic event after another."

On New Year's Eve, Marjorie falsely accused Wilson of domestic violence, and he ended up in jail. Afterwards, trying to figure out what Marjorie was about, Wilson contacted her first husband. This man told him about a second husband. Wilson never knew the man existed.

Marjorie had put her second husband in jail six times. "He told me 'she seeks out men with young children,'" Wilson said. "He had the same situation. Only to find out after the alleged domestic violence lies, that she actually lost custody of her daughter."

Wilson and Marjorie divorced. The next year, Marjorie filed for bankruptcy with $330,000 in debt. Only $175,000 was her mortgage.

Senior sociopaths

Many psychologists and therapists will tell you that sociopaths burn out as they get older and become less dangerous. Don't count on it. It's possible that they may become less physically violent as they age, but they are no less manipulative. By the time they're senior citizens, sociopaths have spent a lifetime perfecting their techniques. I believe they keep exploiting people until they go to their graves.

My con artist ex-husband was 55 when I met him, and was still looking for women to swindle as he approached age 70. A Lovefraud reader told me how her widowed father became involved with a female sociopath whom he met at a grief counseling support group after his wife died. She acted like a sweet little granny, married him and then bled the man of all his money. When the man died, granny already had her next victim lined up.

In the Lovefraud Romantic Partner Survey, 11 percent of respondents reported that the sociopaths were in their 50s when they became involved, and 2 percent — 30 people — said the sociopaths were in their 60s.

"Pamela," a woman in her 40s, had just started working at a golf course, where she met "Bill," a regular golfer in his 50s. Bill was charismatic, educated and well spoken. He told Pamela that he felt a connection with her like he hadn't felt with anyone in years.

They started dating, and Bill paid for everything — dinners, movies, travel. He frequently surprised Pamela with jewelry, although it never came in a box. He hid the pieces behind his back, then placed them on her hand, her arm, or around her neck. Bill even brought her a Rolex watch, and when it didn't fit, had it sized.

"Bill made me feel like a queen," Pamela wrote. "He showered me with attention. I had never felt so beautiful or important in my life. Strangers would tell me, 'You're glowing; what's your secret?'"

The only rough spot for Pamela was that Bill loved to argue. If they disagreed about anything — especially politics — Bill went on a mission to change her mind. "It was a constant source of tension," Pamela said. "He would slowly manipulate everything I said until I would be so confused I would just let him 'win' the issue."

Bill used his skills of manipulation and obfuscation six months into the relationship, when a woman called the golf course to buy a gift certificate for her "husband," who happened to be Bill.

"When I asked him to explain, he went into elaborate detail

about how this woman was not his wife, but had framed him in an embezzlement scheme," Pamela said. "He brought out court documents to prove he was not in any way accountable for her actions. He stated it was all a big misunderstanding and he was trying to take care of the problem."

Well, two years later, Pamela found out that Bill and the woman had embezzled more than $1 million. Pamela ended up cooperating with prosecutors, and more truth came out. Like Bill was still married. Like he didn't actually work, he lived off of multiple women. Like all the jewelry Bill gave her was stolen from these women.

And then there was the sex. Pamela thought it was extraordinary, but apparently it wasn't enough for Bill — he wanted threesomes. When Pamela declined, he put something in her drink, drove her to a secluded house and raped her. She doesn't know how many times this happened; she only has vague recollections. But she did speak with three of Bill's "other women" who experienced the same thing. "If they were not interested in having sex with him and multiple partners," Pamela said, "he would either eventually 'talk' them into it, or he would use the date rape drug."

Bill was convicted of the embezzlement, but served only 15 months in prison. Pamela — depressed, suicidal and suffering from post-traumatic stress disorder — was too weak to prosecute him for the rapes.

Sociopaths in the working world

Along with belonging to all age and demographic groups, sociopaths can be found in all walks of life, and this is apparent by their careers. In the Lovefraud Romantic Partner Survey, 25 percent of the people identified as exploiters were hourly workers, and 32 percent were professionals, including people working in the medical field, the military, education, law enforcement and the clergy. Other employment categories included business owner, student, homemaker and retired. When survey respondents met them, 14 percent of sociopaths had no job at all.

Here is how survey respondents described sociopaths who worked in a variety of occupations:

About a female in the medical profession:

She is a con artist. Lies, distorts, embellishes, mini-mizes, avoids and uses the children as pawns. She also has several "minions" she has convinced that I am bad. She is a social worker/nurse and has used therapists she has associations with and the county system to denigrate me and made up the story that she is "afraid" of me. The only thing she is afraid of is the truth. I know her truth and that scares her for sure.

About a male in law enforcement:

Within a ten-month period, he physically and sexually assaulted me four times. The first time it happened, he cried and begged me to take him back and I did, based on him getting into counseling. He did go to counseling, but would tell me it was my fault. I pushed his buttons. When he assaulted me again, I did press charges. Eventually he was facing some pretty stiff charges and was told he had to retire from the police force. There was also the possi-bility he would lose his retirement, but because he had a "perfect" service record, that didn't happen. Yes, I was stu-pid and took him back each time. The last assault was the worst. He held me hostage in the bathroom for three hours. He punched me repeatedly, spit on me more times than I can count and raped me.

About a female professional:

Everything about her was antisocial and abusive. Once she decided our relationship was over, she continued to string me along with hopes of reconciliation, spending my income without a second thought. The whole time, she was in a relationship with another indi-vidual. She was going to do everything she could to use me up before she threw me away. She would lock herself in the bedroom for hours at a time (I found out later she was videotaping and photographing herself in various sexual acts, then emailing them to her lover), she would intentionally leave me at home with our child and not tell me when she was returning, she lied about trips she was taking to see "friends," etc.

About a male member of the clergy:
Shows absolutely no remorse; his favorite line is, "I don't have to deal with your feelings or emotions." Lies pathologically — for absolutely no reason in some instances. Cheats and steals whenever he thinks he can get away with it and so boldly that often he gets away with it, because no one would believe a "normal" person would be so bold as to tell such a lie.

About a male in the military:
He was a major and I was a private. He was very attentive, charming and handsome. He acted like he was crazy about me instead of just plain crazy. Took a check out of my checkbook and presented it to a car repair place when I went into hiding in an abuse shelter. Beat our son with a strap making welts all over his back. Kept me from leaving the apartment to get help on various occasions.

About a male executive:
Working for same non-profit. He sounded too good to be true. I investigated and it was all true; however, I later learned he blackmailed everyone he stole from or made others legally responsible for his fraud. Very high profile national mainstream media cases. He spent a good year keeping me close. Being a gentleman. Was private, quiet, smart, charming and took over the charity, as I let go of my power to please him.

Sociopaths, in some cases, climb to the upper echelons of their fields, although they often do it by ingratiating themselves with the people who have the power to promote them, and stabbing rivals and underlings in the back. When sociopaths become business executives, they make promises they can't keep, fabricate results, and intimidate or get rid of anyone who might blow the whistle on their actions. Sometimes they get away with it — and sometimes the whole enterprise collapses.

Perhaps the most stunning example of a sociopath who had almost everyone fooled was Bernie Madoff. He was an investment advisor, former chairman of the NASDAQ stock market, and a philanthropist. But Madoff's investment fund was the largest Ponzi scheme in history, in which he generated fake statements indicating steady profits, while using money from new investors to pay returns to earlier investors. When Madoff was arrested in 2008, his fraud was calculated at more than $50 billion. Madoff pleaded guilty and was sentenced to 150 years in prison. Thousands of investors, including major charities, were defrauded.

Although Madoff's case is astounding, he is certainly not the only sociopath among the world's business elite. In 2006, Dr. Robert Hare and an industrial-organizational psychologist, Dr. Paul Babiak, wrote a book, called *Snakes in Suits,* to draw attention to these corporate predators. Dr. Hare, of course, estimated that 1 percent of the general population are psychopaths. But Hare and Babiak evaluated almost 200 high-powered executives using the screening version of the PCL-R. They found that about 3.5 percent of the executives fit the profile of a psychopath.[9]

The conclusion: There are 3.5 times as many psychopaths in corporate suites as there are on city streets.

Where sociopaths meet their targets

When sociopaths are looking for a romantic relationship — meaning an exploitative relationship — they find their targets in all the usual places. In the Lovefraud Romantic Partner Survey, 20 percent of respondents said they met the exploiters in social situations, like bars, clubs and parties. Another 17 percent met because they worked together, or did business with each other. Nine percent were introduced to each other — I'm willing to bet that the friends and relatives who made the introductions later regretted it. Schools, churches, community events — all were mentioned. Nine survey respondents met the sociopaths at the gym, and a dozen met through rehab or 12-step programs. "We met through

Al-Anon Adult Children," one respondent wrote. "I later found out that he did what is known as '13th Stepping.' He went to meetings to meet women."

More meeting circumstances mentioned in the survey: "When I had my car repaired." "Ballroom dance classes." "Libertarian Party Convention." "Met in post office." "Arranged marriage." "Bluegrass music weekly event." "Professional conference." "Beach, where I was a lifeguard." "Met in a store." "My daughter's best friend's dad." "I cut his hair!!!"

Some people didn't even leave the house. A woman whom we'll call "Doreen" was gardening in her front yard when "Roger" walked by and struck up a conversation. Both of them were in their 30s and single. Doreen was taken with Roger's boyish good looks, and his charming, adventurous and spontaneous personality. Still, she wasn't sure.

"My first gut instinct after meeting him was that he was 'off,' and I even said to a friend that he almost seemed like he could be a 'sociopath,'" Doreen related. "My friend said I was just being paranoid, so I brushed it off and continued on. I was in a vulnerable part of my life and was lonely."

Roger piled on the attention with frequent calls, emails and text messages, which boosted Doreen's self-esteem. Within a month of meeting him, she moved into his house. They were together for more than five years, but during that time there were 15 to 20 major breakups.

"It usually was over me finding evidence of something he had done and confronting him," Doreen said. "He would fly into a rage and tell me to 'pack your shit and get the fuck out! This is my house!' I would plead to come back over the following days and eventually, after he'd gotten his thrill out of watching me suffer, he would have me come back."

The danger of online dating

If you think online dating is harmless, know this: 23 percent of Lovefraud survey respondents are like me — we met the sociopaths who exploited us on the Internet. In the Lovefraud Romantic Partner Survey, it was the most common way that sociopaths found their targets.

The predecessor of online dating — personal ads in newspapers and magazines — was once considered the domain of the desperate. But times have changed, and with the Internet being such an integral part of life today, online dating is now mainstream. Research released in 2010 by Match.com and Chadwick Martin Bailey Behavioral Studies found that one in five committed relationships, and one in six marriages, were between people who met online.[10] This, of course, makes online dating big business. According to a report by Jupiter Research, quoted on About.com, online dating is the third largest revenue producer among paid content websites. Revenue is expected to reach $1.9 billion in 2012.[11]

So what do people think about this new way of searching for romance? The Pew Internet and American Life Project released a report on online dating in 2005.[12] Here are some of the findings:

- Of 10 million Americans who are Internet users and single, 74 percent say they have used the Internet in some way to further their romantic interests.
- 37 percent of them — 3.7 million people — have gone to a dating website.
- 52 percent of people who have used online dating services do not think it is dangerous.
- 52 percent of online daters agree that a lot of people on the sites lie about their marital status.
- 43 percent of people who have used online dating services think the activity involves risk to personal information.

The Pew report did not define the term "personal information." It probably refers to a person's full name, address, contact details and credit card information — data that could jeopardize someone's physical safety or lead to identity theft.

But the real risk, Lovefraud readers have found, is the information you provide describing your interests and what you are looking for in a partner. This is what enables sociopaths to snag you. They use the information that you post to portray themselves to be your soul mate.

The problem is not limited to dating sites — Lovefraud readers met exploiters on Facebook and other social networking sites, Craigslist, and other Internet forums. Predators are all over the Internet.

The Internet: custom-tailored for sociopaths

Because of its global reach and anonymity, the Internet is custom-tailored for social predators. It offers an endless supply of potential victims, so the hunt is simply a numbers game. Sociopaths register on multiple dating sites simultaneously. They randomly friend people on Facebook. They just keep baiting their hooks until someone bites.

Anonymity is a core characteristic of the Internet. When communicating via the web, you never really know with whom you are talking, and sociopaths use this to their advantage, pretending to be anybody they want. This has contributed to a surge in blatant romance scams.

Take, for example, the military romance scams. Many fraudsters, based in countries like Nigeria, fabricate identities as soldiers serving in battle zones such as Afghanistan. They steal photos from legitimate soldier web pages, make contact with unsuspecting women, and start online relationships, eventually proclaiming their true love. Then, the "soldiers" ask the women to send money for special international telephones, or to pay for flights so they can meet. The victims, feeling a mix of love and patriotism, often send thousands of dollars, which they never see again. The problem has gotten so bad that military officials have issued warnings to the public about the scams.[13]

It's not just women who lose money this way. I've received emails from many men who have met women on the Internet, believed a pitiful sob story, and sent money — sometimes thousands of dollars — that was gone forever.

How is it possible to fall for such scams? How can intelligent, honest people be so deceived?

Online seduction

The first problem is the electronic communications medium itself. When you meet people in the real world, you notice their height, weight, grooming, voice and mannerisms, and immediately form conclusions about them. Experts believe that 65 percent to 90 percent of human communication comes from nonverbal cues — facial expressions, gestures, body language, tone of voice.[14] None of this information is available in online communication. So what do you do? You fill in the missing pieces with your imagination. The people on the other end of the email or instant message become who you want them to become.

Secondly, deception is easy on the Internet. Someone who claims to be single is actually married. Someone who claims to have an entertainment background really just watches a lot of movies. Someone who claims to be a man is a woman. How would you know the difference?

But because communicating over the Internet is anonymous, it creates a sense of safety. This is enhanced by continuing correspondence. As you send email or instant messages back and forth, you naturally begin to assume that the other person is being honest. Soon, you feel like you can confess your hopes and dreams to your e-buddy — even ideas and desires that you're afraid to share with your family, spouse or real-world friends.

"Emotional closeness and sharing of even negative emotions is one of the hallmarks of computer relationships," said Dr. Esther Gwinnell, author of a book called *Online Seductions*. "Most individuals involved in these relationships have a closeness and connectedness with their correspondent that is painfully missing from ordinary life."[15] Although intimacy is usually slow to develop in face-to-face relationships, Gwinnell says, it's often the first component of a computer relationship.

Dating websites: advertising yourself as a target

Now, let's look at the issues surrounding online dating sites. Your problems begin the moment you sign up. If you are looking for love online, by definition, you are lonely. Sociopaths specialize in targeting lonely people. So simply by registering on a dating site, you are advertising the fact that you are lonely. You are setting yourself up as a target.

Then there's the profile. Besides basics like your age and race, to enhance the chances of a compatible match, dating sites recommend that you describe your education, interests, exercise habits, pets, political views, what you like to do for fun, what you read and other personal details. Although the information seems innocuous, it is exactly what sociopaths use to create a persona to seduce you.

"I see now that he 'studied' me and became the man I wanted in a partner," said "Ruth," about her ex-husband, "Stan." They met on a big, well-known dating site. Ruth soon discovered that Stan was not yet divorced, as he claimed, and uncovered other lies. She even realized Stan had narcissistic personality disorder and broke off the relationship. Still, against the wishes of her grown children, friends and counselors, Ruth let Stan back into her life. "He is VERY, VERY good at what he does!" she wrote.

Ruth and Stan married. "He used my good credit to buy and buy and buy ... including a home on the golf course, in my name only since his credit was so bad," Ruth said. "I lost that house but was able to take what little equity was there to buy myself a townhome (thank God). I discovered an affair after six years of marriage — emails using the exact same words, phrases and LIES he used on me."

In their electronic communications, sociopaths tell calculated lies, based on what they surmise you want to hear. They also shower you with attention, flatter you and offer you a lifetime of happiness. They promise to fill the void — and there must be a void, because that's why you registered for the dating site in the first place.

"Karen" and "Jeremy"

"Karen" and "Jeremy" met on an online dating site. After two months of emails and telephone conversations, when they met in real life for the first time, they immediately kissed.

"It was almost like seeing a relative that I had not seen for a long time," Karen said. "We had this connection, which was formed via email and phone conversations. Jeremy actually told me that night that he was going to make me his wife, that we were soul mates. I am usually careful at initial meetings, and never kiss someone like I did on that evening."

In his emails and phone calls, Jeremy talked about his accomplishments, working for a large, well-known company. "He told me everything that I wanted to hear, that matched my needs and desires exactly, so we seemed matched," Karen said. "What I did not know at the time, was that he acquired this detail on me through our telephone and email communications, and reflected back exactly what I had expressed as my unfulfilled needs."

Jeremy had an overpowering charisma, and kept reassuring Karen that her anxiety wasn't justified, that it was okay to move quickly. "Yes, I was naïve," Karen said. "I wanted the dream of marrying and having a family, a male protector and husband. My biological clock was ticking and he offered me the opportunity I wanted for a family."

They married.

Jeremy did not tell Karen about his criminal convictions. He claimed he had cash flow problems because the renters of his house weren't paying, so Karen paid his mortgage and water bill. At one point, Jeremy tried to apply for a loan using false information about Karen's financial assets, and when she refused to sign the application, he emotionally abused her. When she finally left him, she'd lost more than $50,000, her home and her job. Two years later, Karen learned that Jeremy didn't even own the property she paid the mortgage on — the documents Jeremy had shown her were forged.

20 million to 80 million sociopaths online

Yes, online dating sites have plenty of members who are regular people just trying to make a connection. In fact, after I left my sociopathic husband, I, too, tried Internet dating again, and met a normal man whom I dated for almost a year. Still, the web is full of predators.

More than 2 billion people are on the Internet.[16] It is reasonable to assume that, as in real life, 1 percent to 4 percent of them are sociopaths. That means there are 20 million to 80 million sociopaths online — all trolling for victims 24/7, around the world. These people thoroughly understand the blind spots and opportunities of computer relationships, and use them to take advantage of others. They bait their hooks with fictitious profiles. They work multiple targets at once, until someone actually swallows the bait.

So here's what happens when you look for romance online:

- You notify every predator on the dating site that you are lonely.
- You provide information about yourself by filling out the dating profile.
- You communicate with someone, but 65 percent to 90 percent of the meaning in your communication is missing.
- You pour out your heart and soul, and it feels good.
- The person responds, and you interpret everything to mean what you want it to mean.
- You fall in love with your own fantasy.

Sociopaths are everywhere

Anyplace you go, it is possible to meet a sociopath. They inhabit all segments of society, from the rarified upper crust to the meanest street gangs. Respondents to the Lovefraud Romantic Partner Survey met the people who turned out to be sociopaths in locations ranging from parties to churches, from work to the Internet.

The point is, there are millions of sociopaths among us, and they live to exploit people. These human predators view every social encounter as an opportunity to gain some advantage or snag another target. In the next chapter, I'll tell you how they go about it.

Recap

Sociopaths are in all demographic groups
- Male
- Female
- Rich
- Poor
- All ages
- All races
- All nationalities
- All religions
- All sexual orientations
- All education levels
- All professions

CHAPTER 4

Vulnerable to a sociopath

I have a friend, whom we'll call "Alex," who lost his wife to cancer. After an appropriate period of mourning, he started going out in search of companionship. He knew of my involvement with a sociopath; in fact, he knew my ex-husband. So when Alex had a bizarre experience with a woman he dated for a few weeks, he had questions for me.

The woman claimed to be separated from her husband, although I'm not sure that was the case. She pursued my friend relentlessly, until they had sex. At some point, she made a comment about "a lion needs fresh meat." After that, they spent an entire day together, then she unceremoniously dumped him.

Alex asked, was this woman kooky like my ex?

He told me more, and it sounded like the woman had sociopathic traits, although perhaps not the full-blown disorder. We talked about sociopaths on several occasions. One conversation went like this:

Alex: "What's the first thing sociopaths do when they meet you?"

Me: "Evaluate you to see if you have something they want."

Alex: "What's the second thing they do?"

Me: "Look for your vulnerabilities."

Alex: "And then what?"

Me: "They figure out a way to manipulate you to get what they want."

That's it, the sociopathic MO, or *modus operandi*. First, do you have something he or she wants? Second, what are your vulnerabilities? Finally, how can they manipulate you to their advantage?

Sociopaths specialize in targeting vulnerabilities

Most sociopaths are parasites searching for people to live off of, in one way or another. They plow through life, always on the lookout for targets of opportunity. When they find targets — anyone who has anything that they want — sociopaths work quickly to discover the targets' vulnerabilities. Then they pounce.

With all the email Lovefraud receives, I've heard some truly sad stories: Grief-stricken people who have lost a spouse or a child, and then lose their insurance settlement to a sociopath. Disabled people who are targeted because they get a minimal subsidy from the government. People struggling to care for someone else — like children or elderly parents — who learn that the assistance promised by sociopaths makes their burdens heavier.

And then there are the lonely. Anyone who is lonely for any reason is a walking target for a sociopath.

The Lovefraud Romantic Partner Survey asked the question, "Looking back, did this person appeal to a vulnerability that you had? If yes, what was it?"

Seventy-two percent of respondents said that they did have a vulnerability that was targeted, although sometimes it was nothing more than wanting to be loved, having empathy or being unaware of sociopaths. I analyzed and categorized their answers. Many respondents named multiple vulnerabilities.

Wounded — 20 percent

Respondents said they were vulnerable because they recently ended a relationship or divorced, were in a bad or abusive marriage, or had been abused in their family of origin.

Needed love — 16 percent

Respondents were looking for love, attention and a sense of connection. They wanted to be protected, and needed to be needed.

Lonely — 14 percent

The respondents perceived emptiness in their lives. They had ended a relationship, or had never been in a committed relationship, or their children were grown and no longer needed them, or they had moved to a new community. Whatever the reason, they felt lonely.

Empathy — 14 percent

Respondents were empathetic and caring. They felt compelled to help people, and responded to appeals for sympathy.

Low self-esteem — 11 percent

Some respondents mentioned low self-esteem, a lack of confidence, insecurity, shyness and low regard for themselves.

Wanted a relationship — 10 percent

These respondents felt incomplete. They said they wanted a lover, committed relationship, marriage, family and/or children. For some, the biological clock was ticking — they felt rushed to have a family, before it was too late.

Trusting — 7 percent

Respondents described themselves as trusting, innocent or naïve. Some said they were young and inexperienced. Others said they were honest, moral or religious. They didn't know about sociopaths.

Another 6 percent of respondents had serious problems and needed assistance, like money or a place to live. Or, they had disabilities or medical issues. Five percent of respondents were struggling with their responsibilities as single parents. The sociopaths used the children, by buying gifts or helping to care for them, to worm their way into the families. Finally, 4 percent of respondents were dealing with grief. They had just been widowed, or had lost someone close — a parent, child, friend or relative. They were feeling the void, and the sociopath swooped in.

It's sad, really. When we have problems and need help, we want to be able to trust that offers of assistance are genuine. When we're looking for companionship, we want to be able to believe that the person pursuing us is sincere.

But the truth is that when we're vulnerable, we need to be especially vigilant. Sociopaths are predators, and wounded prey make for an easy kill.

Sociopaths and predatory memory

We are all vulnerable. We all have weaknesses. Somewhere, we all have chinks in our armor — and sociopaths are skilled at finding them. A study published by Canadian researchers seems to indicate that sociopaths have an enhanced ability to spot and remember potential targets.[1]

The researchers created a series of fictional characters using photographs of men and women with expressions conveying that they were happy or sad. They assigned biographical traits to the characters indicating that some were successful and some were not.

Forty-four male undergraduate students participated in the study. They were first given a personality test to determine their level of psychopathic traits. Then they were shown the photos and biographical information about the fictional characters. Afterwards, they were asked to recall the characters. The researchers anticipated that the study participants with high psychopathic traits would best remember useful or vulnerable individuals — the happy, successful male was probably most useful, and the unhappy, unsuccessful female was probably most vulnerable.

Study results indicated that they were partially correct. "Participants with high levels of psychopathic traits demonstrated enhanced recognition for the unhappy, unsuccessful female character; arguably the most vulnerable individual presented in our study," they wrote. "In fact, the high-psychopathy participants demonstrated near-perfect recognition for this character."

The researchers called this "predatory memory."

The study subjects were not criminals in jail, they were college students. The results suggest that social predators go out into the world, spot potential victims and remember them for future use.

Trauma bonds: hurt once, hurt again

One type of vulnerability deserves special emphasis, and that is the trauma bond. This is a psychological phenomenon in which you actually feel attached to, loyal to, even addicted to, someone who has hurt you. According to Dr. Patrick J. Carnes, author of *The Betrayal Bond,* trauma bonds form in situations involving "domestic violence, dysfunctional marriages, exploitation in the workplace, religious abuse, litigation, kidnapping, hostage situations, cults, addictions, incest and child abuse."[2]

If you have experienced any of these circumstances or exploitative relationships in your past, know this: You are more susceptible to being exploited again by a sociopath.

This is what happened to "Stacey." She had just gotten out of a very abusive marriage, and her self-esteem was low, when she met "Don" on a dating website. Stacey just wanted to be loved. Don claimed to be a church elder. "He was very attentive and approached me as he was a counselor and could help me with my issues," Stacey said.

They became romantically involved. "Don told me that once we had sex we were married in God's eyes, and that meant commitment," Stacey said. Actually, it meant that Don was controlling and Stacey was committed — literally.

"Don controlled my life," Stacey explained. "He knew how to do behavioral modification, which means that if I didn't act like he wanted, I was punished, so to speak. I ended up leaving him four times. The first time I went to an outpatient mental health place, but couldn't make it on my own. Second time I was admitted into a mental hospital for major depression, went back to him ... I didn't feel I could make it on my own. Third time, I was gone for a couple of months and felt I couldn't do it on my own ... missed my pets. Fourth time, I had the support of friends who let me live with them for nine months 'til I finally got on my feet."

Don, in the meantime, stole Stacey's house.

Trauma bonds, or betrayal bonds, as Carnes calls them, are complex and destructive, and explaining them is beyond the scope of this book. Here's the point: If you've already lived through a serious betrayal of your trust, you must confront the trauma bond in order to heal and protect yourself from sociopaths in the future. To begin, I strongly recommend that you read *The Betrayal Bond*.

Targeting your best qualities

It makes sense that a human predator will go after your wounds and weaknesses. That's what predators do. But you need to know that sociopaths also target your best qualities, your strengths, and use them to manipulate you.

Compassion, for example, is a vital human quality. Compassion enables us to care about our families and our fellow citizens. Because of compassion, we lend a helping hand, work to make the world a better place, and respond when disaster strikes.

For some people, compassion is central to their character. Maybe this is you. You may consciously perceive yourself as kind-hearted, non-judgmental, altruistic, practicing your religious values or any other variation of a humanitarian nature. Although this approach to life is commendable, it also puts you at risk.

In his book, *Without Conscience,* Dr. Robert Hare writes, "Psychopaths have an uncanny ability to spot and use 'nurturant' women — that is, those who have a powerful need to help or mother others." He specifically mentions women in helping professions, such as nurses and counselors, as easy targets.[3] Compassionate men are also targets. Disordered women are quick to spot, and take advantage of, men who see themselves as riding to the rescue of damsels in distress.

Sociopaths target other parts of our self-image as well. Whatever your strengths — intelligence, reliability, creativity, talent — sociopaths find a way to use them. It may be through flattery, or admiration, or by painting a glowing picture of how well your skills fit into their big plans. They leverage your own character to exploit you.

In my case, I saw myself as a reliable, competent and creative businesswoman. I was perfect prey for my ex-husband's grandiose entrepreneurial plans. He complimented my talents, asked for my opinions, made me part of his projects, and wiped out my bank account.

About the money

Many sociopaths target people in order to bleed money from them. However, when exploiters congratulate themselves on their success, I'm willing to bet that their real source of pride isn't that they got your money. It's that they had the power to control you, so that you gave them your money.

Still, when you have money, it makes you a more appealing target.

In the Lovefraud Romantic Partner Survey, 82 percent of men and 75 percent of women said that they lost money because of the sociopaths. How much? Take a look:

Money lost due to exploitative relationships

Amount	Men	Women
Under $5,000	17%	21%
$5,000 - $9,999	13%	14%
$10,000 - $49,999	17%	25%
$50,000 - $99,999	16%	15%
$100,000 - $499,999	30%	18%
More than $500,000	8%	7%

In some cases, survey respondents were truly swindled by con artists who set out to scam them. One woman and one man each lost more than $500,000 in less than a year. Generally, however, the longer people were with the sociopaths, the more money they lost. Of the women who lost $100,000 or more, 55 percent were with the sociopath for 10 years or longer.

Some sociopaths go after the quick hits. Others sponge off of their targets for decades. The point is, the more resources you have, the more sociopaths believe they are entitled to take.

No apparent vulnerabilities

When asked about vulnerabilities in the Lovefraud Romantic Partner Survey, a small number of respondents — 2 percent — said they didn't have any. Still, they were snagged.

"Leslie," for example, replied to the question about vulnerability by writing, "I am pretty confident in the woman I am; not sure he saw a vulnerability."

Leslie was divorced and in her 40s, already retired and financially secure, when she met "George." He was also in his 40s, and sent her an instant message via America Online. Leslie liked George's personality. "He appeared to be intelligent, attentive, made me laugh, and made me feel like I was the most important person in the world to him," she wrote. She felt an instant connection.

George quickly moved from several states away to be close to Leslie. He told her that he'd owned a successful home remodeling business, and once he became established, he'd do fine financially. Leslie wanted a house remodeled, so she gave him money up front to do the job.

By this time, George had professed his love for Leslie, and they were talking about a future together. So Leslie co-signed a loan for a used truck for George's remodeling business. A week later, Leslie bought a 33-foot motorcoach in her name, so George could rent-to-own it. Then she co-signed for a motorcycle for him — a Harley Davidson. Within a month, he traded the Harley for a bigger, more expensive motorcycle, and later traded up again.

Then George asked Leslie to co-sign for a yacht. Leslie said no.

"When I refused to co-sign for a yacht, he yelled at me that I was NEVER to embarrass him like that again in front of his sons," Leslie wrote. "He was shaking with rage when I told him I couldn't help him get the boat."

Later, Leslie found out that the "sons" weren't even George's sons. One was a stepson and the other was a nephew. And that's not all she discovered.

"Another woman messaged me online to ask me to meet her," Leslie said. "She explained that she'd been seeing George since March ... this was September. She called him on her cell, had him on speakerphone so that I could hear that indeed they were involved. She kept asking him if they weren't getting married. He said, 'So you say.' I, in turn, called him on my phone to ask about the time the next day he'd need to get inside the house he was helping to remodel with me. When he asked if that was all I wanted, he said, 'I love you.' I didn't respond with it back, but the other woman heard all she needed to know that we were both being played. We found other women who had been involved with him at the same time that we were."

Leslie broke off the romantic relationship. When George refused to return the upfront money for the remodeling job, she sued him for fraud.

George didn't pay the loans on the truck or the motorcycle, so because Leslie had co-signed, she was responsible and her credit was ruined. The relationship ended up costing her more than $50,000. And, Leslie discovered that the entire time George was playing her and the other women, he was still married.

Traits in women that increase risk

So how did Leslie, who didn't feel she had an obvious weakness to exploit, end up with George? Why was the predator able to snag a woman who was obviously intelligent and had significant financial resources? Leslie may have had certain personality traits that aren't necessarily vulnerabilities, but did put her at risk of being targeted by a sociopath.

My Lovefraud colleague, Dr. Liane Leedom, used interviews and questionnaires to investigate the personality traits of hundreds of women who had been in long-term relationships with exploitative men. (We do not know of a similar study of men who were in long-term relationships with exploitative women.) The women filled out surveys about their experiences and completed two separate checklists to evaluate whether the men were, in fact, sociopaths. They were.

The women also completed a personality inventory about themselves. Dr. Leedom hoped to discover whether the women had particular personality traits that made them susceptible to sociopathic manipulation. They did — and the traits are not what you might expect.

Dr. Leedom discovered that, as a group, the women exploited by sociopaths were extraverted, invested in relationships and cooperative, and that these traits can be risk factors.

Extraversion as a risk factor

Extraverts are enthusiastic, gregarious and assertive. They like excitement. They don't like boredom. They are energized by other people and don't particularly like being alone. Extraverts are comfortable in social gatherings such as parties, community activities, politics and business groups. They are action-oriented.

Extraverted women turn their outgoing natures into accomplishment. The group Dr. Leedom surveyed included attorneys, doctors, teachers, clergy and business executives. They were powerful women.

When it comes to dating, female extraverts like extraverted men. Because they are so outgoing, in fact, dominant, extraverted women can find more subdued men to be boring, even wimpy. They want a relationship with an equal — a guy who is just as extraverted and dominant as they are.

Who fits the bill? Sociopaths.

Sociopaths, with their charm, charisma and abundant ego, have the type of energy that extraverted women find appealing. And, unlike some men, sociopaths aren't intimidated by the accomplishments of powerful women. Of course, the predators are calculating that the more the women have, the more there is to take, but the women don't know that.

Extraversion, Dr. Leedom explains, becomes the "point of connection" between the sociopath and the woman. This is where they are similar to each other and attracted to each other. A more reserved woman would feel overwhelmed by a sociopath, but an extraverted woman feels like she's finally met her equal.

Extraverted women tend to have a high tolerance for disorder, which enables them to deal with the chaos that sociopaths create. They are also competitive, which, when things go bad in the relationship, tends to make them stay and do battle with the sociopath, when they would be better off cutting their losses and leaving. Some extraverted women are also impulsive, which may cause them to jump into a relationship quickly.

Investment in relationships as a risk factor

Dr. Leedom found that women involved with sociopaths tend to attach deeply. She called this trait "positive sociability and relationship investment." When women have this trait, it means that relationships with other people are important to them, a source of great pleasure and satisfaction. This is especially true of romantic relationships.

Women who are invested in relationships are sentimental. They tend to focus on special moments — and sociopaths, as they are reeling in a target, are experts at creating special moments. Tenderhearted and sensitive to the needs of others, these women listen sympathetically when a sociopath starts telling the sad stories of his life — which may be true, or total fabrications. The women care deeply about how others regard them, especially romantic partners, so they do everything they can to be pleasant and considerate.

Affection is extremely important to women who are invested in relationships. Consequently, they are susceptible to love bombing. When the sociopath pours on the attention and affection in the beginning of the relationship, these women become hooked.

The problem with being cooperative

In her work with victims, Dr. Leedom found that, more than any other temperamental or character trait, the women involved in long-term relationships with sociopaths were cooperative. In fact, they ranked in the 97th percentile for cooperativeness. These women were more cooperative than almost all other women.

What traits are components of cooperativeness? Empathy, tolerance, friendliness, compassion and supportiveness. Women who have these qualities value getting along with others. They are willing to put their own interests aside for the benefit of their relationships, their families and other groups of people that they consider to be important. They see themselves as a part of the whole of humanity. They are altruistic.

This is exactly the type of woman that a sociopath wants and needs. Her abundant empathy, tolerance, friendliness and compassion turn into support for him. He behaves badly, apologizes and blames his actions on the problems of his past. She understands, forgives and resolves to be even more supportive. If she keeps offering unconditional love, she reasons, someday the good that she is convinced lies hidden within the sociopath will blossom, and all her patience will be rewarded with a fulfilling relationship.

And so it goes, around and around. The sociopath keeps manipulating, and the woman keeps cooperating. In fact, Dr. Leedom believes that cooperativeness was the most significant reason why sociopaths targeted the particular women in her study.

What sociopaths really want

In reality, sociopaths only want three things from romantic relationships: power, control and sex. And sometimes, they only want sex in order to enhance power and control.

These human predators keep their true intentions hidden — at least in the beginning. They don't overtly take control by bossing you around. Instead, they almost magically get you to volunteer to pay for dates, support them financially, give them a place to live, boost their careers, invest in their schemes, marry them and have children with them. Despite what sociopaths say, their goal is never to share a life with you. It is to get you to fulfill their needs and desires.

Sometimes, the sociopaths don't even receive sex, money or other tangible advantages for their trouble. That's when the callous objective of power and control is most apparent — sociopaths want control for the sake of control. For example, consider the case of "Suzanne" and "Anthony."

Suzanne and Anthony went to high school together, but neither of them remembered having any interaction when they were young. Thirty years after graduation, they became reacquainted on Facebook. Right away, Anthony sent Suzanne a nude photo of himself, and another photo of his eyes — close up and intense.

Vulnerable to a sociopath

Suzanne was married, albeit unhappily, and Anthony was divorced. "He kept writing me poetry and told me that he would make me fall in love with him," Suzanne recounted. "I thought ... pssst, no way! But he was right; he got way up in my head with his charming personality and deep, emotional poetry."

Anthony swept Suzanne off her feet. He called and sent emails and text messages. He proclaimed that they were soul mates. He asked about her hopes and dreams, and promised to make them come true.

They were in contact for a couple of years. "I stopped talking to him several times and he would always reel me back into talking to him again," she said. "He would tell me to say I would never leave him again. Would accuse me of leaving him for no reason.

"I asked him if we could just be friends, because I could not keep having an emotional relationship with him while I was married," Suzanne continued. "He became furious and subtly hinted at blackmail. I had sent him lots of pictures of me."

Suzanne didn't know what Anthony was capable of. Here's what she did know:

He admitted having sex with hookers. Took drugs and is an alcoholic. Has no contact with his family. Would love to argue and keep me stressed. Talked about wanting to own me. Talked about having sex with me in unnatural ways. Told me I would never be able to get him out of my head. Said I was the only person he had ever loved because there was just something about me. Was always getting whippings as a child for not minding. Buried kittens in the ground with only their heads sticking up and then mowed their heads off with a lawn mower. Had no shame and said whatever he wanted on Facebook, without embarrassment or remorse. Said he wanted to kill my spouse. Said that if I had married him he would have been a better person and would be successful. Has been in prison. Had many women sexually. Talks/flirts with homosexuals on FB. Flirts and becomes very familiar with other people really fast. Has anger is-

*sues, road rage and extreme impatience. Bullies people
and me. Has a Dr. Jekyll and Mr. Hyde personality.*

Here is the amazing part of this story: Anthony did not take
money, sex or anything material from Suzanne. In fact, Suzanne
and Anthony never met in real life during their entire involvement.
It was an emotional affair, conducted via phone and the Internet.
All Anthony wanted was the thrill of seducing Suzanne, and then
controlling her. For him, the game was everything.

Everyone is vulnerable

Many different vulnerabilities, and character traits that are
not usually considered to be vulnerabilities, can set you up for exploitation by sociopaths. You probably saw yourself somewhere
in this chapter's descriptions. At least, I hope you did — it means
that you're human.

The bottom line is, as human beings, we all have some kind of
vulnerability — wounds of the past, dreams of the future, or traits
that enable us to engage in a meaningful way with other people,
but leave us open to abuse.

We don't necessarily want to eliminate our vulnerabilities —
they are also what enable us to have truly fulfilling, loving relationships. But we need to recognize when our vulnerabilities can
be used against us.

That's exactly what sociopaths do, and in the next chapter, I'll
explain how they go about it.

Recap:

Vulnerabilities
1. Wounded
2. Need love
3. Lonely
4. Empathetic
5. Low self-esteem
6. Want a relationship
7. Trusting
8. Need assistance
9. Single parent
10. Grief

Traits in women that increase risk
1. Extraversion
2. Invested in relationships
3. Cooperative

CHAPTER 5

The sociopathic seduction

Sociopaths engage in calculated seduction. When sociopaths overwhelm you with attention and affection, they are not sharing the spontaneous outpouring of love in their hearts. They are employing premeditated tactics designed to achieve their objectives of power, control and sex.

The first step of seduction, of course, is to make themselves appealing to you. The Lovefraud Romantic Partner Survey asked what respondents found enticing, intriguing or captivating in the beginning of their involvements with the sociopaths. Respondents were free to write anything they wanted, and their answers were analyzed for common threads.

The five most prominent themes were:

Made me feel special — 27 percent
    The top response wasn't a trait of the sociopaths — it was how the targets reacted to all the attention they received. Sociopaths piled on affection and expressed their love, which made the survey respondents feel great.

Energy — 26 percent
    The sociopaths radiated a high-spirited energy, an exuberance, a magnetism. Respondents described it as confidence, intelligence, intensity, competence and stability.

Physical appearance — 24 percent

Sociopaths look just like the rest of us—some are ordinary, and others are hot. Physical appearance, of course, is a big part of any romantic attraction. Survey respondents described the sociopaths they were involved with as beautiful, handsome, gorgeous and cute.

Charming — 23 percent

Sociopaths have a way with words. Survey respondents reacted to their charm, charisma, conversational skills, and their seemingly natural ability to always say the right thing.

Personality — 18 percent

Respondents described the sociopaths as pleasant, fun and exciting.

In addition to these themes, 12 percent of survey respondents said that the sociopaths were honest, had good character or shared their values. At least, they appeared that way. Another 11 percent mentioned sexual attraction, and 7 percent said they had similar interests. Four percent of respondents said the sociopaths seemed to be their soul mates, and 3 percent were drawn in by the pity play.

Sociopaths, at first, don't act like jerks

From my personal experience, I certainly agree with the survey respondents. My sociopathic ex-husband, James Montgomery, did his best to make me feel special, and because of his efforts, I was willing to give the man a chance, even though his physical appearance was not all that attractive to me.

Montgomery treated me like gold. His attentiveness started with our initial email correspondence. We met via the Internet, but he lived nearby — I wasn't worried about the pitfalls of a long-distance relationship. During our three weeks of preliminary correspondence — his notes were clever and well written — he made it clear that he was interested in me.

When we did meet, Montgomery was attentive, charming and entertaining. He asked questions and listened to my answers. He was quick to pay me compliments. Yes, he talked about himself a lot, but he was intelligent and intriguing, so I didn't mind — I felt like I was getting to know him.

Significantly, when Montgomery said he would call me, he did. Now, before I met him, I spent a lot of years in the dating game. Many, many times, men said to me, "I'll call you," and then fell off the planet. When Montgomery followed through with this basic courtesy — well, that scored some points.

So, in the beginning of our encounter — I don't want to call it a relationship — he did everything a man who was trying to impress a woman would do. He wore a sport coat when he took me out to dinner. He brought me little gifts. I interpreted these gestures as signs of his budding affection.

Had Montgomery behaved like a jerk — stood me up, acted out in public, flirted with other women in front of me — I would have dumped him. He did none of those things. While he was reeling me in, he was a perfect gentleman.

Of course, I now know that he was on a mission to snag a target, and was simultaneously treating several other women exactly the same way. Apparently, I was the first to bite. He proposed; I accepted. Yes, it was far too soon — but I'd heard all those fairy tales about love at first sight. Why couldn't it happen to me? I didn't realize that all his expressions of affection were empty lies.

It would certainly be easier to spot sociopaths if they always acted like jerks. Unfortunately, they don't, at least not in the beginning. Many of them have excellent social skills. And, they have an inbred talent for seduction.

I was seduced.

How do they do it? How do they get their targets to fall for them? Sociopaths engage in three basic strategies, sequentially or simultaneously, depending on what they discern will work. They may actually test different strategies, and if one seems to be floundering, switch to another. The strategies are attention, mirroring and expressions of love. Within them, you'll see the tactics I described as the *Red Flags of Love Fraud*.

Strategy #1 — Over-the-top attention

Suppose you're an average person in the dating world — not a supermodel, top jock or movie star. As an average person, there are probably times when you feel underappreciated, even ignored. You smile at a girl in a bar, and she walks on by. You have a date with a guy, he says he'll call, and you never hear from him again. Sometimes you may feel that dating is depressing.

Then you meet someone new, and suddenly you're the most important person in the world. Your new friend wants to be with you all the time. Wants to know all about you. Asks questions about your past, your ideas, your desires, and listens carefully to your answers.

Your friend makes no secret of his or her interest in you, showering you with compliments, flattery, gifts and dates. Your friend does everything that a smitten admirer is supposed to do. As one man who completed the Lovefraud Romantic Partner Survey wrote, "She was very attentive. Always sending 'thinking of you' type cards."

If you're an average dater, nursing your share of past disappointments, it's easy to believe such overwhelming intensity is love. You wonder, "Have I finally found my fairy tale romance?" Unfortunately, this constant, over-the-top attention might not signal love, but a sociopath. This is how sociopaths create the whirlwind romance, how sociopaths sweep you off your feet.

"Whirlwind" was, by far, the most frequent description in the Lovefraud Romantic Partner Survey of how relationships with sociopaths began. A total of 28 percent of respondents used the term "whirlwind" or words like it — fast, intense, overwhelming, love at first sight, swept off my feet, an instant connection. Here is how one respondent described the beginning of the relationship — and the end:

> BEGINNING: *Things moved much faster than I thought they should, but I got swept up in it. By the second date, I was his girlfriend. Within a couple of weeks, he'd introduced me to his family. Before a month was over, he'd taken me to his hometown for a weekend visit.*

*THE END: Threats against my life and against the
lives of my friends. Many crimes: PCS (meth), drug dealing (meth), theft, burglary, arson, felon in possession of
a firearm, driving with a suspended license, violating
probation ... I could go on and on. Both his mother and
sister have restraining orders against him and are terri-
fied of him.*

It's enticing to think that someone is so enamored with us that
he or she can't bear to be away from our luminous presence. But
what appears to be enchantment may actually be entrapment.
"Sandra," for example, probably wishes she had known about the
perils of the overly devoted beau before she met "Randy."

"Nobody ever paid that much attention to me in my entire life,"
Sandra said. "Randy lead me to believe we were soul mates, once
he found out how much inheritance money I had stashed away."

Randy bought her a ring within the first month, although they
couldn't marry because he was evading taxes. He moved in with
Sandra within three months. They bought a house within six
months, although it was in Sandra's name, because he was evading
taxes.

What was the deal with the taxes? "He said point blank that he
was evading taxes because they had taken enough from him," Sandra recounted. "That he was Robin Hood taking from the rich and
giving to the poor by getting his employee's job under the table."

Sandra's friends thought buying the house was a bad idea, but
Sandra decided she would take a chance on love. Still, she had apprehensions, which she shoved aside.

That was her mistake. It turned out that Randy was a financial
wreck. He had no bank account and his address was a post office
box. Along with evading taxes, he had committed fraud. In less than
a year, Sandra lost the house and a big hunk of her inheritance.

Strategy #2 — Mirroring your image

Any dating coach or marriage counselor will tell you that for a
romantic relationship to be successful, the partners must be compatible. The two people need to have comparable outlooks on life,

shared values, mutual interests, similar backgrounds — enough in common so that they can get along, keep each other company and grow together.

Sociopaths understand the importance of compatibility. They understand it so well that they make themselves just like you.

This is the "chameleon" aspect of their character, or lack of character. Since sociopaths have no real internal substance — no beliefs, no values, no emotional connections to people or principles — they can put on a new persona as easily as you put on a new coat. They mold the persona to match you.

How do they do this? First, they study you. Today's social media make this easy. Be aware: If you post frequently on Facebook, or write your own blog, you may be giving potential predators all the information they need to seduce you.

"Lucy" met "Amir" on the Internet. The relationship lasted less than a year — Lucy found out that Amir was abusive, deceitful and created drama out of thin air. But that's not how their involvement started. In the beginning, Amir seemed to share her interests and values. Lucy found out why: He had added her as a friend on Facebook so he could discover what was important to her.

"He blatantly lied about his interests so I would think we had something in common," Lucy said. "Mirroring my values, always agreeing with me when I had strong opinions about something, mirroring my interests, being physical very quickly, acting like a know-it-all, lying about everything."

The Internet and social media make it easy for sociopaths to research you, your connections and your interests. Still, sociopaths usually get all the information they need for seduction directly from you, through conversation and correspondence. It happens early in the relationship, under the guise of "getting to know you." It goes something like this:

"So," the sociopath asks, with pitch-perfect sincerity, "what do you really want in life?"

"I want to have a family before I get too old," you reply. (Or, "I want to live on the beach on a tropical island." Or, "I want to send my kids to a top college." Or, "I want to retire while I'm still young enough to enjoy it.")

"That's what I want," the sociopath replies, with a touch of feigned surprise. "We have so much in common. We must be meant for each other."

Respondents to the Lovefraud Romantic Partner Survey put this phenomenon into their own words:

> *Simply convinced me that he was just like me by emulating what I said, what I believed and how I acted. He was my twin!*

> *He and I enjoyed the same activities. We shared similar stories and feelings. We seemed to have the same perspectives on life and love. He became everything I wanted.*

Marriage counselor Gary Cundiff, MFT, believes that sociopaths select targets based on their best qualities. Then, the predators morph themselves into copies of their targets, so that they appear to be perfect partners. In an article on the Lovefraud Blog, Cundiff explained how they do it:

> Using each piece of information, they create the disguise — a mask carefully constructed to look like their prospective target. Flawlessly, they weave a canvas picture of their mark, a tapestry precisely reflecting the brightest, most honorable aspects of your personality, sewing in the most desirable and wanted details, literally stealing your persona, mirroring this image back, without the defects of character, flaws and shortcomings.

> The pathological relationship is a one-dimensional interaction. You fall in love with yourself as presented by this reflecting object. The attraction is irresistible. People are attracted to those who are similar to themselves. By transforming themselves into a reflection of their prospective prey, the sociopath becomes the most alluring figure imaginable, and the propensity to trust that person becomes compelling.[1]

As a result, Cundiff says, "You experience a sense of oneness like none other. At the emotional center of this connection is intensity never felt before, making the appeal and apprehension addictive."

This is exactly what one survey respondent described. She wrote, "Tons of stuff in common, never felt that close to someone before, never felt that kind of attraction and intensity of feelings so fast or strong."

Sociopaths intentionally create the mirage of oneness. To do it, they go after your deepest desires. In their probing, disguised as "wanting to know what's really important to you," sociopaths sneak into your inner sanctum, the core of your being.

They target your dreams.

Fifty-six percent of respondents to the Lovefraud Romantic Partner Survey agreed that the sociopaths asked about their hopes and dreams, then promised to make them come true.

This is perhaps the biggest reason why the deception of the sociopath is so painful. Sociopaths steal our dreams and use them against us. In those heady early days of the relationship, as the sociopaths listen intently, we spill our guts, telling them what we really want, what is really important to us, our most profound desires in life. We think they're listening because they truly want everything that we want. In reality, they're listening to discover the deepest places within us where they can set their hooks.

What better way to draw us in than to promise to turn our most heartfelt aspirations into reality? How can we resist someone who believes as we believe, wants what we want, and seemingly has the capacity to achieve it?

It's a brilliant tactic on the part of the predators. They use our dreams to hook us, promise to make our dreams come true, and we believe them. Then, because we cherish our dreams, we can't let go.

Strategy #3 — Expressions of love

When you and another relatively healthy person begin dating, you are both testing the waters. You are spending time with each other to see if you like each other enough, or have enough in common, or get along well enough, to keep going. Yes, one of you may be more interested than the other, but neither of you has made a decision.

Hesitation is normal in the beginning of romantic relationships. So is reticence. You may be willing to talk about your interests, work and adventures. Maybe even your political and religious views. But early on, you don't usually tell the secrets of your heart, whether they're loving or painful. And you don't really expect your date to spill his or her guts, either. Women, in fact, are accustomed to men who are "tough guys" or "the strong, silent type," and rarely reveal their emotional natures at all.

So when your new romantic interest engages you in deeply personal conversation, confesses the sorrows of his or her past, and professes that you are the person who can heal the wounds, in fact, with you, true love is finally possible, well, what do you think?

You think, "Wow! This person is really opening up to me! I've never seen anything like it! It must be love!"

These predators know that talking about feelings is a sign of trust, trust is crucial for love, and love means they can get what they want. So they talk fluently about feelings — especially their feelings of appreciation and affection for you, the target. And they demonstrate their feelings as well. Sociopaths are masters of the "grand gesture." In the Lovefraud Romantic Partner Survey, 41 percent of respondents agreed that the sociopath "did something extravagant to demonstrate love for me."

It's not that they actually feel the emotions they share with you, or feel them the way the rest of us do. Rather, sociopaths have learned that if they mouth the words of emotion and do a sufficiently convincing acting job, you believe them, which means you are primed for manipulation.

For example, "Bridget" met "Victor" on a dating website. After two weeks of email communication, they met in person. From that point on, Victor called Bridget almost every day, and they chatted online every night for hours. He couldn't wait to see her again.

"Within a couple of weeks he asked me to be his girlfriend," Bridget said. "At that time we started spending every weekend together. He would come over on Thursday nights and stay 'til Monday mornings ... even without being asked or discussing it. He just was there all the time."

Never before had Bridget felt such an instant connection and ease. "Victor made me believe that he loved me more than anything, ever," Bridget wrote. "He had a hard past and had never been loved unconditionally, but he saw that heart in me. I remember my sister asking me once if I loved him and I paused and answered, 'He loves me soooooo much.' Then she asked again, 'But do you love him?' After a long pause I said, 'Of course.' Looking back, I was hesitant ... there was always something that I held back about. He even would say that he was always a few steps ahead of me, but that was okay because he knew I would catch up. I guess I felt like he loved me so deeply that I couldn't give that up."

Bridget always wanted to be married, and that's exactly what Victor promised — he would spend forever with her. Even when Bridget got upset with him, Victor made sure they talked things through so they could move on. After all, they were "forever" — theirs was a special endless love that other people never found.

Bridget's family all liked Victor — everyone except her grandfather. When Bridget's mom told him about Victor, Granddad said, "Sounds like a con man to me."

Bridget learned that Victor wasn't working — he explained that he'd lost his job in a large layoff. He also had bad credit, which was why he didn't have any credit cards. Then, when his sister kicked him out, Victor moved in with Bridget.

At the time, she was having the roof on her home replaced, and Victor got a job as a salesperson with a roofing company. As a favor to him, Bridget allowed him to bid, and his company won the job. Sort of.

"After our relationship ended, I needed some insurance documentation from the roofing company and I discovered he had not worked for the company," Bridget said. "Victor hired guys off the street and pocketed the money. He even provided me with a fraudulent invoice. He also used my credit card without my approval and I discovered he had a warrant for his arrest in another state for credit card fraud."

The relationship with Victor, who promised "forever," lasted a little over a year and cost Bridget more than $10,000.

Research on sociopaths and love

Many professionals in the mental health field are under the impression that sociopaths do not express love. In fact, the first draft of the American Psychiatric Association's *Diagnostic and Statistical Manual of Mental Disorders,* Fifth Edition (DSM-5), reflected this viewpoint.

The draft included a definition of antisocial personality disorder that was substantially revised and improved from the previous edition, DSM-4. However, the introductory description of the disorder contained the following sentence:

> Their emotional expression is mostly limited to irritability, anger, and hostility; acknowledgement and articulation of other emotions, such as love or anxiety, are rare.[2]

Dr. Liane Leedom and I were seriously troubled by the statement. We had both been married to sociopaths, and we were both subjected to abundant professions of love. So were thousands of Lovefraud readers. We were concerned that if this sentence became part of the official diagnostic description, sociopaths could fool clinicians into thinking they were not disordered simply by talking about love. So in the Lovefraud DSM-5 Survey, we asked if the sociopaths expressed love or caring.

The answer was a resounding "yes!" Fully 85 percent of survey respondents stated that the individuals they were involved with verbally expressed love or caring. Not only that, 44 percent said the individuals expressed love every day.

Sooner or later, these proclamations of love usually stopped. Seventy-two percent of respondents agreed that eventually, the sociopaths' emotional expressions were, indeed, limited to irritability, anger and hostility. But first, virtually all sociopaths pursuing romantic relationships seduced their targets with expressions of love.

The updated draft of the DSM-5 further revised the description of antisocial personality disorder. I am happy to report that the statement about these individuals not expressing love is no longer included.

More on how sociopaths express love

The Lovefraud DSM-5 Survey asked respondents to describe how the individuals they were involved with expressed love, and how it changed over the course of the relationship. Again, the survey respondents could write whatever they wanted, and an analysis revealed recurring themes. Many of them have already been highlighted as *Red Flags of Love Fraud.*

Love bombing — 18 percent
Sociopaths lavished attention on the respondents early in the relationship — calling all the time, sending texts and emails, wanting to spend time together, quickly proclaiming love and rushing the relationship along.

Love early then stopped — 17 percent
Many respondents reported that initial loving behavior ended, either suddenly or gradually.

Love through spending money — 16 percent
Respondents frequently reported that the sociopaths spent money on them, buying gifts and flowers, going out to dinner, concerts and on vacation. This, of course, is normal courtship behavior, so sociopaths know what they are supposed to do in order to reel their targets in.

Expressing love through sex — 14 percent
Many respondents mentioned plentiful and satisfying sex, especially in the beginning of the relationship.

From love to hostility — 11 percent
Respondents described how they had been idealized in the beginning of the relationship, but eventually subjected to outright hostility, characterized by rage, abuse, humiliation and degradation.

Lying about love

Hundreds of comments in the Lovefraud DSM-5 Survey made it clear that the undying love proclaimed by the sociopaths was, in fact, only a temporary phenomenon. So when sociopaths speak the words "I love you," are they lying?

The answer probably is that some are lying, and some don't know what they're saying.

When we learn language, our brains learn to associate particular items, processes and concepts with particular words. Most of us have learned to label our warm feelings about a person, and our desire to be with and take care of that person, as "love."

Sociopaths may have learned to label something else as love — perhaps sex, or the pleasure they experience by getting you to do what they want, or even predation. So when they say, "I love you," they may not be lying. It's just that in their minds, the word "love" has a different definition.

Remember, the core problem of sociopathy is an inability to love. If they feel no connection to other human beings, no empathy, they can't possibly understand the feeling of love, nor know what the word means. Some sociopaths even admit this.

> *She confessed she didn't really understand the concept of love and had trouble classifying love; i.e. romantic, platonic, familial, etc. She didn't seem to understand what love was, and stated that. She said she loved everybody. She started telling me she loved me after I told her first, then rarely said it. It became an issue of contention. I'd never experienced this with a woman before — very odd. Usually women are the first to state love and it usually comes after several physical, sexual sessions. She was being honest! She didn't know what the emotion love was.*

But even if sociopaths don't truly know what love means, other stories from the Lovefraud DSM-5 Survey indicate that they clearly know that they are using the expression of love to manipulate their targets.

The sociopathic seduction

One of the most shocking results of the survey was the number of respondents who reported that the minute they were committed — moved in, married or pregnant — the sociopath's behavior towards them drastically changed. Any pretense of love and caring was dropped. This complete reversal of behavior was reported by 2 percent of spouses and romantic partners. Here is how some of them described the startling change:

Affection, sex, expressions of love, gifts, everything seemed almost perfect. Once I moved in with her everything changed. I almost left the first week but hung in for 6 months of hell.

At first, he'd call me a dozen times an hour to tell me he loved me, couldn't live without me, needed to hear my voice; then when we got married, that stopped ... and he didn't tell me he loved me ever again. He "won his prize."

Love was expressed only when I was ready to give up on the relationship and had shown signs of seeing thru her. Later, after she got pregnant and we married, she never expressed it ... she had me right where she wanted me.

Continually professed "love at first sight." Admitted after marriage it was all an act to see if he could "get/catch" me.

In these cases, expressing love was obviously nothing but manipulation. The problem is that some sociopaths can say words of love with so much apparent emotion that they seem to be genuine. "A convincing way of expressing love, such that I was 100 percent sure she experienced it," one survey respondent wrote. They can also keep the charade going as long as they think it necessary.

Many sociopaths, however, eventually get tired of playacting. Then, they may speak the words, "I love you," but they can't be bothered adding the appropriate emotion. As one survey respondent wrote, the sociopath "would say 'I love you' almost robotically, like he was saying good morning, but his actions never matched his words. He would do something so cruel and then say 'I love you' as if nothing ever happened."

Bait and switch

In the end, sociopaths pursuing romantic relationships engage in classic bait-and-switch scams. They seduce you with overflowing attention. They engage in impression management to present themselves as everything you are looking for; in fact, they are just like you. They whisper words of unending love. And once you are well and truly hooked, committed, cohabitating, pregnant or married, or, once the sociopaths are bored, everything changes.

"Julie" and "Ken" both moved thousands of miles from home to take jobs with a particular project. They were both in their 40s and neither knew anyone else in town, so they started hanging out together.

"I did not rush into anything, but within a couple of months I thought he was my best friend," Julie wrote. "I thought my romantic ship had finally come in. Boy, was I ever wrong."

The project was located on an island, and the waters around it were magnificent. Julie and Ken had great fun exploring it together. Although Julie felt misgivings about Ken, she ignored them. "I made excuses for him in my head, mainly because I wanted him to be the man I thought he was, not the man he really is," she explained. "When he said things to me like, 'I use people,' I thought he couldn't possibly be serious, and that no one would say that about themselves. Actually, he was right — he does use people."

Ken told Julie that he had been separated from his wife for six years, but they hadn't divorced. Then, when Ken had been spending six nights a week at Julie's house, his wife came to visit for Christmas. He was obviously still married.

"I broke up with him the first time then," Julie said. "He wormed his way back into my affections and became increasingly mean and manipulative. I broke up with him again after he tortured a cat in front of me. He followed me, actually stalked me, for a couple of months, and then became his 'great' self. Once he lured me back in — it took eight months of very hard work on his part —

he then discarded me in the most hurtful, brutal way possible.

"He fooled me," Julie continued. "He pulled the bait and switch on me. He made me believe he was everything I had been waiting for in a man. He claimed to like the same things I did and to have the same values. He was a liar."

Winning through persistence and pursuit

So how do they do it? How do sociopaths convince their targets to enter romantic relationships? The Lovefraud Romantic Partner Survey asked exactly that question. Love bombing was the most common tactic, which I've already described. The next most common tactic, experienced by 12 percent of respondents, was simply persistence. The sociopaths pursued their targets, wined and dined them, never gave up.

"Cheryl" was subject to both love bombing and persistence. She worked with a man, "Todd," who pursued her for more than a year, even though she wasn't interested. "He didn't stop," Cheryl said. "Just wore me down, even though there were red flags all over the place. Told me we were meant for each other, how rare it was to find the mental, spiritual and physical attraction. I thought, regardless of the red flags, that if this man continued to pursue me with no success for more than a year, he must have a true interest in me."

Finally, Todd's persistence won her over, although Cheryl still intuitively felt something was wrong. "I kept stuffing it down because he seemed so genuine and earnest about working hard to become a better person," she said. "My sister said he was the devil. Others said he was no good for me. I gave him the benefit of the doubt. People can change if they really want to. He said I was such a good example in his life of the right things to do and he needed my guidance."

Still, periodically she tried to break off the relationship. "I would work up the courage to end it, then felt bad — he didn't have a job, or didn't have money, or he was all alone," Cheryl wrote. "I would think, 'What kind of person am I to just leave someone I care about in that kind of situation?' So, after about a week I would jump back into the relationship."

It lasted a few years, then "creepy stories" about Todd slowly started leaking out. "Jail, lifelong therapy, addictions, drugs, medications, being checked into a mental institution," Cheryl related. "I believe there was quite a bit more on a more disturbing level, but by then I didn't stick around to find out."

Cheryl also figured out why Todd seemed to know her so well, and was so similar to her — morally, ethically, spiritually and even similar hobbies. "Guess having access to my emails to family and friends (via work servers) helped with that," she said. Todd had surreptitiously read her emails.

The sociopathic objective

Sociopaths like power, including the power of conquest. They seduce you, pulling out all the stops to make their affection seem genuine in order to exploit you, or entertain themselves, or prove that they still have what it takes to hook a target. As one survey respondent wrote, "He said on a forum (incognito) that he manipulated women until they loved him, then he was done and could leave them."

Essentially, sociopaths want to win, although what exactly constitutes winning changes with their circumstances and mood.

People with normal human emotions find such behavior impossible to understand. How can someone do this? Bewildered targets of sociopaths often ask Dr. Leedom, "What did he really feel? What did he want from me?" She addressed these questions in a post on the Lovefraud Blog:

> This question is easy to answer intellectually, but very hard for victims to accept emotionally. There are three pleasures we get from our love relationships. The first is pleasure in affection. The second is sexual pleasure. The third is pleasure associated with dominance and control. Sociopaths experience sex and dominance as enormously more pleasurable than affection. Therefore, they are in relationships to get sex and power, pure and simple.[3]

Take, for example, the case of "Felicia" and "Tom," who met

on a dating website. Felicia was divorced after a 30-year marriage in which she was both ignored and verbally abused. She was starved for affection, and Tom, who was in his 40s, provided it. Here's how Felicia described his attention:

"Intense/multiple daily emails, quickly sent me phone numbers of his parents and sister for 'references,' sending Xmas gifts, having a ton of expensive flowers delivered (sigh, my weakness ...), calling me 'just to check in,' chatty, sharing hopes/dreams that mirrored mine, had manners, was highly educated, appeared responsible, claimed to be an open book, had same job for 30 years, acted caring, warm, decent and loving."

But even with all the attentive emails, Tom respected Felicia's boundaries. "Tom always wanted me to feel 'comfortable,' so he never really rushed/forced me into the next phase," Felicia said. "This so thoroughly disarmed me, I fell head over heels completely and thoroughly!"

Felicia was attracted to Tom's intelligence, along with his manner of writing and speaking. "He was getting a second master's degree in theology," she wrote. "He was industrious and capable. Used a lot of 'we' statements ... I had catapulted into a state of extreme limerence such as I've never known before. I wanted to die in his arms someday and even have his baby, despite the fact that I was 54 and had had a hysterectomy! I thought/talked about him *constantly*!!!"

Felicia felt this incredible passion for Tom — even though she didn't meet him in real life for more than a year. And, before they met, she discovered that Tom was not faithful to her.

Tom actually forwarded to Felicia an email from the dating site where they met that suggested his newest matches. He told Felicia that since he had met her, the "woman of his dreams," he was no longer interested in anyone else. Tom didn't realize that at the bottom of the email was his password to the dating site. Felicia debated — momentarily — then decided to access Tom's account. She discovered that Tom was lying. He was, in fact, corresponding with several other women, even trying to meet one of them.

Felicia was crushed, confused and furious, but didn't accept what she had learned. "I was just heartbroken over the lie/betrayal, yet I mentioned nothing to him except that I had had a 'bad dream' that he was cheating/lying to me," she said. "His response was anger/denial. 'Why, how could you think of such a thing when I call you constantly, I truly love you and would never hurt you?' Blah, blah, blah. And, foolishly over another six months, I shelved what I had found out. We met in person. He appeared to still be The Man of My Dreams!!! I was in love! He was in love, too. We got married two months later ... DUH!"

After they married, Felicia discovered that Tom was, in fact, cheating on her — with both women and men. He was secretly into pornography, and his sexual demands made her uncomfortable. Felicia became so anxious, depressed and sick that she considered suicide.

Tom didn't take any money from Felicia. In the end, the seduction was nothing but a game.

Recap

Why targets found the sociopaths enticing
1. Made me feel special
2. Energy
3. Physical appearance
4. Charming
5. Personality

Sociopathic seduction strategies
1. Over-the-top attention
2. Mirroring your image
3. Expressions of love

CHAPTER 6

Sociopathic sex and bonding

"Young, handsome, attentive — Best. Sex. EVER." That's how "Jane" explained why she found "Kyle" so appealing. Jane was a professional in her 30s and unhappily married. Kyle, in his 20s, worked sporadically. Jane didn't care. "We began as 'friends with benefits.' Very intense. Best. Sex. EVER." Yes, she wrote it again.

Jane's intuition told her that the relationship with Kyle was not a good idea. "I brushed it aside as being paranoid," she said. "Besides, it was just sex — at first." Friends also warned her not to get involved. Her reply: "I know I'm stupid, but the boy can f*ck."

The relationship continued for more than five years. Oh, there was a break for a year and a half, after Kyle's newest baby mama called. Jane and the woman talked for hours, finding out plenty about Kyle's adventures that neither was aware of. But then Kyle remembered Jane's phone number, and they got back together. Bad idea.

The relationship cost Jane more than $10,000. She incurred debt. Kyle cheated on her. She became infected with a sexually transmitted disease. The stress of the relationship made her ill.

Eventually, Jane had to admit the truth. Kyle was a "huge liar. Even about things that didn't matter. Sex/porn addict. Huge user. If you didn't serve a purpose for him, then he didn't need you."

Rating sex with sociopaths

People who have had sex with sociopaths almost always rave about it. "Swept off my feet by the most intense sexual experience," wrote one respondent to the Lovefraud Romantic Partner Survey. The sentiment was echoed over and over again, as can be seen in the answers to the survey question, "If you had sex with the individual, how would you rate it?"

Sex with sociopaths

Extraordinary	30%
Satisfying	15%
Dissatisfying	6%
At first satisfying, later dissatisfying	30%
He/she was satisfied, I was not	12%
Abusive	4%
Not applicable	3%

These responses show that 75 percent of survey respondents rated the sex as satisfying or more than satisfying, at least in the beginning of the relationship.

Why are sociopaths so hot in bed?

First of all, they're born that way. Sociopaths have a lot of energy. They crave excitement and stimulation — it's an integral part of the disorder. They're always looking for the next thrill. Sex, of course, is one of the most stimulating activities a human being can enjoy. Sociopaths want it. They want it early and often. So they start young and engage frequently.

The flip side of relishing excitement is that sociopaths get bored easily. So although conventional sex with a steady partner is okay for a while, what they really want is variety in their partners and sexual experiences. So they push the boundaries of what their partners find acceptable. If the partners won't do what sociopaths want, they find someone who will. When normal sex is no longer interesting, they seek the taboo.

And, they seek aggressively. All sociopaths, both male and female, have high levels of testosterone. This hormone affects behavior in many ways. One is that it drives people to compete for sex partners and then mate with them. In sociopaths, high testosterone means high pursuit of sex.

Here's another way in which sociopaths are hard wired for sex: Besides craving excitement, they are also born without fear or shame. Consequently, they fail to develop guilt, inhibitions, a conscience or a sense of morality. Social proscriptions against particular acts mean nothing to them. They don't care about the discomfort of their partners either.

So what does all this mean for sociopaths and sex? They have voracious appetites, they get a lot of practice and anything goes. In pursuit of their desires of the moment, some engage in coercive sex, including rape.

No such thing as "just sex"

Jane was sleeping with Kyle, against her better judgment. She rationalized it as "just sex." Here's what you need to understand: "Just sex" doesn't exist.

"Martin," a man in his 30s, went through a terrible break-up. Afterwards, he met "Brenda" on Craigslist for NSA sex — that's no strings attached. But their involvement turned into a dating relationship that progressed much faster than Martin wanted.

"Brenda appeared to have a big, open, loving heart," Martin said. "She was very funny and charming, with a sharp, sarcastic sense of humor; she seemed to want the same things out of life and a relationship that I wanted."

Two months into the relationship, Martin broke up with Brenda — he knew he hadn't recovered from his previous girlfriend. "She gave me three weeks of space, then showed up at my job one day, looking like a million bucks, and made a date with me," he said. Nine months later, they married. They were together for more than five years, but it didn't go well for Martin. The relationship cost him more than $100,000. He lost his home, incurred debt and declared bankruptcy. He suffered post-traumatic stress disorder.

"I am an old-school Southern gentleman, and I need a woman to support, worship, protect, even fight and die for," he explained. "She was happy to be all those things in order to 'get' me, but unwilling to allow me to indulge in them once we were married — total false advertising."

Even the sex didn't last. Martin was one of the survey respondents who rated it as at first satisfying, later dissatisfying. Brenda's sexual demands actually made Martin uncomfortable. She cheated. So how was he drawn into the relationship in the first place?

"I can't even say," Martin related. "I just fall back on an old cliché: She got her hooks in me and didn't let go."

One of the hooks was certainly sex. Sex is a big part of the human bonding process, which is a normal part of life, love and the continuation of the species. Sociopaths instinctively know how to hijack the bonding process in order to capture and eventually control their targets. That's why it is important to realize that sex is never just a physical function. Sex helps to create a connection between you and your partner, a connection that may be wonderful — or may be manipulated to your detriment.

Three stages of love

So how do human beings bond? How does a connection between people progress into love? Scientists have learned that several psychological and biological processes are involved. My colleague, Dr. Liane Leedom, explained the processes in multiple articles on the Lovefraud Blog. The following information summarizes her explanations.

First of all, love has three stages: attraction, pleasure and bonding.

In the attraction phase, you are looking for a partner, or at least receptive to the idea of finding a partner. Attraction involves the senses, primarily sight and smell. When you like someone's physical attributes, it's a big step toward considering that person as a potential partner. This doesn't mean everyone has to be a supermodel in order to be attractive — luckily, we all have different ideas about what is physically appealing. In fact, you may not be able to identify why someone is attractive to you — perhaps the person reminds you of an important individual from your past. As Dr. Leedom points out, "The unconscious mind plays a big role in our partner selection process."[1]

Next, if things go well, comes the pleasure. Because of your attraction to Mr. or Ms. Right, you feel excited, your pulse races, you have butterflies in your stomach. You want this person to be part of your life. Now, suppose the person also wants you. Mr. or Ms. Right agrees to spend time with you; in fact, he or she showers you with attention and affection. You are thrilled — you have obtained the object of your desire. This provides you with pleasure, which is the second stage of love.

The third stage of love is bonding. Your desire for an individual has been rewarded, and you have experienced pleasure. Then, just like a laboratory rat pressing a bar for food, you become motivated to keep repeating the pleasure. You develop a compulsion to be with your new romantic partner. This is called attachment — you unconsciously feel compelled to seek proximity to your love interest. Of course, you want to physically spend time with the individual, but any form of contact is considered proximity, such as phone calls, texts and emails. The more contact you have, the more you feel rewarded and the more you keep repeating the behaviors that bring what you want — the attention of Mr. or Ms. Right. And each time you are rewarded, the bond that you feel with the person is strengthened.

The biology of bonding

The stages of love are associated with certain chemicals and activities in the brain. Testosterone is important in the attraction stage. This hormone is the lust drug — it drives both men and women to pursue and compete for mates.

The pleasure stage involves brain chemicals such as endorphins and dopamine. Endorphins are produced during excitement, love and orgasm, and generate a feeling of well-being. Dopamine has many functions in the brain. In relation to bonding, dopamine creates feelings of enjoyment, and the motivation to engage in behavior that will provide enjoyment. Dopamine is released by rewarding experiences such as food and sex. Cocaine increases dopamine, which is why the drug produces feelings of well-being and euphoria. Therefore, dopamine is closely associated with reward-seeking behavior, including addiction.

In the bonding stage, another hormone becomes important. It's called oxytocin (not to be confused with OxyContin, the pain relieving drug). This neurotransmitter has been called the "cuddle chemical" and the "love hormone." When oxytocin is released in the brain, it increases feelings of trust, contentment and calmness, and reduces fear and anxiety.

Oxytocin has long been associated with female sexuality and childbirth — it is released during orgasm and labor, and it facilitates breastfeeding. This hormone serves a normal and important function in the human bonding process — it makes us feel calm and trusting with our mates. Nature probably gave us oxytocin so that we want to stay with our partners to raise children, thus helping the survival of the species.

But scientists have found that oxytocin plays important roles in other human interactions. First of all, both males and females have oxytocin, and experience its effects. Secondly, sex and childbirth are not required for oxytocin to be released — hugging, touching and social interactions involving trust also cause oxytocin to enter the brain.

And what does oxytocin do? "Researchers studying rodents have actually pinpointed the molecular mechanism responsible for oxytocin's action in another area of the brain responsible for memory, the hippocampus," Dr. Leedom explained. "Oxytocin binding to its receptor induces production of another protein, pCREB. This protein acts to enhance plasticity and long-term memory. The long and the short of it is that oxytocin produces a rewiring of the brain! When you love someone, your love changes the wiring in your brain."[2]

What does all this mean? Trust, love, intimacy and sex change your brain. That's why there is no such thing as "just sex." Anytime you are emotionally intimate with someone, and especially when you have sex, you are building a bond with that person. The more intimacy and sex you have, the stronger the bond. You are flooding your brain with endorphins, dopamine and oxytocin. These chemicals increase your pursuit of the reward — Mr. or Ms. Right — and change your brain to be more trusting of that person.

Now, here's the scary part: This information does not apply to sociopaths. Research suggests that the oxytocin system in sociopaths may be dysfunctional. Sociopaths do not trust and do not bond. But they are very good at pretending that they do.

Believing in love

You've probably heard of the "placebo effect." When drug companies are testing new medicines in clinical trials, they give some patients the actual drug, and others a "sugar pill," or placebo, that has no pharmacological effect. Then, by comparing the effects on those who took the real drug and those who took the placebo, they can measure what the real drug actually does.

Physicians and researchers have long known that people in clinical trials frequently experience the benefits of the drug, even though they are taking the placebo. Because patients *believe* they are taking the drug, they *believe* they will get better, and they do.

This is not just an imaginary improvement. Research has shown that when people believe they are receiving medication, their brain chemistry changes, even though they aren't actually receiving the drugs. In other words, belief can be just as strong as actual medication. Your thoughts affect the structure of your brain.[3]

Why am I bringing this up? Because the same thing happens in romantic relationships. If you are attracted to Mr. or Ms. Right, and you feel the pleasure of having your interest reciprocated so that you form a love bond, you experience all the psychological and biological effects of attachment — even if the object of your affection is a sociopath who is toying with you.

"Sociopaths and psychopaths are con artists," Dr. Leedom wrote. "They entice others to form attachments to them through deception and trickery. The problem is that our unconscious minds do not distinguish between attachments made after deception and those made legitimately."[4]

Therefore, the sociopath says, "I love you," and you believe it. The experience is very real to you, you form a love bond, and your brain is rewired — even though the sociopath doesn't love you at all.

From love bond to addiction

Sociopaths pour on the charm, proclaim their love and get you into bed. Then, as you become more and more attached, they disappear. Or they ignore you. Or they pick a fight. What are they doing? They are intensifying your love bond.

Just as sociopaths instinctively know to hook you with pleasure in the beginning of the relationship, they also know that they can make you even more attached by threatening the relationship.

This seems counterintuitive. If someone is giving you a hard time, why would you want to continue your involvement? The answer comes from addiction research. Scientists have discovered that although pleasure is required to establish a behavior pattern, it is not required to maintain it.[5] So once a love bond is formed, it stays in place, even when the loving behavior disappears. This is Nature's way of keeping people together. If parents split up at the first sign of trouble, the survival of children would be in doubt. But it also explains why victims of domestic violence find it so hard to leave — even though they are being abused, the original love bond is still in place. Victims feel the compulsion to stay with the abuser.

Even without violence, sooner or later, relationships with sociopaths get rocky. Perhaps the sociopath engages in lying, stealing or cheating. For you, the sociopath's callous actions create fear and anxiety. But instead of driving you away from the sociopath, *anxiety and fear actually strengthen the psychological love bond.*

What do you do? You turn to the sociopath for relief. You ask what is wrong. You try harder to make him or her happy. Your goal is to get back to the heady pleasure that you felt in the beginning of your relationship.

In response, the sociopath may blame you for whatever the problem was and accept your offer to try harder. Or, he or she may apologize profusely and promise to change. You, feeling bonded to the sociopath, want to believe the reassurances, so you do. Then the two of you have make-up sex, which releases all those feel-good brain chemicals, relieving your fear and anxiety and reinforcing the love bond again.

Then the whole cycle repeats. Eventually your relationship becomes a vicious circle of bonding, anxiety, fear, relief, sex and further bonding. The longer it goes on, the harder it is to escape.

For you, the love bond becomes an addiction. Dr. Helen Fisher, who researches love extensively, believes that all romantic love is addictive.[6] But being addicted to loving a sociopath can only end badly and painfully.

This is what happened to "Bonnie." For two years, she and "Ray" acted together in a local theater group. Then the theater director, who was Ray's friend, wrote an original play. Ray told the director that he was in love with Bonnie, so the director coerced her to play Ray's romantic opposite.

Although she was 29, Bonnie felt naïve and introverted. Ray was the first man to pay attention to her. She was starved for affection, and believing that Ray really did love her, focused more on the fact that he wanted her, rather than on asking herself if she wanted him.

They moved in together. Then Bonnie discovered that Ray went back to his ex for sex, and moved out. But Ray cried and begged until Bonnie returned. This became a pattern — roughly every two weeks, Ray would leave, then return, claiming to be confused. Bonnie chose to believe him. Years later, however, she realized what Ray was doing.

"He was deliberately 'training' me to have to go through the feelings of loss, and the relief of his coming back," Bonnie explained. "This process was like being a yo-yo, and it wreaked havoc with my self-esteem, but ultimately, he knew I'd rather be relieved than depressed. This is how he coerced me not to break it off forever — it was too painful to go through that every time!"

So what happened? Bonnie and Ray married and had a child. In the 10 years they were together, Ray forged her name on tax returns and used her social security number to commit identity theft. After Bonnie left him, he made death threats and hired thugs to beat her up. He broke many restraining orders, and when their daughter was 12, coerced the girl away. The daughter was sexually and physically abused by her half-brother, Ray's son, but this didn't bother Ray. She also attempted suicide several times and became addicted to heroin.

"He had absolutely no conscience or feeling, such as empathy, for others," Bonnie said. "Ray has worked diligently to destroy our lives, until Child and Family Services started an investigation on him. After that, the sociopathic behaviors stopped."

Sociopaths and sex

Because sociopaths do not experience the emotion of love, many of them assume that sex is love. So when they say, "I love you," what they may really be saying is, "I want to have sex with you." Or the statement "I love you," coming from the mouth of a sociopath, is just a strategy to manipulate you into bed. They've learned that the phrase is more socially acceptable — and also more likely to get the result they want, which is sex.

"He saw sexual intercourse as love," commented a respondent in the Lovefraud DSM-5 Survey. Another wrote, "He expressed love in a sexual nature. Nothing else at all. All gifts, cards, expressions of love were intended to get me in bed. That is it!!"

Sociopaths want the physical sensation of sex. Most human beings want and enjoy sex, and at certain times of our lives — like the young adult years — many of us may think it's an end in itself. But sociopaths never emotionally mature, never experience the joy of truly caring for someone else. So after they've been with you for awhile, many simply stop pretending that they feel love and go directly for sex. In the Lovefraud Romantic Partner Survey, 28 percent of respondents agreed with the statement, "It seemed that the individual only wanted sex."

Here's how one woman described her experience:

For the first three months of the relationship we were "committed." He did and said a lot of sweet things and totally included me in his life with his friends and family. Then, three months later, he downgraded me to a booty call by saying that he doesn't want to be in a relationship at this time, it doesn't fit with his lifestyle. But we could still be friends and still see each other.

I agreed to try things his way (never again) because

*by then I had some feelings for him. He stopped doing all
of the "sweet" things he did at the beginning and stopped
taking me out on dates or spending ANY time with me
other than to have sex. At my place on HIS timeframe.*

*He stopped being nice overall and whenever I ob-
jected to this type of treatment, he would always say he's
sick of hearing my "mouth." Tried to flip the script by saying that my "mouth" was the problem and that's why he
stayed away and didn't do those things anymore, forget-
ting it was his bad treatment of me on the front side that
caused the "mouth" to activate. He would say sweet
things to stop a fight to further his sex agenda with me.*

Search for sexual variety

In their pursuit of sexual variety, sociopaths seek all kinds of
partners, and all kinds of experiences.

We used to call people who slept around "promiscuous." Researchers Steven W. Gangestad and Jeffrey A. Simpson developed
a concept called "sociosexual orientation." They said that in regard
to sexuality, human beings generally fit into two groups: Those
who require a relationship and love before engaging in sex with a
person have what the researchers termed a "restricted sociosexual
orientation." Those with an "unrestricted sociosexual orientation"
are quite comfortable having sex with one-night stands, multiple
partners and with strangers.[7]

Some people who have an unrestricted sociosexual orientation
are simply free spirits. It was a popular approach to sex during the
"free love" years of the 1960s and 70s, before AIDS became a
worry. Further research on this personality type, however, has
shown that unrestricted sociosexual orientation tends to be associated with grandiosity, a lack of agreeableness and a tendency to
lie, especially in men.[8]

Not surprisingly, sociopaths have unrestricted sociosexual orientations. Because they also have no conscience and lie to the extreme, they frequently engage in deceptive sexual strategies.

In today's society, most people make their own decisions

about what they want out of sex. If some people enjoy activities that are different from typical sexual experiences, and their partners agree, that's fine — as long as everyone involved is a consenting adult. But when individuals are not honest about their proclivities and desires, and engage in behaviors surreptitiously, unknowing partners are betrayed and damaged. And, due to sexually transmitted diseases, their health and very lives are at risk.

This is what I experienced. While seducing me, my sociopathic ex-husband, James Montgomery, admitted that he'd cheated on previous romantic partners, and had sexual relations with many, many women. But after meeting me, he declared, he was certain that he would never feel the need to stray again. And before we ever became intimate, I asked Montgomery if he had been tested for AIDS. He claimed that he had tested negative, and added, "There's not a gay bone in my body!"

Well, he lied. When I left him after two and a half years, I learned a lot about his sexual activities:

- He had sex with at least six other women during our relationship.
- He was heavily into Internet porn.
- He solicited gay male prostitutes.
- He tried to arrange threesomes and looked for swinging couples.
- He advertised online for sex. He wrote that he was jaded about sex with women, and desired a man who wanted to experience sex like a woman — the thrill of the totally forbidden.
- He was not tested for AIDS.

While we were married, believing that my husband was monogamous, I consented to unprotected sex. I did not consent to the risk that I was subjected to due to his cheating.

It is a common problem with sociopaths. In the Lovefraud Romantic Partner Survey, many respondents reported that their sociopathic partners were deceptive about sex:

- 75 percent said their partners cheated on them.
- 46 percent found that the individuals were secretly into pornography.
- 40 percent said that the sociopath's sexual demands made them uncomfortable.
- 20 percent became infected with a sexually transmitted disease.

Almost half of survey respondents reported that the sociopaths they knew were "secretly into pornography." An interest in pornography does not automatically make someone a sociopath. Plenty of people — men and women — enjoy looking at pornography from time to time. With sociopaths, however, the interest in pornography is often extreme, both in quantity and the level of deviance. "Sick stuff," commented one survey respondent. "He was very heavy into pornography and his habits surrounding this just kept getting more extreme," wrote another.

Always looking for the next thrill may translate into more and more deviance and risk-taking. Many survey respondents were severely disturbed to discover what their partners were really doing sexually, such as:

He would answer Craigslist ads for sex, not just with hookers but trannies and all sorts of strange types of sex.

He was exploiting women on lesbian sperm donor sites, offering sperm when he was having unprotected sex with men on swinging sites.

Sociopaths, sex, power and control

With all this discussion of intense desires for sex, you might be thinking that sociopaths are slaves to their sexual urges. They're not — sociopaths are quite capable of abstaining when it suits their purpose. Sometimes, they even lose interest in physical relations. Many men and women who completed the Lovefraud DSM-5 Survey said that, after the initial sexual exuberance, the sociopaths withheld sex from them.

This happened to "Vanessa." When she first met her husband, "Keith," he expressed his love verbally and physically. Six months after moving in with her, he refused to have sex, refused to seek counseling and wouldn't tell his wife what was wrong. Vanessa thought it might be impotence, so she learned to live without. Then she discovered his affair. It turned out that Keith had cheated throughout their 17-year marriage — while refusing to touch her.

Why would Keith do that? Maybe all he ever wanted from Vanessa was a place to live. Or maybe he decided that denying his wife sex would enhance his ability to get what he wanted from her. Because as much as sociopaths want sex, they want control more.

For sociopaths, sex always has an agenda. Sometimes the agenda is simply finding a partner who will enable them to release their physical urges. Sometimes they embark on a sexual conquest to entertain themselves. But often, sociopaths view sex as a means to an end. When you can give them something that they want, sociopaths know that if they hook you sexually, they have a much better chance of getting it. Sex is just something to be used in order to achieve their objective, whatever that is.

"Margaret" explained that when her husband, "Hank," was in full manipulation mode, he told her how much he loved her and was sexually seductive. Then, when Margaret asked him to contribute to their marriage — perhaps by getting a job — Hank would get angry and take off to be with other women, leaving Margaret with all the financial responsibilities.

"When he wanted to come back, he would do a full-court press to show how much he loved me by crying and saying how he knew he was in the wrong," Margaret said. "Called all the time, constant sexual expression of love and when he had me hooked again, he would stop being sexually expressive."

Hank would get bored, leave, and sooner or later, beg to return again, promising his love to Margaret. The cycle repeated over and over.

"He kept me constantly off balance by loving me so much and then taking off, but coming back and begging me to take him back," Margaret said. Hank, it seemed, just wanted a place to live between his flings with other women. He used promises of love and sex to convince his wife to provide it.

The pregnancy trap

When they really want to lock you in, both male and female sociopaths use the pregnancy trap. Female sociopaths view pregnancy as a lifetime meal ticket — once they have a child with a man who takes his responsibilities seriously, the father is obligated to either stay with the woman and support her, or send child support payments for the next 20 years. As Dr. Liane Leedom wrote, "In most states, if there is a separation or divorce, custody of children is handed to mothers. She who gets the kids, gets money. Professional mother is the perfect occupation for a female psychopath. All she has to do is have sex, get pregnant, and she's got it made! For her, kids aren't a liability; they are an asset she can use in the next con."[9]

Many sociopathic males also want to trap their partners with pregnancy. I've heard of multiple cases of men who claimed they were sterile — due to cancer, childhood mumps, whatever — and convinced their partners to have unprotected sex. Then, when she got pregnant, he was ecstatic, claimed it was a "miracle baby," and they were meant to be together.

William Allen Jordan is profiled as one of the "True Lovefraud Stories" on Lovefraud.com. Jordan, who also goes by the name William Allen, pulled this scam repeatedly. He engaged women with flowery poetry and promises, told his sad story of infertility, wishing that, because he loved them so much, they could have a child together. The women had sex and got pregnant. Jordan ended up with 13 children by seven different women. His real objective: Money. Jordan conned hundreds of thousands of dollars out of the women, and used the money to pursue his next victim.

The dangers of sexual deception

In the Lovefraud Romantic Partner Survey, 19 percent of respondents said that the sociopaths lied about their sexual orientations. Nine percent of the sociopaths pretended to be straight, but had gay sex as well. Eight percent had no sexual preferences — they would have sex with anyone.

To analyze the data further, I combined the last two groups — sociopaths described as pretending to be straight but having gay sex also, and those who would have sex with anyone. Then I compared this sexually deceptive group — 17 percent of the total — to the sociopaths whose sexual preferences were described as straight, gay or bisexual. The results were shocking.

The sociopaths who engaged in deceptive sex were the most pathological in the survey. On every measure, they were the most disordered and caused the most harm to their partners.

Survey respondents who were involved with sexually deceptive sociopaths experienced all of the following at higher rates — often much higher rates — than people who were "only" involved with run-of-the-mill sociopaths:

- Lost money
- Lost their homes
- Lost their businesses
- Lost their jobs
- Incurred debt
- Declared bankruptcy
- Physical abuse and injury
- Sexually transmitted disease
- Lives threatened
- Thoughts or attempts at suicide
- Pets injured or killed
- Isolation from family and friends
- Lawsuits
- Criminal charges

Surprisingly, even though the sexually deceptive sociopaths wanted both straight and gay sexual experiences, or were willing to have sex with anyone, they weren't any better in bed than the other individuals. But their partners experienced more cheating, more disturbing sexual demands, and were much more likely to discover that the individuals were secretly into pornography.

This group of sociopaths exhibited all of the *Red Flags of Lovefraud* at higher rates than those who were not sexually deceptive. Interestingly, 71 percent of the sexually deceptive group engaged in intense eye contact, compared to 57 percent of those who were not sexually deceptive. And 70 percent of the sexually deceptive group were described has having eyes that sometimes seemed lifeless, compared with 58 percent of the rest of the sociopaths.

And then there's the antisocial behavior. Survey respondents described truly horrific behavior from these individuals:

One time during sex he wanted to put a gun to my head. I said no way and he didn't push the issue but later made me feel like I was not satisfying to him. He also had an explosive fight with me when I wouldn't kiss him goodnight after he made a rude remark to me. He was driving so crazy, we almost died in a car crash. He became someone I had never seen before. Extreme rage.

I did not realize it at the time, worked it out afterwards from a diary note of a "memory hole" — he drugged me throughout the relationship. Date rape drugs, sleeping drugs. So he could literally bed hop, control me, make me ill, have sex with me, etc.

Towards the end he started to get rough with me. One time he exploded and looking at his eyes I didn't know who he was. They were dark and empty; it scared me.

Here is the bottom line: If you discover that you are in a relationship with someone who has lied about his or her sexual orientation, or is willing to have sex with anyone, get out of the relationship immediately.

Sexual predators

The beginning of this book makes the case that most sociopaths do not live up to the media hype. They are not all sadistic, sexually violent serial killers. However, the hype is founded on truth, and some sociopaths do fit the depictions that you see in TV crime shows. These predators are truly scary.

Sex crimes and sexual offenders get a lot of attention in the United States. This is certainly justified — there is no excuse for sexual violence. Some, but not all, sex offenders are psychopaths, diagnosed according to the PCL-R. About half of serial rapists are psychopaths.[10] Child molesters, however, can be diagnosed as psychopaths, or they can have other mental problems.

The most important thing to understand about sex offenders who are diagnosed as psychopaths is that chances are high that they will recidivate, which means they will commit offenses again after being released from prison or treatment.

One study of sex offenders found that within six years of release from prison, more than 80 percent of the psychopaths, but only 20 percent of the nonpsychopaths, had violently recidivated. Many of the offenses were sexual in nature. Another study of sex offenders released from prison found that the violent recidivism rate was 90 percent for psychopaths and 50 percent for nonpsychopaths. This study also found that 70 percent of the sex offenders who exhibited both psychopathy and deviant sexual arousal committed another sexual offense, compared to 40 percent of other groups.[11]

When a sexual offender is a psychopath, having him (or her) released from prison is bad news for the community. They don't change. Neither do the sociopaths who are never arrested for sex offenses.

Recap

Three stages of love

1. Attraction
2. Pleasure
3. Bonding

Survey respondents on their partners and sex

*   75 percent said their partners cheated on them.
*   46 percent found that the individuals were secretly into pornography.
*   40 percent said the sociopath's sexual demands made them uncomfortable.
*   20 percent became infected with a sexually transmitted disease.

CHAPTER 7

The reality of the relationship

"Roxanne" came from a home full of addiction and abuse, so as a young woman, she really wanted someone to love her and accept her for who she was. "Darren" poured on the charm, took her on dates, swept her off her feet and promised to make her dreams come true. The sex was extraordinary. In a whirlwind romance, she quickly became pregnant.

"He claimed that I was his soul mate," Roxanne said. "He had never met anyone that he felt that way about." Those were Darren's words, even though he was still in his 20s and on his second wife. He kicked his wife, and his 18-month-old daughter, out of the house, convincing Roxanne that he had married the woman because it was the right thing to do when she, too, became pregnant, but she was crazy.

Darren's wife tried to warn Roxanne. "She said that Darren would make you think that he would save you, but that he can't," Roxanne wrote. "I didn't believe her, because she was acting crazy, like he had been describing all along."

Three months into the relationship, however, Roxanne's honeymoon was over. Darren didn't want to go anywhere, and she was not allowed to go out and do things, especially without his permission.

Their daughter was born with multiple handicaps. One day Darren threatened the child, and within six hours, Roxanne left him.

"I was able to stay away for two and a half years," she said. "We decided to get back together; the abuse started then. I was given choices of performing certain sexual activities or he would leave. Then another two and a half years later, he stated he wanted a divorce, at which time I moved out and began my life."

But Darren initiated another love bombing campaign, calling all the time, trying to make Roxanne feel special. "We once again tried to be together," Roxanne said. "This time though, the abuse, from mental, to emotional, to physical, of my daughter and myself, as well as the sexual abuse, got REALLY BAD. He hurt me so bad during sex that I cried all night long from the pain, and had to drive myself to the hospital the next day. All of no meaning or concern to him. It felt like he really hated me, and loved having such power over me. I tried to fight him off several times, but that only increased his pleasure and determination."

Roxanne is finally out of the relationship, and now realizes what happened. "Darren was VERY EFFECTIVE with his love bombing," she explained. "He masked care and concern to learn everything he could about me, and then used it all against me later in the relationship."

Looking for the traits of a sociopath

None of the people who completed the Lovefraud Romantic Partner Survey understood what they were getting into when they became involved with sociopaths. If any of the respondents had heard of sociopaths or antisocial personality disorder, they certainly did not know what it really meant. Only after enduring their partners' lies, manipulation, betrayal and abuse, interspersed with proclamations of undying love, did respondents go looking for answers. So when they completed the Lovefraud surveys, it was with the clarity of hindsight.

As explained in Chapter 2, several survey questions were based on the description of antisocial personality disorder in the first draft of the American Psychiatric Association's fifth edition of the *Diagnostic and Statistical Manual of Mental Disorders* (DSM-5). The official description of antisocial personality disorder has since changed. However, the preliminary version identified a list of traits that did a good job of summarizing the negative aspects of the disorder: callousness, aggression, manipulativeness, hostility, deceitfulness, narcissism, irresponsibility, recklessness and impulsivity. The degree to which individuals exhibited each trait was indicated along a continuum, ranging from "not at all like that" to "extremely like that."

In the case described above, Roxanne rated Darren as "extremely like that" for every single one of the nine traits. In my opinion, he was probably a sociopath. But Roxanne, like most targets of sociopaths, did not see his abusive and destructive behavior right away.

Sociopaths are often good at hiding their negative traits, at least in the beginning of a relationship. So in the Lovefraud DSM-5 Survey, Dr. Liane Leedom and I wanted to find out not only how well the people with whom Lovefraud readers were involved matched the proposed DSM-5 description of antisocial personality disorder, but also how long it took for the survey respondents to see the sociopathic traits.

In the Lovefraud DSM-5 Survey, respondents could answer the questions in reference to anyone who they thought was a sociopath — a spouse, romantic partner, family member, friend, or associate. The following information compiles the data related to spouses and romantic partners, which comprised most of the survey — 1,096 responses. The traits are presented in the order of most observed to least observed.

Lovefraud DSM-5 Survey
Assessment of traits exhibited by spouses and romantic partners of survey respondents. N = 1,096.

Manipulativeness
Using others to their advantage through seduction, charm, glibness, ingratiation, cunning or subterfuge.

Extremely	90%
Moderately	8%
Mildly	2%
Very little or not at all	0%

Deceitfulness

Dishonesty, fraudulence. Misrepresenting themselves. Embellishment or fabrication when relating events.

Extremely	88%
Moderately	10%
Mildly	2%
Very little or not at all	1%

Callousness

Lack of empathy, concern, guilt or remorse. Willingness to be exploitive.

Extremely	81%
Moderately	15%
Mildly	3%
Very little or not at all	1%

Narcissism

Vain, boastful, self-centered. Exaggerating achievements and abilities. Feeling and acting entitled. Preoccupied with unlimited success, power, brilliance or beauty.

Extremely	74%
Moderately	18%
Mildly	6%
Very little or not at all	2%

Irresponsibility

Failure to honor obligations, commitments, agreements or promises, financial or otherwise. Failure to keep appointments or complete tasks. Unreliable. Careless with possessions belonging to themselves or others.

Extremely	70%
Moderately	17%
Mildly	7%
Very little or not at all	7%

Impulsivity

Acting on the spur of the moment in response to immediate stimuli without a plan or consideration of outcomes. Difficulty following plans. Failure to learn from experience.

Extremely	61%
Moderately	23%
Mildly	10%
Very little or not at all	7%

Recklessness

Pursuit of stimulation without regard for consequences. Prone to boredom and unnecessary risk taking; lack of concern for limitations or danger. High tolerance for uncertainty and unfamiliarity.

Extremely	56%
Moderately	24%
Mildly	12%
Very little or not at all	8%

Hostility

Irritable, hot tempered, unfriendly, rude, surly or nasty. Responding angrily to minor slights and insults.

Extremely	56%
Moderately	24%
Mildly	11%
Very little or not at all	9%

Aggression

Mean, cruel, abusive, humiliating, demeaning, belligerent or vengeful. Willfully engaging in violence. Using dominance and intimidation to control others.

Extremely	55%
Moderately	26%
Mildly	11%
Very little or not at all	8%

The reality of the relationship

The predominant traits noted by survey respondents were manipulation and deceitfulness, with respondents saying that the individuals were "extremely like that" at rates of 90 percent and 88 percent, respectively. The next most prevalent trait was callousness, with 81 percent selecting "extremely like that." The order of prevalence for all sociopathic traits was almost identical in the Lovefraud Romantic Partner Survey, which took place a year later.

Interestingly, the traits that people generally associate with sociopaths and psychopaths — aggression, hostility and recklessness — were not the dominant traits identified in the survey. Fifty-five percent of respondents said their partners were extremely aggressive, and 56 percent said the sociopaths were extremely hostile or reckless. They are nasty dudes and dudettes, for sure. But this is further evidence that the common understanding of sociopathic behavior is only half correct. Sociopaths are much more likely to engage in deception than aggression.

Given the degree to which survey respondents selected "extremely like that" or "moderately like that" for almost every trait to describe the individuals with whom they were involved, I believe that most of those individuals were sociopaths.

Generally, psychology and mental health professionals say that untrained people such as the survey respondents should not be making diagnoses. I agree that lay individuals cannot make a diagnosis to be used in therapy or a court proceeding. But anyone certainly can — and should — use information about sociopathic behavior to evaluate whether an individual is suitable relationship material. Anyone who realizes that a spouse or romantic partner matches the list of sociopathic traits should end the involvement.

The problem is seeing the traits. The data on when survey respondents noticed each of the traits proved what almost all targets experienced: Sociopaths do not show their true, destructive selves right away. In fact, if they want, they can keep the charade of love, care and respectability going for a long time.

So when do sociopaths reveal themselves? Averaging together the responses for all nine traits, here is when survey respondents noticed the negative behaviors:

When survey respondents saw sociopathic traits

Right away	7%
In the first month	14%
In the first six months	29%
In the first year	19%
After one year	30%

These data help explain why people get stuck in relationships with sociopaths. Only 21 percent of survey respondents saw sociopathic traits early in their relationships — within the first month. On the other hand, 30 percent did not see the dangerous behaviors until after they had been involved for a year or more.

Take, for example, the trait of deceitfulness. Although it was one of the two most identified traits in the survey, 36 percent of survey respondents didn't know that the sociopaths were lying until at least a year into the relationship. So because they weren't aware of such behavior for a year or more, when they finally did see the lies, the targets thought the false statements were aberrations, not the true characteristics of their romantic partners.

By that time, of course, the survey respondents had already bonded with the sociopaths. As I discussed in the last chapter, human love bonds are designed not to dissolve at the first signs of trouble, so even when the targets realized there were problems in the relationships, they stayed.

Signs of trouble in the relationships

So what are signs of trouble? The survey asked about behaviors that, if respondents were able to view them objectively, would clearly indicate an individual was an unsuitable relationship partner. Below are the percentages of respondents who agreed that their partners engaged in the behaviors:

Objectionable behavior from partners

- Disappeared for extended periods of time without explanation — 43%
- Manipulated me to pay for dates and things we did together — 47%
- Promised special dates or occasions, but they never materialized — 50%
- Switched love on and off — 57%
- After hurtful words or actions, acted like they never happened — 73%

"Vivian" experienced all of these behaviors from "Dan" — but not, of course, in the beginning of their relationship. Dan approached Vivian at her job — she held a master's degree and worked as a librarian. Dan — well, he talked a lot, and worked sometimes.

Dan became Vivian's swimming partner and companion. "He doted on me," Vivian said. "He brought me food and gifts at work that impressed my co-workers. He showed up in the parking lot at work or at my home, announced or otherwise. He made sure I sat straight, made me a neck rest for my commute, insisting that I use it, even salted my food for me. I felt dominated, but rationalized it as care."

Dan reflected Vivian's beliefs in loyalty, fidelity and partnership. He said they were soul mates. Within a month, he declared that he was falling in love with her.

"Dan supported my dream of motherhood and a better job," Vivian said. "He was a handyman, he took the weight off my busy life in the beginning and my walls came down for him. He used many words, spoke with conviction, shared my values, did all things to support me and convince me that he was 'on my side' and that he loved me and needed me and wanted me."

Dan impressed Vivian as confident, assertive, highly intelligent and well read. She admits that he was "extremely eccentric" — other people thought he was creepy. Vivian's mother didn't like how fast Dan moved in on her, and her father said the man had "massive problems."

But Vivian was loyal to her boyfriend. "I was convinced that they could not see what I saw, and that I would be the one person that believed in him," she said. "I was terribly attached."

They were romantically involved for six and a half years, although the relationship began to deteriorate in one year. After two years, Dan disappeared, but later returned, and Vivian was determined to love him more than ever. In the fifth year, Dan disappeared for three weeks.

"This knocked me to my knees emotionally, like something was trying to break into my consciousness that something was terribly wrong," Vivian said. "I lost my emotions. He told me everything was fine. I thought, how can I help him? What is wrong? Why am I in so much pain? Why am I so confused? Why does he determine my sense of well-being? My body was breaking down from the stress. When I tried to break up, he would not."

In the sixth year of their relationship, while Vivian was driving in busy lunch-hour traffic, Dan suddenly turned on the cruise control of her car. Vivian freaked out, and Dan didn't care. Once again he disappeared, apparently prompted by her stressed reaction. Vivian could not make sense of his indifference to her feelings.

"After one month, he popped up at my work unannounced and came into the staff room, where I was by myself," Vivian said. "He said, 'What it is, Viv,' and I hugged him and wept. He did not shed a tear. I was bewildered. I felt so abandoned. He told me I was not abandoned. Also during this time he started calling me 'little shit' and 'motherfucker' when I did not do something he wanted me to do, like give him my car keys while we went for a walk. What was happening? I told him I did not like what he was saying, how he was acting. He said if I walk away, I am walking away from love.

"My body was filled with adrenalin, more than once," Vivian continued. "I knew I needed to get away. I could no longer reason, but my body knew things my mind was not ready for. He hated my questions. He hated my increasing suspicions. He hated when I did not behave as he expected."

It turned out that for more than five years, Dan had been living with another woman, whom he was conning along with Vivian. He was also sponging off of a single mother who had a trust fund.

Dan himself had no mailing address except for a homeless shelter. When he disappeared, he was most likely spending time with the other women, then returning to Vivian as if he'd done nothing wrong.

Sociopaths are professional cheaters

In the Lovefraud Romantic Partner Survey, 75 percent of respondents said that the sociopaths they were involved with cheated on them. However, it is quite possible that you, like Vivian, may never know it.

Lovefraud once received a very nice email from a website editor, suggesting that one of her articles about cheating spouses would be of interest to Lovefraud readers. Although the article provided information that would be useful in most normal, or semi-normal, relationships, it described cheating by mere amateurs, not sociopaths.

According to the article, all of the following should raise a woman's suspicions that her guy might be cheating:

1. He improves his personal appearance.
2. He finds fault with you.
3. Your sex life changes.
4. He uses a new phone or other new technologies.
5. Your intuition tells you something is wrong.
6. His routine changes, or he has new interests.
7. His work or financial habits change.
8. You find evidence of another woman.[1]

The key here is that something about the guy's behavior is different. I'm sure this is what happens if a man who is bored or unhappy, but not personality disordered, strays. But it's not the case with sociopaths. For sociopaths, cheating is a way of life, so there is no change to notice.

Sociopaths — both men and women — are professional cheaters, liars and manipulators. So let's take a look at the list in the context of a sociopath.

Red Flags *of* Love Fraud

1. There probably won't be a change in personal appearance. Either they're always obsessive about how they look, or they rely on their skills of seduction.
2. After initial flattery to get you hooked, a sociopath will at some point start finding fault with you. In time, the sociopath blames you for being the source of all problems.
3. Sociopaths always have plenty of sexual tricks and incredible stamina, so if they want to, they'll continue to get sex from you, even if they're getting it from someone else at the same time.
4. A new phone is simply another new toy, and sociopaths love toys. In fact, they'll get you to buy the toys.
5. Your intuition has probably always been telling you that something is wrong. But sociopaths have so many glib explanations that you no longer trust your own perceptions.
6. Sociopaths are always coming and going, and they're always starting something new. After awhile, you accept this as normal.
7. A sociopath is always irresponsible. Jobs and money just disappear. This, too, becomes normal.
8. When you find direct evidence of cheating, the sociopath either explains it away, or accuses you of being paranoid.

The problem about being involved with a sociopath is that he or she is always erratic, and you are always off balance. So it's difficult to see the signs of cheating, especially as the sociopath continues to profess his or her love and concern for you.

In fact, you may never find out the extent of the cheating until the sociopath discards you. Only then, when the sociopath no longer bothers to spin a web of deceit, might you learn what was really going on.

But while you are still useful to the sociopath, they keep you around by establishing power and control over you. Strategies that they use include nonstop communication, possessiveness, isolation and gaslighting.

Constant phone calls, emails and text messages

One of the *Red Flags of Love Fraud* is love bombing — constant attention, praise, flattery and declarations of love. Sociopaths engage in love bombing while physically with you. They also do their love bombing via communications media, overwhelming you with a constant barrage of phone calls, emails, text messages, and even old-fashioned cards and letters. Some Lovefraud survey respondents reported receiving 20, 30 or more communications a day.

When sociopaths do this, it seems, at first, like an outpouring of affection. They tell you how wonderful you are and how much they love you. They call you just to hear your voice. They paint shimmering verbal pictures of the wonderful future the two of you will share. It all sounds so enticing, and you believe the sociopaths are expressing the deepest feelings of their hearts. But what they are really doing is exerting control.

Sociopaths inundate you with calls and messages so that they can keep tabs on you. For example, when "Patty" was 19, she met "Vince," who claimed to be 26, although he was actually 30 and married. "A casual friendship was all I was interested in," Patty said. "He had other plans.

"Vince became instantly fixated on me, frequent phone calls, charming letters, notes, cards, and he called and left voice messages, although I stated I would not be available at particular times," she continued. "He claimed he was single and lonely. I felt sorry for him. I was flattered and I thought I could handle what was going on. He seemed like a nice guy for the most part, so I overlooked his obsessive behaviors. After a few weeks, he stated that he loved me and wanted to be with me. I was very resistant, and had a feeling he was not going to back off."

He didn't. But Patty, who had a toxic and dysfunctional family life, got caught up in the attention and flattery.

"Vince was very persistent and made it very clear that he wanted me," Patty said. "The stalking began very early on and I didn't know how to handle the situation, so I went into denial and it became worse. The relationship was a cat and mouse game. He chased me until I gave in."

Patty dated Vince for more than 10 years. Even when she wanted to break it off, she couldn't.

"I would begin to feel very bad and emotionally drained, depressed and at one point, suicidal," Patty said. "Whenever I brought up my feelings and hoped to talk about them as if he might care, I was told I was 'crazy,' 'weak,' 'fucked up' and needed 'to see a shrink.' There were many times that I did leave the relationship, and his obsession and stalking became very scary. He would usually begin romancing someone else, yet still continue to harass and pursue me. I realize now that the frequent obsessive contact was to emotionally break me down, and it worked. We would end up getting back together after many empty apologies, promises, begging and, of course, sex."

Patty finally did get out of the relationship. She recognized the real Vince — he engaged in stalking, harassment and physical violence, towards herself and others. Shortly before Patty filled out the Lovefraud Romantic Partner Survey, she found out even more — Vince made the local news for first-degree murder.

Possessiveness is not love

To a sociopath, you are nothing but an object. So while you feel like you are building a relationship, caring about your partner and becoming emotionally bonded, he or she considers you to be a possession, like a flat-screen TV.

Possessions, of course, are not only utilitarian, they also indicate status. Sociopaths may like the idea of a good-looking or successful romantic partner, because it conveys status to them. In fact, just having a partner enables them to appear to be normal members of society, which is a useful image that helps them pull off their scams. So they may actually take care of you and the family — providing a home, food, other necessities, even luxuries — viewing the effort as maintenance of their property. As one survey respondent wrote, "He treated me like a prized possession. I foolishly thought that was love."

The reality of the relationship

Sociopaths will keep you around as long as they view you as useful. But when they decide that you are no longer appealing, or want to trade you in for a newer model, they feel perfectly entitled to get rid of you, as they would any possession.

Their children are also nothing more than possessions. Sociopaths do not love their children. They do not care about their children's welfare, growth or happiness. They may be pleased when their children are attractive or accomplished, but only because it makes them look like father- or mother-of-the-year.

Kids do, however, offer something special to sociopaths: a tool for controlling their partners, whether they stay together or not. Many mental health professionals are under the impression that sociopaths abandon their children, and some of them do. But many sociopaths, both male and female, hold on to their children, using them to torment their partners or ex-partners for years — even for the rest of their lives.

She has used my son as a pawn since the day he was born.

He physically assaulted me and our daughter, then blamed me when he filed for sole custody (he got that, then lost our child to CPS) ... but he won the child, the object. Everyone is an object to entertain this man.

He went after our minor kids and stopped at nothing until he got them 5 1/2 years later. I had no idea that he was capable of such pure evil. I also never really realized what a skilled liar he was. He told horrendous stories about me, had me arrested, harassed and stalked me, used our kids as pawns, and never, never ever showed an ounce of regret or remorse; in fact, he seemed defiantly indignant and justified in his awful behavior and no one seemed to notice but me!!!!!!!!! He has done enough to me that I am sometimes surprised that I am still here! I am trying to move on, but he has the kids and I had to move out of state to try and rebuild some semblance of a life for myself. He ruined me in every way. The mind games still haven't completely stopped.

Systematic isolation

To make you easier to control, sociopaths systematically isolate you from your family, friends and support network. In the Lovefraud Romantic Partner Survey, 61 percent of respondents reported that the sociopaths separated them from the people in their lives.

How do they do it? Sociopaths are unpleasant, disagreeable or insulting to your friends and family, so that the people you've known all your life no longer want to be around you. Sociopaths lie to drive wedges between you and everyone you know. They go into a jealous rage if you talk to someone of the opposite sex, or sometimes if you talk to anyone at all. If you defy them and spend time with your friends and family, they retaliate by making your life miserable.

Here is how some survey respondents described their partners' isolation campaigns:

> *Got rid of all my friends, would not allow me to have friends, tried to have sex with my friends, which drove them off.*

> *She didn't want to be around my friends nor family. One time she told me, "I LET your family come over." It was my home—I built it in 2001—and she tells me she LET my family come over. On 2 other occasions that I recall she was adamant that I DO NOT go out and see friends. One was with a friend whose wife was friends with my first wife. The other was a get-together with high school friends (my twin sister and her husband were there), but I couldn't go. I guess I could have, but it wasn't worth the hell I would have received.*

> *He told people that I did not like them. He told me that other people didn't like me and left the impression*

that, if confronted, the other person had volunteered that they would deny what he had said, so there would be nothing gained by confronting that other person.

The isolation strategy works — over time, all your friends and family are no longer part of your life. The dismal result is that when you've finally had enough, and realize that you must get out of the relationship with the sociopath, he or she has burned all your bridges. When you need help the most, to escape the predator, you feel like you have no one to turn to.

Gaslighting: Are you going crazy?

The word "gaslight," when used as a verb, means "to manipulate someone into questioning their own sanity; to subtly drive someone crazy."[2]

The term is a reference to the 1944 movie *Gaslight*, starring Ingrid Bergman, Charles Boyer, Angela Lansbury and Joseph Cotten. It's set in Edwardian London, where an accomplished singer is mysteriously strangled in her home. The crime is discovered by the singer's young niece, Paula Alquist (Ingrid Bergman).

Ten years later, Paula falls head-over-heels in love with a handsome and suave pianist, Gregory Anton (Charles Boyer), and they quickly marry. The couple returns to the London house, which Paula inherited. Then Gregory begins a slow, calculated campaign to make Paula believe she is becoming forgetful, then hysterical, then insane.

Gregory moves things and asks Paula what she did with them. When Paula is understandably confused — after all, she didn't move anything — he feigns concern, while making more and more items disappear. Then he shames his wife in front of their servants, and gradually convinces them that there is something wrong with their mistress. He lets it be known in society that Paula is not well, and contrives to make his wife have a very public breakdown.

Throughout the movie, Gregory shows flashes of rage, then quickly shifts to solicitous manipulation. He becomes more and more dominant — telling Paula what to do and where to sit — while his wife crumbles. It's behavior that many Lovefraud readers recognize.

Several film reviews call the villain of the movie, Gregory, a psychopath. Most movies that are supposedly about psychopaths do not, in fact, portray them accurately. *Gaslight* does a fairly good job. Even though Gregory's disordered behavior seems theatrical, some real-life sociopaths do exactly what he does. Here are examples from the Lovefraud Romantic Partner Survey:

> *She would move my possessions from where I left them and tell me I was forgetful. When I sometimes talked about our experiences together, most of the time she would tell me I was wrong and it never happened. She also denied telling me things that she told me in the past.*

> *He had a mask he wore in public, which dropped in private and he'd turn into a monster. He lied all the time, would secretly hide my keys, then claim I was mentally ill because I kept "misplacing" them. He'd call me a nasty name in the middle of a good conversation for no reason — completely unexpected — then deny it and call me crazy and "hearing things."*

Sociopaths employ gaslighting to make you doubt your own perceptions, and then your own sanity. Why? Because when you feel like you're losing your mind, you are more pliable and easier to control.

Exerting power and control

The control sociopaths exert over their targets takes many forms: They shower the target with affection and then engage in extreme cruelty, creating emotional unbalance. They keep the targets trapped by withholding money. They threaten to take the children away if the partner has the audacity to leave. Through psychological manipulation, they make their targets feel helpless and unable to function on their own.

Respondents to the Lovefraud Romantic Partner Survey experienced all of these tactics. Here is how some described the manipulation:

> *He conned me into thinking that we had something special, and then once he got me hooked, sexually assaulted me until I psychologically rolled under so he could totally exploit me for his own egotistical and sexual gratification without any regard for my feelings or needs. Once he had "won" and used me up, he then discarded me like I was a piece of trash and said bad things about me behind my back when I started fighting back. He told people that I had a mental problem and low self-esteem (the same thing he said about his wife) and got people to shun me like I was a nothing nobody. He cut me off from friends and family by spreading lies and insinuations, while all the time lying profusely to me by telling me to my face that he "loved" me and wanted me back.*

> *Because he would turn his love ON and OFF — during the OFF periods I would sober up, so to speak, and begin to see things more clearly and gain courage to break it off, only for him to come back showering me with love, gifts, promises to change, etc. It was a yo-yo! Over time he did gain control over me in one way or another in an effort to push me into submission, making me feel as though I could not leave him — I was dependent on him and could not stand on my own. As time went on things escalated and the circumstances got worse and worse. The final breaking point was the mental abuse and public threats to kill me, using a high school classmate as an example for murdering his family.*

These anecdotes may sound far-fetched to you, like something out of a psychological thriller movie. But this is exactly what happens in many relationships with sociopaths. Remember, this is the same disorder that produces cult leaders. They instinctively know how to manipulate people, even brainwash them. Sociopaths cause incredible psychological damage to their victims.

That's why so many victims seriously consider suicide. I have heard from family members of victims who, because of the sociopath, finally did kill themselves.

Aggression and violence

Aggression and violence are not, according to Lovefraud's research, the defining characteristics of sociopathy — that distinction is held by manipulation and deceit. Still, plenty of sociopaths are aggressive. In the Lovefraud Romantic Partner Survey, 57 percent of respondents said the sociopath was "extremely" aggressive, and an additional 24 percent said the person was "moderately" aggressive. Therefore, 81 percent of the sociopaths described in the survey exhibited aggressive behavior, including "willingly and willfully engaging in acts of violence."

When asked to explain the antisocial behavior that they witnessed in their romantic partners, 15 percent mentioned abuse and domestic violence, and 20 percent mentioned stalking, violence and threats of murder. Respondents reported being intimidated, threatened, restrained, beaten, punched, kicked, choked, sexually assaulted, and having guns pointed at them.

"Julia," for example, owned a retail store, and "Tim" was a banker who worked across the street. Tim kept coming into her store, even showing up when Julia was working late to help her move items around. He was attentive, kind, generous, exciting and good-looking.

"Tim started calling constantly, sending flowers, leaving love notes and gifts," Julia said. "Very persistent. Presented himself to be a true gentleman, opening doors, lighting cigarettes and very flattering. It was like a fairy tale and he was my prince."

Tim proposed after six months of dating, but Julia had just come out of a 20-year marriage, so she didn't want to rush into anything. She dated him for four years before they married, but during the courtship they never lived together, so she never saw the real Tim. She was in for a shock.

"Three months after marrying him, he began squeezing my head with both his hands so as to cause damage without leaving a mark," Julia related. "He was a body builder, so was very strong. When I started fighting back, he punched me in the eye. I ran and got a pistol, which I pointed at him. He left and I called the police. When they arrived I was hysterical, and he was at the neighbor's, calm, cool and collected. I looked like the lunatic and I was taken to jail.

"When I got out the following day, I was driving my car out of the state when he telephoned me. I recorded him screaming and telling me he was going to put me in the trunk of a car and have me disappear. I took the recording to the prosecuting attorney and all charges against me were dropped."

That turned out to be one of many incidents. Every time Tim became violent and Julia broke up with him, he then turned on the charm again, telling her something that he knew would draw her back, like he was turning his life over to God. He even started reading his Bible and going to church.

But he didn't change, and after 10 years of rage, manipulation and violence, Julia divorced him.

"Ernest" and "Athena"

Female sociopaths can also be violent, as illustrated by the case of "Ernest" and "Athena." They were both professionals working in the same department, and they started driving into work together. Then they dated after work, and eventually became more involved.

Athena admitted that she had previous legal and financial problems, but was eager to begin her life again with fresh hopes and dreams. "She was trying to do something with her life after revealing she had a bad childhood and a bad previous marriage," Ernest said. "We purportedly had a lot in common, such as we were both trying to move up professionally."

They married, but the honeymoon ended after six months. "We had a few spats which involved a few days apart," Ernest said. "Then we separated for six months, tried to reunite. Finally, we separated for two years and tried to reunite one more time."

It didn't work. "Athena would start fights for no reason, and then throw things as well as get physical," Ernest said. "She would make up lies to the police to build a case against me, as my state is an anti-man one when it comes to domestic abuse." After more than five years, Ernest finally divorced her.

With sociopaths, inevitable harm

Sociopaths are the most destructive people on Earth. If you are involved with a sociopath, sooner or later, you find this out.

From early in my relationship with my ex-husband, James Montgomery, I was stressed. We had only been dating a few weeks when he started asking me for money. Of course, he didn't just ask for a handout; he presented the requests as investments in our future. Then he wanted me to pay for a two-week trip from New Jersey to Australia with my credit cards, promising to repay me as soon as the bills came in. That never happened, and his business ventures — more like get-rich-quick schemes — never panned out. He wiped out my earnings, my savings, and ran up my debt. My finances, once stable, disintegrated.

Montgomery wanted a place to live, reliable sex and someone to finance his dreams of grandeur. All his love notes, his little gifts, his forever promises, were designed to make me provide what he wanted. It worked. Two and a half years later, when I was used up, he moved on.

The magnitude of his betrayal was staggering. As I started to unravel what really happened, each day revealed another fabrication, another treachery. I coped as best I could with the legal and financial consequences, but emotionally, all I could do was collapse. It was painful. It was ugly.

All relationships with sociopaths are harmful. At the very least, if you're lucky enough to get out of it quickly, you feel slimed. At worst, you lose all your money and everything you own, your emotional and psychological stability, your children, or your very life. Yes, some sociopaths are murderous.

Respondents to the Lovefraud Romantic Partner Survey catalogued the harm that they suffered. A staggering 76 percent lost money, ranging from a few hundred dollars to over $1 million. But that was just the beginning of the pain.

Harm caused by the sociopath, as reported by Lovefraud survey respondents

Health issues
Became anxious or depressed	92%
Stress of the relationship made them ill	77%
Suffered post-traumatic stress disorder	65%

Financial and property losses
Lost money	76%
Incurred debt	60%
Lost home	27%
Lost job	26%
Lost business	11%
Declared bankruptcy	10%

Sexual issues
Individual cheated on them	75%
Individual was secretly into pornography	46%
Sexual demands made them uncomfortable	40%
Infected with a sexually transmitted disease	20%

Violence
Considered or attempted suicide	38%
Physically abused or injured	36%
Life was threatened	34%
Individual threatened or committed suicide	21%
Pets were injured or killed	14%

Legal issues
Lawsuits filed against them	19%
Criminal charges filed against them	12%

This list of statistics, although shocking, doesn't begin to communicate the real-life trauma of an involvement with a sociopath. Since Lovefraud.com launched in 2005, I've spoken with hundreds of people tangled in these abusive relationships, and

I've heard some truly appalling stories. Still, I was unprepared for the tragedies that people recounted in the Lovefraud Romantic Partner Survey.

Following are three of those stories:

"Andrea" and "Scott"

"Andrea" and "Scott" were both professionals in their 20s when they met. Scott was charismatic and charming, and surprised Andrea with tickets to shows, plays and romantic dinners. She enjoyed his company, his calm nature and his sophisticated lifestyle.

They eventually married, and once they did, Andrea learned that her husband totally expected to get what he wanted. When they had "date nights," Scott took Andrea home to relieve the babysitter, and then went out again to listen to live music. He did this when he brought Andrea home from the hospital after she had emergency surgery. He complained about getting her prescriptions, told her that she ruined his good time, then went out. "He did the same thing on the night of our third daughter's birth," Andrea said. "You could feel the seething rage inside of him, along with the pained silence as he said to me, 'Ya know, it's just not so special the third time around.'"

In his efforts to control Andrea, Scott read her mail and email. Then, when she took steps to protect her privacy by getting a post office box, Scott broke into it. When Andrea objected to anything, Scott ignored her for a month. Later, when Andrea disagreed with him, Scott became physically abusive.

In their fifth year of marriage, Scott had an affair. "I nailed him on everything," Andrea said. "This tapped into his anger at being caught, though he only showed remorse superficially. His rage got the best of him, and he tried to strangle me. But when the babysitter walked in, he stood up and greeted her as if nothing happened."

Scott was arrested and Andrea left with the children. They separated, with him living 3,000 miles away. Before he left, though, he tapped Andrea's phone and cleaned out the bank account, leaving her penniless. Two years later, he returned, manipulating Andrea into rescinding the divorce papers, but the relationship was rocky. They went for counseling.

"He 'seduced' each and every therapist by remaining calm and highlighting every little annoyance I caused him," Andrea said. "He told the therapist that I had post-partum depression, was sullen and displeased with everything, when actually I was displeased with his selfishness, and he wouldn't accept even positive criticism. He made me feel like a nanny."

Things got worse. "During an argument, I tried to leave the house and he pulled one child after another out of the car, pulled the phone lines out of the wall, and told me I'd never see my children again," Andrea said. Scott was arrested and subject to a new restraining order. He left for more than a year.

When he returned, Andrea found her mammograms among his belongings. She had been looking for them frantically, because due to her family history, she was at high risk for breast cancer. Scott claimed to have no idea how he ended up with the mammograms. Then, Andrea found out that she did have breast cancer. Scott's parents were visiting when she learned the terrible news, but Scott didn't want her to say anything about it, because it would ruin their visit. When Andrea lost her hair due to chemotherapy, Scott called her a lesbian.

Later, when Andrea had yet another restraining order against him, Scott broke into the house. Andrea had changed the locks, which enraged him. The police took him away once again.

A year and a half later, after their fifth round of counseling, they divorced. "He tried to pollute all my relationships, with my family, my children, my employer," Andrea said. "He threatened that I would 'go down, further than I ever thought an individual could go,' if I didn't give him our vacation property."

The relationship cost Andrea more than $500,000.

After the divorce, when Andrea's oldest daughter came home from college, the other girls were with Scott. "He wouldn't let her see her sisters, physically lifting her out of the house and telling her, if she didn't leave, he would call the police and tell them that she hurt him," Andrea said. "Then, he started screaming, 'Oh, you HURT me ... Stop that!' He disowned her, saying that she reminds him of her mother. The children cannot speak my name in his house."

"Valerie" and "Katrina"

"Valerie" and "Katrina" were both in their 30s when they met on an Internet dating site. Valerie was attractive and self-confident, but she considered Katrina to be exceptionally beautiful. "She could walk in a room and every man, woman and child would take notice of her," Valerie said.

"I described what I wanted in an individual and she described exactly the same thing I did and said, 'We must be soul mates,'" Valerie recalled. "We decided to meet and did. Within 30 minutes of us meeting, Katrina pulled out her phone and was texting a good friend to tell her that she had finally met the woman she wanted to spend the rest of her life with."

The two women seemed to have so much in common, although Katrina had been through some rough times. By the time Valerie learned that, though, she was already captivated — and willing to help.

"She couldn't believe she met someone that was willing to help her get her life back in order," Valerie said. "I told her she could move in with me until she got back on her feet, and I sent her two grand for the move, which she agreed to pay back, but I never got. Which was the beginning of thousands!"

Seven months later, Katrina's stories weren't adding up. Valerie questioned Katrina, but the answers didn't make sense, so she dug deeper. "The more I dug and asked questions, the more violent this person became," Valerie said. "Over a period of two years of me 'digging' into her business, my back was broken in two places, I was dragged 100 feet down my driveway by her car and both my eyes were blackened. I never tried to press charges until the last time she hit me."

When Katrina punched her in her eyes, Valerie called the police. But at that point, Valerie had no visible injuries, while Katrina had a scratch on her finger. The officers told them to calm down and sleep in different rooms.

The next morning, both of Valerie's eyes were black, and she flipped out. Livid, she stormed into the guest bedroom, where Katrina was sleeping. Katrina refused to acknowledge her, so Valerie grabbed her face and made her look at her black eyes. Valerie then left for work, and Katrina called the police, claiming that she'd been assaulted.

"She just happened to get a gay cop that put a warrant out for my arrest!" Valerie said. "I had no idea ... I left work at lunch that day and called the police station to say that I still wanted to press charges because my eyes were black. The officer I talked to told me to change the locks on all doors except for the entrance to the home and the room she slept in. I did so and called a friend over to take pictures of my black eyes. The locksmiths were at my home, as well as my friend taking pictures, when Katrina arrived. With papers in her hand she said, 'Wait 'til you see what I am doing to you! You are going to jail!' I said, 'What?' She said, 'Yeah, there is a warrant out for your arrest.'"

Valerie freaked out. Katrina pretended to freak out. Katrina said she didn't want Valerie to go to jail, and said, "Let's run." Valerie, who had never seen the inside of a jail, panicked and went with her.

After sitting in a car in a church parking lot for two hours, Valerie and Katrina returned home — and the police showed up. They hid — Katrina held Valerie as they sat on the kitchen floor, out of view. But Valerie had had enough of the running around. She got $3,000 from her credit card for bail and called the police station, wanting to turn herself in.

Katrina drove Valerie to the police station. "The officer took one look at me and literally said, 'Oh shit, you have a black eye. We will discuss your options later,'" Valerie said. "I was handcuffed. At intake the officer asked me, 'Why are you going to jail? You have the black eye!' My response was, 'Funny how your system works!'"

Valerie was released three hours later, the case never went to court, and Katrina was gone — until she wasn't.

Valerie went to work in another state, and eight months later, around Valentine's Day, Katrina called, wanting to get together. Valerie agreed, and Katrina promised to fly to see her.

"I knew she was seeing someone else, but she said I was her heart!" Valerie said. "Valentine's Day came and went, and then she confided that the 'other girl' showed up, and she didn't turn her away. I told her to leave me alone forever!!!"

Valerie found out through mutual friends that Katrina purchased a home with yet another lady. Valerie looked up the new target's Facebook page and cringed. Her post was, "I AM THE LUCKIEST PERSON IN THE WORLD TO FIND MY GIRLFRIEND!!!"

Valerie felt bad for the newest woman. "Katrina cheated on me seven times," she said. "This was her premise: I would come home from work, and if she wanted to f*** someone else, she would pick a fight with the buttons she knew how to push on me, and got results every time. She would leave and do her business, and as if nothing ever happened, come back to me."

The new woman, Valerie was sure, would eventually find this out.

"Charlotte" and "Juan"

"Juan" looked like "Charlotte's" father when they met, but importantly, Juan didn't act like her father. "I actually had been scared of my dad's temper, and this guy never fought with me, so I thought he was gentle," Charlotte remembered.

Both Charlotte and Juan were in their 20s and working as professionals. Over several months, Juan charmed Charlotte into dating. Eventually they married and Charlotte got pregnant. That's when she saw Juan's abuse — although it was often subtle.

Juan never again took Charlotte out on dates, but would sometimes go to an event if she planned it. Or, he would ruin it. "He would pick fights with me if he ever accompanied me to one of my functions," Charlotte said. "He would make me late, or threaten my pet or children — threatened to throw them out of the moving car. And then laugh and pretend it was a joke, much of the time — so you never knew."

Juan used anger to keep Charlotte walking on eggshells. If she asked questions, he exploded, so she stopped asking questions. She now knows that Juan was leading a double life — seducing other women and doing drugs. He always had a woman on the side — he even went after Charlotte's best friend and her mother.

"My mother was having a long-term extramarital affair,"

Charlotte said. "In retrospect, I think she desired my husband and was using him as her own gigolo, traveling with him. I never dreamed they would cross a boundary and have a non-platonic relationship. I was naïve."

Charlotte worked hard to raise their children, and Juan sabotaged her efforts. When Charlotte was trying to put the children to sleep, he started playing with them, exciting the kids and throwing off their bedtime. Or, when Charlotte was getting the children ready for school, and told their son to put on his pants, Juan turned on the TV to mesmerize the child, so he was not dressed and they were late for school. "It was sabotage on every level, but so tricky that some of it has taken years for me to figure out," Charlotte said.

When Juan insisted on watching the children, all Charlotte asked was that he kept them away from the rocks. But as soon as Charlotte was out of sight, her son hit his head on a rock, and she was rushing off to the emergency room for stitches and a concussion.

"At the time, I had to consider this and many other things 'accidents' or 'negligence,'" Charlotte said. "He would stretch the severe ones out, so the hospital was not a daily occurrence. I could not imagine it was intentional, until years later when he admitted to certain things. I could see a pattern. He was not trying to hide his intentions on certain things, but was, at this point, trying to scare and terrorize me blatantly."

Charlotte pieced together that none of the incidents were accidents. All were carefully planned, although sometimes opportunistic as well. And 20 years later, Juan was still at it.

"Now he uses custody to make sure every plan the children and I ever make, anything dear to us, is ruined, sabotaged, even if it is just that he takes us to court or calls the sheriff for a bogus complaint, so our holiday or family event is negated," Charlotte said. "I am intimidated out of planning anything, for I know he will find a way to ruin it. My children haven't dared celebrate a birthday for years!"

No heart, no conscience and no remorse

As these stories illustrate, there is no such thing as a normal relationship with a sociopath. Even mundane events of day-to-day life are opportunities for gamesmanship, exploitation and sometimes violence.

This is the truth about sociopaths: They have no heart, no conscience and no remorse. If you're involved with a sociopath, you'll never see real growth or improvement. Oh, there might be temporary changes, in which sociopaths return to their love bombing behavior, just to keep you around until they're done with you. But once sociopaths are adults, they do not change.

If the information you just read sounds like your relationship, the only real solution is to get out of it. I'll tell you how in the next chapter.

Recap

Sociopathic strategies to establish power and control
- Nonstop communication
- Possessiveness
- Isolation
- Gaslighting

Harm caused by sociopaths
- Health issues
- Financial and property losses
- Sexual issues
- Violence
- Legal issues

CHAPTER 8

Escaping the sociopath

We all thought we found love. When my ex-husband proposed to me, I thought I found love. When their "soul mates" swept into their lives, Lovefraud readers thought they found love. Our romantic partners pursued us; swooned over us; promised the happy, committed futures we always wanted; fervently declared that they did, indeed, love us, like they had never loved before.

We know what we experienced. It all seemed so real — but it was not. Why?

To answer the question, let's first look at the concept of romantic love from a psychological perspective. Drs. Philip R. Shaver and Mario Mikulincer, social psychology researchers, have explained romantic love in a way that is helpful for people involved with sociopaths to understand.

Psychologists have come to believe that human beings have innate motivational systems, also called behavioral systems, which have evolved over millennia to help the species survive. Shaver and colleagues suggest that three of these systems are involved in the experience of romantic love. They are the attachment, sexual and caregiving behavioral systems.[1]

We've already discussed attachment — it's the desire to seek proximity to a particular person. This behavior starts when we're infants, when we want to be with our mothers and other comfort figures. Shaver proposed that romantic love is a grown-up version of the same innate need.

Obviously, sex is a component of romantic love, both for the closeness it engenders between partners and for conceiving children.

Then there's the caregiving system. Human beings are social animals, and caregiving evolved to help the group survive. Not only do parents care for their children, but we are biologically predisposed to respond to others who are in need.

Romantic love involves all three systems — attachment, sex and caregiving. Here's what you need to know: Sociopaths are only capable of two of these systems.

Sociopaths experience attachment — they want to be close to you, at least for awhile. And, sociopaths certainly want sex. But in sociopaths, the caregiving brain system doesn't work. They will never feel empathy for you. They will never be concerned with your welfare. They will never put your needs before theirs, unless they're trying to set you up for exploitation later. And no matter what you do, you will never be able to fix this.

What you experience with sociopaths is not real love, but empty love. Real love — attachment, sex and caregiving — is impossible with sociopaths. Therefore, if you realize that you're involved with a sociopath, the healthy thing for you to do is leave the relationship.

Waiting for clean and sober

Even when you know that you're being treated poorly, and you're aware that your romantic partner has issues, you may believe that he or she has a problem that can be fixed. This often happens when you're involved with an alcoholic or drug user. You keep hoping, praying and believing that once the individual becomes clean and sober, everything will be fine.

If the person is a sociopath, it isn't going to happen.

Remember, the core traits of sociopathy include recklessness and a need for excitement. For this reason, sociopaths are always looking for thrills, and often find them in partying. As a result, many sociopaths become addicted to drugs and alcohol.

Addicts and sociopaths exhibit similar behaviors. They are callous. They have low impulse control. They feel entitled to do what they want and pursue their addictions, regardless of who gets hurt. But when addicts who are not sociopaths recover, these negative behaviors diminish, and they can be genuinely loving and caring. When sociopaths overcome their addictions — and some of them do — they are still sociopaths.

Even when clean and sober, sociopaths remain deceitful, manipulative and callous. The abusive behavior they engaged in while using drugs or alcohol will probably continue. All that changes is the excuse. Before they could blame their behavior on the drugs or drinking. When sober, it's quite possible that they'll just blame their behavior on you.

"Leslie" learned this the hard way about "Gary." They were both in their 20s, and both had daughters, when they met. "He was 'everything' I wanted ... looks were perfect, charm, 'bad boy' image," Leslie said. "I was going to help make him into this great man ... with no addiction issues ... How wrong was I!!!!"

Deep inside, Leslie knew from the very beginning that Gary wasn't good for her. But she saw herself as the "good girl" with the big heart. She imagined that she could fix him, help him overcome his drug and alcohol addictions. Then, with their daughters, they'd become the perfect family and live happily ever after. "He needed someone to 'show him the way,'" Leslie said. "So I continued for years, hoping to 'change' him ... I lost myself in the process!"

Leslie was always taught to see the good in people, so she chose not to see the bad — the addictions that took over Gary's life. Even though she was warned that Gary had a temper and was violent, she married him, and for 17 years gave and gave, expecting nothing in return. That's exactly what she got — nothing. Gary was emotionally and physically abusive. He stole to support his drug habit. And he never quit his addictions.

"I can't count how many times I left and came back to him, hoping he would 'see the light,'" Leslie said. "He chose addiction and friends over me!!!"

If you are involved with someone who has substance abuse issues, look carefully for the other *Red Flags of Love Fraud*. If you see indications that the person is a sociopath, there is no point waiting for clean and sober. Even if your partner does kick the addiction, he or she will never offer you the loving, committed relationship that you want and deserve. The sooner you extricate yourself from the involvement, the better.

The biggest battle in breaking up: yourself

The most difficult part of breaking up with a sociopath is often dealing with your own emotions. Remember, you have psychologically bonded with this person. Even though the sociopath was not really in the relationship, you were. The sociopath did not form a love bond. You did.

It started in the beginning of the relationship, when you were attracted by the sociopath's charisma, charm, magnetism, looks — whatever you found appealing. Then, when the sociopath expressed interest in you, or reciprocated your interest, you achieved the object of your desire, which gave you pleasure. Your pleasure was enhanced when the sociopath treated you like gold, showered you with attention, proclaimed undying love. You became attached to the sociopath, feeling a compulsion to be with your new Mr. or Ms. Right. You were swamped by all those brain chemicals released during intimacy and sex — endorphins, dopamine and oxytocin. The psychological love bond solidified.

You, at the time, did not realize that the sociopath was incapable of love. So when the sociopath withdrew, disappeared or cheated, you felt anxiety and fear, which had the perverse effect of strengthening the love bond. Then when the two of you reconciled, you felt relief, had sex — and the cycle started all over again. With each turn of the wheel, the bond became tighter and tighter. In the end, you felt addicted to the relationship, and from the perspective of your brain, you were.

This is what happened to "Laurie." She and "Ed" were both in their 20s, working together in the medical field. Ed was handsome, people liked him, and he made Laurie feel alive. She wrote:

"We met, we dated, I slept with him, he dumped me, I found out I was pregnant with his child, he ignored me 'til the end of the pregnancy, when he claimed to love me and convinced me to give the baby up and live happily ever after with him, got pregnant again, he told me to have an abortion or he would kill himself, I did, we got married, he lied, cheated, manipulated and abused, we got divorced, he came back claiming he made a mistake, got remarried, he lied, cheated, manipulated, abused again, we got divorced again ... I am trying to get over 20 years of life with him and the aftereffects of the time with him."

The relationship went around and around. "From the engagement, he would lie and cheat and I would leave," Laurie said. "Initially he would beg and cry and try to get me back. This went on for years. At some point he stopped even acknowledging my leaving, because he knew he had total control over me and I would come back because I was totally incapable of being without him. This happened at least 100 times ... makes me sound pathetic, but truly it was up and down, hundreds of women, etc., but somehow he led me to believe that they meant nothing and I was his soul mate, and ultimately, if I hung in there long enough, it would eventually maybe stop."

Laurie was addicted to the relationship. In the very beginning of the involvement, Laurie was warned about Ed. Co-workers knew of his past with other female employees. But Laurie believed that love could change everything. She ignored the warnings.

Ignoring the warnings

Many respondents to the Lovefraud Romantic Partner Survey felt the same way that Laurie did. They believed in love, the goodness of people, that change was possible. Half of the people who completed the survey were warned by someone not to get involved with the sociopath. Twenty-one percent said they ignored the warning. Why?

Following are the reasons given by the survey respondents:

Misunderstood — 14 percent
Respondents believed that their romantic partners were misunderstood, and no one knew the individuals like they did. They defended the sociopath and rationalized his or her behavior.

Own decision — 9 percent

Respondents didn't want to be told what to do. They thought they could handle the situation and wanted to make their own decisions. When warned about the sociopath, they became angry, defensive, and told other people to stay out of their business.

Denial — 7 percent

The warnings were just too outrageous. Respondents didn't believe what they were told; the sociopath couldn't possibly be that bad.

Jealousy — 7 percent

Respondents believed that whoever gave them the warning was jealous, lying or had an ulterior motive.

I can help — 7 percent

Respondents believed they could change the sociopath. Perhaps the individual had difficulties in previous relationships, but their love was different from all the others. Or respondents admitted problems, but believed the relationship would get better.

I'm in love — 7 percent

Respondents heard the warnings and continued the relationships anyway. They were in love, addicted or enjoyed the sex. The sociopath's grip was too strong for them to leave.

Why did this happen? Why did so many people hear warnings and disregard them? Because they didn't know about sociopaths.

We are not taught about human predators. We are not taught that there are people in the world who look and seem to act just like us, but spend their lives exploiting others. I've spoken to hundreds of people who have been targeted by sociopaths. Over and over, they said to me, "I didn't know such evil existed."

The Lovefraud survey respondents experienced attention and

adoration from the sociopaths. They did not see the nefarious behavior described by whoever tried to warn them. Without the understanding that sociopaths exist, and an awareness of their behavior patterns, the warnings didn't make any sense.

Changing our world views

We all have a certain *Weltanschauung,* a word borrowed from German that means "world view." We have ideas and beliefs about how the world works, the nature of things, and the nature of people. Perhaps we are idealistic about helping people, making the world a better place. We may believe that "people are basically good," "everyone deserves a chance," "love can change anything." These are the lenses through which we interpret everything we see and experience in life. These are also the lenses through with we approach our relationships.

Many of us begin our relationships with someone who turns out to be a sociopath assuming that, if we see an abusive exterior, there must be a "poor, unloved child" underneath it. We try to nurture that inner individual, offering unconditional love — only to discover that under the shell, there really is nothing. The person is hollow inside. The truth is revealed, and we learn that our romantic partner never loved us; in fact, everything we believed about him or her is a lie.

When this happens, we experience much more than the loss of a relationship. We are thoroughly betrayed. The lenses through which we viewed the world are shattered, and we are shaken to the core of our beings. We question all our deeply held beliefs about people, life, and how it should be lived. We are deceived and emotionally destroyed, and we are forced to admit that our view of the world is deeply flawed.

Yes, our experiences with sociopaths are devastating. But I don't believe that once we've encountered these predators, we have to totally give up our ideals. We do, however, need to recognize that our ideals cannot encompass everyone.

There are people who have been dealt a bad hand in life, and with understanding and assistance, can turn their lives around. They are worthy of our efforts. Sociopaths, however, will continue to do what they do, no matter how we persevere in our attempts to help them, save them, reform them.

We must learn to discern which people have a heart and a conscience, and which people do not. Then, we can lavish our time, love and idealism on those who can benefit from our efforts. The others, we leave behind.

The disappearing act

Sometimes sociopaths end the relationships themselves. Usually, it's emotionally brutal — they simply decide that you are no longer necessary in their lives and either leave or throw you out — the "devalue and discard" routine. At one time you were ensconced on a pedestal, with the sociopath singing your praises. Then suddenly, you aren't worth a return phone call.

Perhaps, when this happens, trouble has been brewing in your relationship for awhile. You may have been standing up to the abuse. Or, you may have been running out of money and demanding that the sociopath honor all the promises to repay you.

Sometimes, however, you have no inkling at all that your partner is dissatisfied. One respondent to the Lovefraud Romantic Partner Survey wrote about her husband, "He walked out after nine years without a word ... I came home, after being out only 45 minutes, to find his closet empty."

Generally, when a sociopath disappears without notice, he or she has been cheating on you for some time, and has decided to cut over to the new target. If you've been providing the financial support, and you've run out of resources, the new soul mate probably has more to offer. Or, the sociopath's reason may be as flimsy as a desire for a change of scenery, meaning a change of partner.

What should you do? If the sociopath leaves you, never to be heard from again, let him or her go and count your blessings. As painful as the disappearing act is, the faster you can get the parasite out of your life, the better.

Sometimes, however, the disappearing act isn't permanent. Sociopaths may leave, and then months or even years later, initiate contact again. They tell you that leaving you was the biggest mistake of their lives. After being apart, they realize how much they miss you, they're truly sorry, and can you please forgive and try again?

Make no mistake — it's just another scam. No matter what they say, sociopaths are not capable of an actual change of heart. Probably their most recent romantic interest kicked them out and they need a new source of money, sex or housing. They're probing to see if they can bleed you again.

Don't fall for those new-and-improved words of love and contrition. They are just as empty as they always were.

Breaking up and reuniting

Many targets try to end their relationships with sociopaths, but keep getting drawn back in. The Lovefraud Romantic Partner Survey asked respondents to describe any history of breaking up and reuniting with the person who they now realize is a sociopath. Seventeen percent of respondents described a never-ending roller coaster, a continuing cycle of breakups and hookups. Here is how one woman explained it:

> *There was constant drama. His temper would flare and I would leave or attempt to leave him. He would cling to my car and cry. Sometimes it was difficult to get away. I always had an escape plan but it didn't always work. Those episodes would be followed by extensive apologizing on his part and begging for my forgiveness. He always promised to change. Of course, he was incapable of sustaining any positive change, so it was a constant cycle of abuse and apologizing. It wore me down.*

Sociopaths often want to hold on to you — not because they truly love you, but because they're still using you. So when you break away, they embark on a campaign to win you back. They pressure you directly, or they go to your family and friends, acting distraught at the prospect of losing you, and wanting them to "talk to you." Sociopaths usually employ some or all of the following strategies: Crying and pleading, the pity play, blaming you, threats of violence and threats of suicide.

Tactics to win you back

Groveling on their knees, with real tears streaming down their cheeks, sociopaths who are begging for another chance are capable of Academy Award-winning performances. They weep, apologize and promise, all to worm their way back into your life. Eleven percent of Lovefraud readers saw this act. Here is how some described it:

> *She continually asked me back, promising things would be different. They never were. They got worse.*

> *He lies, he cheats, I discover it, there is a blowout, we go to counseling, he lies to the counselor, I stop going, he cries and pleads and states he will be a "new man" and all of "it" will never happen again ... and of course, it always does.*

> *He was very emotional, extremely so and after breaking up he would turn on the tears and be like a dog with his tail between his legs. Once he realized he had been forgiven, the "act" came to a halt.*

Sociopaths seem to be hurting so bad, and seem so genuinely upset, that you may feel sorry for them. Know that this is their objective. Perhaps, in the beginning of the relationship, they hooked you with the pity play. If it worked once, they assume that it will work again.

Some sociopaths, when you try to leave, counterattack by blaming you for all the problems in the relationship. They even blame you for their own atrocious behavior. "He would tell me that I always started our fights and I knew what to say to get him upset and he would lose control," one survey respondent wrote.

The woman had been subjected to threats of violence and physical assault. Amazingly, threats of violence can be a powerful tool not for driving someone away, but for keeping a target in a relationship. Why? Because of fear.

"Cecelia" learned this the hard way with "Kenny." They were

both in their 40s when they met on Facebook. Within a month, they met in person, and Kenny made their involvement fast-paced and dynamic. "I hadn't even known him one day and he wanted to purchase me lingerie," Cecilia said. "Kenny spent the entire weekend dating me intensely, doing things — cinema — that were never repeated."

After that first weekend, Kenny moved to be close to Cecelia. She was actually uncomfortable with the situation, but told herself it was just nerves. "I used to be physically ill," she said, "but later learned to control my nerves by drinking before his arrival to my home."

Cecelia should have listened to her body, and to her friends who instantly hated Kenny. She eventually found out that Kenny had a long criminal history, and she knew she had to end the relationship.

"There were lots of breakups," Cecilia said. "I ran away but he used guilt and tears to get me back. There were several breakups and he often used violent threats against my family, friends, my home, etc., saying he would NEVER allow me to have a life without him. I was so scared I believed this was true and feared for the safety of my friends and family, so went back to him."

Cecilia finally did break free of Kenny. The nightmare lasted less than a year.

Threats of suicide

If you try to end the relationship, some sociopaths threaten to kill themselves.

This is what "Janet" experienced with "Will." The threats were surprising, because what she found so attractive about Will in the first place was "his lust for life and magnetism." She described the beginning of their relationship as "passionate, intense, fast-moving and all-consuming."

In just four months, though, it started to change. "Will was very much emotionally and verbally abusive," Janet said. "He would start fights that lasted for as long as eight hours, not letting me sleep and saying horrible things. He never actually hit me, but it was verging on physical abuse, with restraining and shoving. He threw objects towards me and punched the wall next to my face.

"We broke up at least five times, but he always managed to pull me back in through mind games, suicide threats, and promises to change," Janet continued. "I finally managed to escape. As I was leaving, he threatened to kill our pets."

When it comes to threats of suicide, most people interpret them as signs of a troubled soul, someone so filled with despair that he or she simply can't go on. Usually this is true. Research shows that 98 percent of people who completed suicide had at least one mental disorder. Mood disorders, such as depression, accounted for 30 percent of the diagnoses, followed by substance abuse issues at 18 percent, and schizophrenia at 14 percent. People diagnosed with personality disorders, including antisocial personality disorder, accounted for 13 percent of suicides.[2]

When sociopaths commit suicide, however, it's not because they're overwhelmed by the pain of life. Sociopaths either want to go out in a blaze of glory, or commit suicide as their final act of contemptuous superiority.

Steve Becker, LCSW, explained this attitude in an article on the Lovefraud Blog:

> Let me start with a bit of crude, brutal logic: For many sociopaths, as we know, life is very much a game; hence, when *game* over, *life* over. No more game, what's left? The answer may be, nothing.
>
> And yet it may be less "despair" and "depression" with which the sociopath is left when his act has been shut down, than his preferring *no longer to deal with* an existence he knows will cease supplying the gratifications to which he's grown accustomed, perhaps addicted and certainly privileged.
>
> In the face, then, of this massive problem, the sociopath, with his notorious penchant for escaping inconvenient situations, may consider "checking out" out of life — suiciding — when *it,* too, becomes insolubly inconvenient.
>
> Some sociopaths, recognizing that their run of exploitation has ended, may use suicide as a final act of re-

bellion and contempt, as if to express, "*See!* You may have apprehended me, but *watch!* I'll *kill* myself, and so I'll escape again! *Nobody* gets me. *Nobody* makes me account! I am accountable to *myself* only, and *now* I choose to disappear, permanently. *Ha!*"[3]

So if you're romantically involved with a sociopath, and he or she threatens suicide when you try to leave the relationship, what should you do?

Leave anyway.

Recognize the suicide threat for what it is — a brutal bid for control over you. Go ahead and report the suicide threat to the police or to an appropriate mental health organization, but do not go back.

If the person is truly suicidal, you should let people who are trained to deal with the situation handle the problem. But if the sociopath makes good on the threat, know that he or she was not pining away with love; the intention of the act was to hurt you and make you feel guilty. It's not your fault. The sociopath made the decision, and he or she can die with it.

Domestic violence

Among the most difficult relationships to end are those involving domestic violence. This seems hard to believe — why would anyone stay in a relationship when they are being physically assaulted? The answer has to do with the progression of sociopathic manipulation and control.

Domestic violence is perpetrated by both males and females. A study of young adults — aged 18 to 28 — by the Centers for Disease Control and Prevention found that almost 24 percent of intimate relationships had some violence, and half of those were reciprocally violent, meaning both partners used physical force. In relationships where only one person was violent, women were the perpetrators in more than 70 percent of cases. Men, however, were more likely to inflict injury.[4]

Men who engage in intimate partner violence are often sociopathic. According to Dr. Liane Leedom, "studies of male perpetrators of domestic violence reveal that 50 percent are sociopaths and another 25 percent have sociopathic traits but not the full disorder."[5]

Relationships that become physically abusive do not start out that way. When the abusive partners are sociopaths, they are, as always, charming and charismatic in the beginning. They pour on the attention. They engage in constant communication. If the target notices that they seem a bit possessive, the behavior is interpreted as a sign of love, not control.

"Bonnie" and "Sid," for example, worked together when she was 15 and he was 18. Sid was a catch — good looking and fun. They started dating.

"He treated me well, took me out a lot, bought me gifts, was a good and dramatic dancer, which I loved because I was a dancer," Bonnie said. "He wanted exclusivity and that made me feel loved. He was very possessive, but at 15 I thought that meant he loved me and wanted me only!"

Bonnie was flattered by Sid's loving attention — especially since her home life with her narcissistic mother was miserable. A few months into the relationship, Sid told Bonnie that he wanted to marry her. When she was 18, in part to escape her mother, Bonnie went ahead and married Sid.

"He turned cold and indifferent HOURS after getting married," Bonnie said. "On our ONE night honeymoon at a nice motel, he stopped to pick up two hoagies on the way to the motel and said, 'There's a good movie coming on tonight, so DON'T BOTHER ME!!!' Can you imagine? I was shocked and so hurt, and STUCK! I had nowhere to go, so I had to stay and endure."

Bonnie endured for 10 years. "Sid was antisocial to me, our two children, neighbors, friends, outside people, law enforcement officers, court judges, lawyers, people walking along the road, pets, neighbor's pets," she said. "He was destructive verbally, emotionally, psychologically and physically to ME. He even destroyed items I earned or won in school — trophies, yearbooks, etc. He had a very bad temper and broke items in the house and punched the wall weekly!!! ... He was abusive at the courthouse when we were going through a separation and later divorce. It was terrible.

But he got away with it."

Bonnie finally escaped — but why did she stay so long? She had no family support so she was trapped, with no place to go. Sid actually may have selected her for that reason. Sociopaths want control, and with no one to help her, Bonnie was an easy target.

Another respondent to the Lovefraud Romantic Partner Survey told a story that was similar, but much worse, involving extreme manipulation, brainwashing and physical abuse.

When "Sheila" was 20, she went to a dance with her female cousin, where she met "Leon," who was also in his 20s. "He was very handsome and he was very fit, and he was a keen board surfer like me," Sheila remembered.

After dancing all night, Leon asked Sheila for a date. "He was a bit pushy about it," Sheila said. "Because I was taking my time to decide, so I would not appear over eager, he demanded I make up my mind right then."

Shelia said yes. She should have said no.

They dated, then married. The day after the wedding, Leon told Sheila that he hated brunettes and did not know why he ever dated one. Sheila had waist-length black hair. Leon demanded that she bleach it. She did, and Leon told her it was not blond enough. It became brittle and snapped off at the roots when she brushed her hair, so Leon got the scissors and hacked her hair off at chin level. It was just the beginning of his controlling behavior.

Leon began beating Sheila in the first month of marriage. "I was so ashamed and unable to tell anyone," she said. "He always claimed it was my fault, because I upset him when I knew he had been drinking." Anything that went wrong was her fault. "If I greeted him at the door with hugs and kisses, he said, 'You make me sick the way you slobber all over me.'"

Leon became more and more physically abusive. Eventually, Sheila had a heart seizure at work. Her boss took her to the emergency room at the local hospital. "My arms and legs went black to the elbows and knees because my heart had stopped," Sheila said. "I got such severe palpitations my whole body shook. The doctors did tests and could not find the cause, until one started to question me, and found that I was so tense that I had literally stopped my own heart from beating."

Leon demanded that Sheila not scream or cry when he was hurting her. She had learned such strong self-control to avoid more beatings, that her tension had no way of release other than a mental breakdown or a physical collapse, which was what happened when her heart stopped.

On the doctor's advice, Sheila left Leon, and tried to release tears to get rid of the tension. But three months later she had a traffic accident. Leon found her new address from the hospital, and used every trick in the book to emotionally manipulate her into returning. Then he convinced Sheila that her parents were ashamed of her, and doubted her sanity.

"I was so broken I swallowed every tranquilizer the doc had prescribed, as well as my painkillers and antibiotics," Sheila said. "I did not really want to die, but I could not see any way of escaping the torment of his cruel words, and the way he always tracked me down and found me and harassed me. I was out of it for 36 hours, and so glad when I woke and I was still alive. I swore I would never let anyone get me that low ever again."

So when Leon conned her into returning, Sheila endured.

"Over nine years, we had three children — when he was not beating me up and causing me to miscarry. I lost about 30 pregnancies," Sheila said. "I kept hoping against hope that his crying and pleading and saying he would change and never hurt me again would be true this time. 'God will never forgive you if you don't give me another chance.' He played every line on me, and he would go to all my friends and family, crying heartrending, 'genuine,' remorseful sobs, and telling everyone how much he loved me, and there would be a lot of pressure from others, because 'How can you take three little boys away from their father?'"

Eventually Sheila realized that any sort of emotional reaction to his cruel words or physical abuse only excited Leon more. "I became a blank page and would stay totally calm as he bounced me off walls and kitchen cupboards. That way his rage soon ebbed," Sheila said. "Just having a stack of clean folded nappies on the lounge was enough to trigger him off, if he came home from drinking at the pub with his mates. I was isolated from friends and family, unless he wanted to visit, to bum a meal.

"No one knew what was happening, as I was too afraid to disclose it due to his skill at lying and covering up and then punishing me for speaking out," Sheila continued. "He could twist my arms and really hurt me without any marks showing. He never hit in a way to bruise me where it would show outside my clothing. He would load his rifle and point it at me and tell me that accidents do happen, and he would tell the police he was cleaning his gun and it went off. He threatened to kill me in such a way that no one would know."

Sheila was always receiving electrical shocks from household appliances. One morning, while making her husband's toast and coffee, she was electrocuted by the kettle. Power ran through her arm and into the sink, and melted the metal plug chain onto the stainless steel sink. Sheila was wearing rubber flip flops, because Leon never gave her money for shoes. They saved her.

That day, she called the state electricity inspector to check her home. He found that the ground wire for the stove was cut and tucked up into a brick cavity. The washing machine had no ground, and the vacuum cleaner had a faulty ground.

"The inspector said that if he didn't know better, he would think someone was trying to kill me!" Sheila said.

"I invited a neighbor over for coffee at the time I knew my husband would come home," she continued. "He was furious that someone was in the house, but he just looked daggers at her and me, and she felt uncomfortable. I cheerfully told him about the inspector's visit, and what he had said. I said, 'You're an electrician and you had better fix everything or it WILL look like YOU'RE trying to kill me.'"

Leon panicked and fixed everything that day.

Finally, they divorced, but Leon still didn't let Sheila alone. He used the courts to harass her, trying to take her children away. One time, after the divorce, Sheila spent the night at a friend's house. When she arrived home, she found her tiny teacup poodle had been bashed to death, swung around on its leash against a fence until all of its bones were broken. The police were horrified, and had the phone company connect a phone that day so Sheila could call them if necessary.

Leon still had visitation with the children, and for 14 years, he continued harassing her at every access handover, even while he was living with another woman. "He spent great effort each time he had the children, poisoning their minds against me so they would resent me and blame me for not having their dad living with them," Sheila said. "As they became older he refined his brain-washing, so the boys would not notice the subtle way he manipulated their thinking. They would come back from a three-week holiday with him and treat me horribly. Then eventually reality would kick in, and they would be so sorry and apologetic and ask me to forgive them. They would resent him for telling them lies."

Cycle of abuse

What Sheila endured was domestic violence. All of the literature about domestic violence says that what the abusive partner wants is power and control. This, of course, is exactly what a sociopath wants. Domestic violence, therefore, is sociopathic behavior taken to an abusive extreme.

People who inflict domestic violence use all the typical sociopathic strategies: gaslighting, coercion, intimidation, blaming, guilt and all manners of abuse — verbal, psychological, emotional, financial, sexual and physical. Typically, the relationship becomes a predictable pattern, first described by Dr. Lenore Walker in her 1979 book, *The Battered Woman.*[6] The "cycle of abuse" begins with tension building, which explodes into an act of abuse, which is followed by reconciliation, which leads to a period of calm — until the tension builds again.

This is essentially the same pattern that creates psychological bonding, as explained in Chapter 6 — except that when perpetrators instigate fear and anxiety, they do it with abuse and violence. Because the cycle of abuse creates such strong bonds, and because mental manipulation weakens the victims' internal strength, they often find it extremely difficult to leave.

If you are in a situation involving domestic violence, know that you are probably dealing with a sociopath. Sociopaths never change. If you want to have any kind of life, and in some cases, if you want to save your life, you must escape. If you feel like you can't do it on your own, ask for help.

How to end the relationship: No Contact

Once you realize that you must end a relationship, how do you do it? You cut the sociopath out of your life. That means no phone calls, no emails, no texts, and certainly no in-person meetings. It means No Contact.

There are times when this is difficult, such as if you work with the sociopath, or if you have children together. In these cases, you need to implement No Contact as best you can. But let's talk about situations where it is possible to get rid of the person, such as a dating relationship. What is the best way to establish No Contact? Clearly, firmly and permanently.

An excellent book called *The Gift of Fear,* by Gavin de Becker, devotes several pages to the topic of rejecting an unwanted suitor, and these pages are among the most helpful of the entire book.

De Becker discusses the situation in which a woman decides she doesn't want to be involved with a man. The same advice applies to men who need to end relationships with women. Do not, the author says, worry about letting them down easy. Here's what he writes:

> One rule applies to all types of unwanted pursuit: Do not negotiate. Once a woman has made the decision that she doesn't want a relationship with a particular man, it needs to be said one time, explicitly. Almost any contact after that rejection will be seen as negotiation.[7]

So what does this mean? After you tell the person one time — repeat, *one time* — that you do not want a relationship with him or her, you cease all further contact.

Expect sociopaths to try to win you back. When this happens, you must not engage with them. Don't keep telling them that you don't want to talk, because guess what — even when you're saying, "Leave me alone," you *are* talking to them. Don't ignore 40 text messages, and then, on the 41st message, reply with, "Stop texting me!" You've just given the sociopaths what they want — a response. They will continue to text until they get another response.

Even if it is contrary to your nature, if you're dealing with sociopaths, you may need to be brutal. Watering down your message is counterproductive. If you try to be nice or delicate, sociopaths may see your niceness as an opening. Do not explain why you don't want a relationship. An explanation just gives sociopaths something to challenge, and they love to debate. If you say, "I'm not up for a relationship right now," sociopaths will keep after you until you give in.

Hanging on like a leech

It's important to be firm, because sociopaths are capable of dogged pursuit. In the Lovefraud Romantic Partner Survey, 12 percent of respondents said that the sociopath convinced them to enter the relationship simply through pursuit and perseverance.

"Rachel," for example, went on a first date with "Marco," but didn't want to see him again. "I told him I didn't want a second date over the phone," Rachel said. "He said, 'I want you to tell me to my face,' so he came and sat outside my work until I came out. I didn't tell him no to a second date."

Marco was handsome and outgoing. Rachel thought of herself as average, so she was surprised that a good-looking man like him would choose her. "I learned later that he was so ugly on the inside, but I felt powerless to leave him," she said.

Only five days into the relationship, Marco proclaimed his love. Then he wouldn't leave Rachel alone. "He was like a leech," she said. "He would not give me a second of free time to breathe and evaluate the relationship."

Rachel didn't have a lot of family, and Marco quickly isolated her from her friends. She did run into one of Marco's former girlfriends, who asked, "Has he hit you yet?" At that point he hadn't, but later, he did.

Rachel can't explain how she got involved with Marco. "I thought I was such a strong woman," she said. "He took that strength away." So what happened? Rachel told her story:

"I moved in after five months, moved out but still dated, got pregnant, moved back in. Moved out with child. Broke up for three days then succumbed to him again. Got pregnant and cried. Got married at the courthouse and moved back in, feeling stupid and trapped. Bought a house together, he lost his job due to drinking and threatening a co-worker while house was in escrow. I was the breadwinner with two young children. He played golf and paid a sitter to watch our children every day for nine months. Three and a half years later, I saved up enough money on the sly to leave him and relocate closer to work. Custody battle began."

Do not have sex with a sociopath

Rachel's story brings up an important point: If you realize, or even suspect, that you are involved with a sociopath, do not have sex with the person.

As I wrote in Chapter 6, there is no such thing as "just sex." Sex releases all those chemicals that increase your trust of the sociopath, strengthen the psychological love bond and rewire your brain. Sex makes it easier to get caught in the sociopath's web of deceit, and harder for you to escape.

A consequence of sex, of course, is children. Having children with a sociopath is a nightmare that can create trouble for you for the rest of your life.

If you are very lucky, the sociopath will abandon you and your children, and you'll be left to raise them alone. If you are not lucky, the children will bind you to the sociopath forever, and he or she will use them to manipulate, exploit and control you.

There's something else to consider as well. The sociopathic personality disorder is highly genetic. That means when you have children with a sociopath, they may inherit a genetic predisposition to become sociopaths themselves. Whether the disorder actually develops is influenced by their childhood environment and the parenting they receive.

Sociopaths make terrible parents. At best, they neglect their children. At worst, they actively try to make the children into miniature copies of themselves. If the sociopath remains a part of the children's lives, it will be extremely difficult for you to raise them to become healthy adults.

No Contact breaks the addiction

When you have a relationship with a sociopath, the sex and psychological love bonds change your brain's chemistry, and the structure of your brain, much like drug or alcohol addiction does. Therefore, you need to view breaking off the relationship as if you are breaking an addiction. In cutting the sociopath out of your life, you need to ramp up your willpower and go cold turkey.

That's what No Contact is all about. Do not agree to meet the individual for any reason. Do not answer phone calls from him or her. Most people think they should get a new phone number to avoid unwanted calls. However, in *The Gift of Fear,* Gavin de Becker recommends a different strategy — don't change your phone number, but get an additional number. Give your new phone number to people you want to talk to, and forward all calls on the old number to voice mail. This way, the sociopath doesn't know that you have a new phone number, but does know that you are not responding to his or her calls.[8]

You can apply a similar strategy with email. Create a rule in your email client software — such as Microsoft Outlook — to send messages from the sociopath's email address directly to a special folder, without you even seeing them. Of course, it's easy to get new email addresses, and sociopaths often do this, so you may need to keep adding addresses to your mail filtering rule. Just do it, and don't respond.

Eliminating contact with the sociopath enables the changes that the relationship made in your brain to unravel. The longer you maintain No Contact, the more you heal, and the stronger you become.

What happens if you're wishy-washy about No Contact? What happens if you give in and respond to the sociopath? It's just like an alcoholic who falls off the wagon and starts drinking again — you'll have to start the healing process all over.

This is what happened to "Lenore," who told her story in a letter to Lovefraud.

> *I literally had to count the days that went by as I re-fused contact with him, and on Day 120, I celebrated be-*

cause I felt healed. Well, on Day 121, he emailed me, and against my better judgment, I emailed him back. He told me he had been in therapy, he realized what he had done wrong, he was on medication.

I was cautious and wary, and decided, amidst warnings of concern from my friends and family, to perhaps work on a friendship again. We worked on being friends for a few weeks, and everything was great and fine. I felt in control of the situation.

Then his old behaviors started creeping in. He installed a GPS app on my phone so he could track my whereabouts. He began calling and texting incessantly, and flipping out if I didn't answer right away. The verbal and psychological abuse had begun again. Fortunately, this time it did not escalate to physical abuse. He began lying again, gaslighting and acting erratically, and began seeing other women on the side. Last night, it once again became too much and I told him not to contact me again because my heart and my spirit couldn't take any more pain, and his inconsistency is so bad for my son.

So today begins Day One again without him. I am writing you today to tell you that your No Contact advice was the best advice I didn't take. For 120 days I went without him. It took a while, but by day 90, I was happy and free and at peace. Now I am back to square one.

No Contact is the path to healing from an entanglement with a sociopath. The stronger you can be about No Contact, the faster you will recover.

If you're living with the sociopath

Sociopaths do not want to lose control. If you're living with the sociopath, and he or she has been abusive, escaping the relationship can be difficult and dangerous.

Perhaps the home is yours, and was yours long before your relationship. You may ask the sociopath to leave, and he or she may flatly refuse. Some sociopaths educate themselves on exactly how to establish legal residency in your home, and how your local laws protect them against eviction. Then they use the laws against you.

Do not let the individual stay — do what you must to get the sociopath out. If necessary, initiate eviction proceedings. One respondent to the Lovefraud Romantic Partner Survey, whom we'll call "Nanette," described even more drastic measures.

Nanette, who was in her 50s, had been widowed for two years when she met "George" on a religious dating website. George was also in his 50s and widowed. "We had instant chemistry on meeting," Nanette said. "He made me feel like the most special person in the world."

It was a whirlwind romance — too good to be true, Nanette thought, but she pushed her hesitation aside. When her family and friends urged caution, Nanette told them, "You just don't know him like I do. When you learn, then you'll see how great he really is."

They quickly married, and George moved into Nanette's home — raising suspicions in Nanette's family that her home and car were all he wanted. Apparently, they were right, because in a month, the honeymoon was over, and George became a controlling monster.

The entire involvement lasted less than a year. How was it resolved? "My children came and got me away from him, at gunpoint," Nanette said.

Nanette's children may have known what all domestic violence experts know: Victims of abuse are in the most danger when they leave their abusers.

Some sociopaths react with rage when their targets leave the relationship. Will the rage turn to violence? According to Dr. J. Reid Meloy, author of *Violence Risk and Threat Assessment,* the best predictor of future violence is a history of past violence.[9]

If you know that the sociopath you're leaving has a history of violence, be extremely cautious. The violence need not have been directed towards you. Consider any violence towards any person, animal or property to be a warning sign that it could occur again.

When you decide to leave, do not reveal your plans. In fact, you should make coffee and turn on the charm — whatever it takes to keep the individual calm — until you're ready to go. Carefully plan your escape — you'll need to outsmart the sociopath. Figure out where you can go — whether it's to a domestic violence shelter or to a friend or relative the abuser doesn't know. You may want to contact the police.

Put together an escape bag. Abuse survivors recommend you include the following:

- Cash.
- Spare house and car keys.
- Medications, copies of your prescriptions, multiple pairs of glasses.
- Several changes of clothing.
- Important documents — birth certificates for you and your children, passport, driver's license, health insurance card, mortgage, phone numbers and anything else you can think of. If you can't take the originals without raising the abuser's suspicions, make copies.

The best time to leave is when the sociopath is not at home. Avoid confrontation if possible. But if the sociopath flies into a rage and you know it's going to be bad, you may have to run with just the clothes on your back. Don't hesitate. As long as you're alive, you can sort out the rest later.

Should you warn the next target?

Many, many people, realizing that they've been involved with a sociopath, are horrified. They've been deceived and betrayed. They've lost money, their jobs, their homes. The sociopath smashed through their lives like a battering ram — and has nonchalantly moved on to the next target.

Many Lovefraud readers don't want anyone else to suffer what they suffered. So they ask me, should I warn the next target? If you're considering warning others about the sociopath, here are factors to think about:

1. Can you warn safely?

The first thing to consider, of course, is your physical safety. If the sociopath you were involved with has a history of violence, be careful.

But safety involves more than worries about violence. Consider your legal and financial status. If you are in the midst of a divorce or custody battle with your ex, you do not want to do anything that will jeopardize your case, your job, or anything else that he may damage through accusations. No matter how badly you may feel for the next target, you must put yourself first.

2. What is your emotional state?

Relationships with sociopaths inflict severe emotional and psychological damage. As I explained above, to escape and recover from the damage, you must have No Contact with the sociopath.

Tracking a sociopath's actions may feel gratifying because you are no longer being deceived. You've seen through the mask. You know what he or she is up to, and in a way, it's a boost to your trampled self-esteem. If you were honest with yourself, you probably would have to admit wanting a taste of revenge by ruining the sociopath's game.

But even if you're not talking to the sociopath, or sending email, remember that keeping tabs, tracking on the Internet and warning others are all forms of contact. As Lovefraud readers say, the predator is still renting space in your head.

So, before you do it, think about where you are in your recovery. Can you warn the next target and continue to heal?

3. Will the target's reaction affect you?

You know how good the sociopath is, because you were fooled. Think of how the sociopath described his or her romantic involvements prior to you. Did he say his ex-wives were mentally disturbed? Did she say her ex-husband was a stalker? Well, you can be sure the sociopath is now saying all the same things about you.

The sociopath is already running a smear campaign to discredit anything that you may say. At the same time, the sociopath is love bombing the new target. The latest conquest is primed to disbelieve you. If you attempt a warning, and the new target ignores you, can you just walk away?

In my personal opinion, if you can warn the next victim without jeopardizing your own safety and recovery, I think you should at least try.

I've heard of cases where the next victim was grateful for the warning and got out. I've heard of cases where the victim refused to listen and stayed with the sociopath. And I've heard of cases where the victim stayed for awhile, then started to see the bad behavior, remembered the warning, and got out.

I know that since I've posted the information about my ex-husband, James Montgomery, on Lovefraud.com, at least seven women have contacted me to thank me for the warning. They Googled his name, found my story, and dumped him. This makes me happy.

However, James Montgomery is on the other side of the world. I've recovered and moved on. He can't damage me.

So if you feel like you need to warn others, remember this: Your first obligation is to yourself. Do what you must do for your own recovery. If you can assist others without hurting yourself, that's a bonus.

More importantly, use what you've learned about sociopaths to protect yourself in the future. I'll explain how in the next chapter.

Recap

Responses to warnings about sociopaths
1. Believed the sociopath was misunderstood
2. Wanted to make their own decisions
3. Denial
4. Believed the warnings were made in jealousy
5. Believed they could help the sociopath
6. Too in love to listen

How sociopaths try to hold on:
- Crying and pleading
- The pity play
- Blaming you
- Threats of violence
- Threats of suicide

How to end a relationship with a sociopath:
- No contact

CHAPTER 9

Protect yourself from predators

Sociopaths are hazardous to your health — your physical, emotional, psychological, financial and spiritual well-being. Any romantic involvement with one of these human predators has the potential to damage you, and possibly destroy you. So how do you protect yourself from the danger? How do you prevent yourself from becoming involved with them in the first place?

Safeguarding yourself from sociopaths involves three steps, and, by reading this book, you've already taken the first two.

Step 1 — Know that evil exists.

As much as we want to believe that all people are basically good, this simply is not true. There are people in the world who are devoid of human caring. There are people in the world who live their lives by exploiting others. They're called sociopaths, they live among us and they are evil.

Step 2 — Know the signs of sociopathic behavior.

The *Red Flags of Love Fraud* are warning signs that someone who is angling to be your romantic partner is, in fact, a sociopath. One or two signs, of course, do not make a predator. If you meet someone who is charming and sexy, feel free to get acquainted — unless the individual also lies, engages in the pity play, blames others for everything, stares at you like you're the next meal and tries to move in on you quickly. When an individual exhibits most or all of the *Red Flags of Love Fraud,* put your guard up.

Step 3 — Trust your intuition.

Instinct, intuition, a gut feeling — whatever you want to call it, we all have an innate sense, honed over millennia, that enables us to instantly know, without knowing how we know. Sometimes it enables us to know the mundane, like who is on the phone before we look at the caller ID. But it's when we really need information, when we face critical danger, that our intuition is strongest and most effective.

The whole point of Gavin de Becker's book, *The Gift of Fear,* is that fear is Nature's strongest survival signal, and it's based on intuition. Your intuition is designed to warn you about predators. Your intuition will almost always tell you when someone is dangerous, or at least not to be trusted.

The Lovefraud Romantic Partner Survey asked the following question: "In the beginning of the involvement, did you have a gut feeling or intuition that something wasn't right about the person or the relationship?" A whopping 71 percent of respondents answered yes.

I want to repeat that — *71 percent of survey respondents knew in their hearts that the sociopath was bad news.* Most of them proceeded with the involvement anyway.

Some of the intuitive warnings were blatant, visceral and dramatic. Unfortunately, the warnings were ignored.

For example, "Janice" and "Carl" were both students in a college town when they met at work. Carl seemed to be kind, intelligent, genuine and unpretentious. Still, Janice was reluctant to date him. Carl pursued her relentlessly.

"I had a sense of impending doom, but remote," Janice said. "I felt that if I let myself fall in love with him, I would regret it."

She did fall in love, and was married for 20 years. She regretted it.

The sex was extraordinary and they got along okay, until their child was born. Then Carl became passive aggressive, emotionally abusive and seriously angry. "He continually verbally abused me in private and public and within hearing of our child," Janice said.

In the end, Janice suffered post-traumatic stress disorder. She lost her business, her home and more than $100,000. She incurred debt and declared bankruptcy. She considered suicide.

"Carl blackmailed me and destroyed me financially and emotionally in the divorce," Janice said. "He acquired a new family and he is very rich now. It is very difficult for my child and myself."

"Amanda" and "Josh"

"Amanda" and "Josh" were both college students when they met at a party. Josh insisted on walking her home. That's all Amanda let him do; she didn't even give him her phone number. Josh got it from a mutual friend and pursued her.

Josh was affectionate and complimentary. By the end of the second week of dating, he told Amanda that he'd never been with anyone like her, and he wanted to be with her forever. Josh said they were soul mates.

It all sounded good, but Amanda was hit with a stark warning that it wasn't.

"I remember seeing a picture of him while we were first dating," she said. "He looked like a blackness amidst a group of happy people. It scared me. I initially wanted to run, and felt as if I would barf when I thought about spending my life with him."

Amanda disregarded that extremely visceral flash of intuition and continued to see Josh. Three weeks into the relationship, she became ill. Since they barely knew each other, Amanda asked Josh to give her some space. He came around anyway. She asked him not to smoke in her house, because it made her sick. He smoked anyway. She asked him not to drink beer because the smell made her sick. He drank anyway. After a week of such disregard, she started ignoring Josh.

Then Amanda found out she was pregnant. She told Josh, and he promised her the world — a beautiful house, financial security. But at the same time, he restarted his relationship with his ex-girlfriend, and continued to see the woman for the duration of Amanda's pregnancy. Then, when Amanda had the baby, Josh came on strong, again promising security.

"I never wanted to get together with him, but was very afraid of being a young single mom," Amanda said. Again, she disregarded her own feelings and married him.

Josh's family was thankful that Amanda was with him. "His mother used to talk to me a lot about how grateful she was that he had found me," Amanda said. "She would thank me for being with him, while coaching me as to how hard it is and would be. She would be very intense about this and often cried."

Josh's mother must have known that her son had serious problems, which Amanda found out as soon as she moved in with him. Despite his promises of togetherness, Josh treated Amanda and the baby with anger, blame and disdain. Amanda stayed for five years, then found the strength to leave.

"Elena" and "Craig"

"Elena" was at work when "Craig" walked into her office with a single rose. "By unanimous decision," he said, "this is for the loneliest secretary on Broadway."

Elena froze, petrified with fear.

Craig walked out, and Elena chided herself for her illogical reaction. "I told myself that I really overreacted and I should have more composure, instead of being silly over nothing," she said.

The next day Craig came back and asked Elena for a date. She turned him down, but he kept bringing her coffee and flowers. So they dated.

Because he was so charming, Elena's family liked him. Craig's family was cordial to Elena — except for his father. "Only met him once and my heart was beating a mile a minute the entire time I was in his home," Elena said. "It was horrifying. He was an old man and barely said anything. It was as if he was an object that breathed. But my instincts tried to warn me. I, of course, ignored my instincts and put it down to my own social phobia."

Elena and Craig were married for 25 years. Although she didn't learn it until much later, Elena's initial instincts were correct. Craig was a predator.

"Let me count the ways," she said. "EVERYTHING HE DID had to be illegal even when he could have done it legally much easier. He sold drugs, he bought hookers, he raped children, he committed murder by arranging accidents, he lured others to break the law for him, then killed them. There's no end to his evil. I never knew what he was doing because I believed his stories about what actually happened. All lies."

Ignoring the internal warnings

Of the 71 percent of survey respondents who felt intuitive warnings to steer clear of the sociopath, 40 percent ignored them.

"I pulled down the red flags, I silenced the alarm bells, I smashed the red lights!" wrote "Rita" about her involvement with "Paul."

When they met, Rita was married, but felt like she had been emotionally abandoned by her husband. Paul swept in and paid Rita more attention than she'd ever known.

"He seemed to be completely rapt in finding love with me! (gag)," Rita wrote. "He was highly intelligent, funny, witty and bewitchingly charming. To me he was worldly and wise and I was immensely flattered by his attention, by his compliments — for him, I was the most brilliant, sexy, smart, amazing woman in the world! (puke). He promised me, well, the world! (retch). Love, a new life for all of us (I had a young daughter — hmmm), away from where we were living.

"That person declared his love for me early and frequently," Rita continued. "He told me he was 'there' for me forever, that he'd look after us (shudder). I was depressed, alone and lost. He came into our lives and swept us up in an unforgettable (regrettable) adventure!"

Rita left her husband, married Paul, and they were together for more than five years. During that time, she lost her home, was physically abused, her life was threatened, she suffered post-traumatic stress disorder, and she considered suicide. She also learned the truth about Paul:

"Pathological liar," Rita wrote. "Kleptomaniac. Used false names. Used my identity to conduct business. Spread vicious and untrue rumors about me. Fraud. Assault. Stalking. Threatened injury to others."

So why did Rita and so many other people ignore their own internal warnings to leave the sociopaths? Some were simply uncomfortable listening to their intuition. "Ignored it since I couldn't base it on anything concrete," wrote one respondent. "Ignored it, rationalized it, saying to myself I cannot base my judgment on a mere gut feeling," wrote another.

Yes, you can base judgments on your instincts and gut feelings. Pay attention — here is one of the most important points of this book: When it comes to assessing danger, rational judgment is vastly overrated. Your intuition will tell you instantly, or very quickly, that someone is a predator. Intuition works really well. Listen to it.

"Anna" certainly wished she had listened to her own misgivings about "Henry." They met at college. Anna had been raised in an abusive environment, and had no outside support. Henry brought her food, and, because Anna didn't have transportation, he brought her to and from work.

"He provided physical help when I needed it," Anna said. "He attended church regularly, did not drink or smoke, seemed to be everything I wanted in a partner." Still, her intuition told her that something was off.

"I wrote it out," Anna said. "Then I destroyed the writings, since they appeared to be based only on gut feelings, which I was taught to discount."

Anna married Henry, and the honeymoon ended, literally, on the night of the honeymoon. Henry raped her. "I tried to get help to get out, but all my friends were of the same religious persuasion, and stuck to what the church told me. I was stuck with him for life."

Anna stayed for more than 10 years. Henry neglected the children while forcing Anna to work to support the family. She lost money, lost her home and business, was physically abused, her life was threatened, she considered suicide, Henry threatened suicide, even the pets were injured or killed.

"All of it was done in secret and away from public scrutiny," Anna said.

Anna had actually written down what her instincts told her about Henry. If she had listened to herself, her life would have been much different. In the Lovefraud Romantic Partner Survey, many respondents who ignored internal warnings about the sociopaths explained why. Following are some of their reasons:

Doubted themselves — 18 percent

The biggest reason why people disregarded their intuition, expressed by 18 percent of respondents, was that they doubted themselves. These respondents brushed away the trepidation, assuming they were the ones with the problems — social phobias, residual pain from past breakups, paranoia.

I told myself I was just being paranoid, and that I had to open up and trust him completely if I ever expected him to love me in return.

I ignored it because I loved him. After a time he convinced me there was something wrong with ME and convinced me to go on antidepressants. The drugs mellowed me and I lost that feeling.

I subdued it. I'm the one with the problem, I said. I'm the one who just had my heart broken, and I shouldn't let that stop me from having something wonderful in my life — what I'd always wanted, in fact. It never occurred to me to answer these feelings as warning bells.

Gave the benefit of the doubt — 12 percent

These respondents excused, rationalized or explained away the sociopath's peculiar or hurtful behavior. They gave second, third and fourth chances — a multitude of opportunities, in fact — because they believed everyone deserved the benefit of the doubt.

I pushed it aside because I believe that there is good in everyone. And everyone deserves a second chance. At the time he made me so very happy.

I ignored it, because when he was "on," the relationship felt like a dream come true. It never entered my mind that all these people could be right that were coming down so hard on him. I saw him as the victim.

I responded by trying to learn more, to be patient and understanding, to be accepting so that whatever it was in him that seemed like damage, or made me afraid, would get the chance to heal. I ignored my guts and rationalized very creatively.

Questioned the sociopath — 11 percent

Many respondents actually raised their concerns about the relationship with the sociopath. Some sociopaths addressed the concerns with seemingly plausible explanations. Other sociopaths reacted with hurt or anger, making the respondents feel guilty for bringing the issues up.

I told her about my doubts, she told me I was overly paranoid because of past relationships and I should trust her, so I did.

I brought my concerns to his attention saying, "maybe this just isn't right for me — I think I need to slow down." He became enraged — calling me names and throwing things — saying I had gotten him to trust me and now I was abandoning him. I ended up apologizing and feeling horrible for "hurting" him. After that I ignored my gut feelings.

On our third or fourth dinner date, I vividly remember asking her, bluntly, "What do you want?" She looked at me, startled, and I went on, "You seem too good to be true — you must want something from me." She didn't react harshly, but recovered quickly and sweetly explained that she wanted nothing but to be with me, etc., etc. My objectivity tanked after that and never resurfaced until it was way too late. My instincts gave me a fighting chance but I squandered it.

Wanted to believe — 9 percent

Some survey respondents wanted to believe the sociopath, believe in the relationship and believe in love. So they chose to accept the explanations, overlook the negatives and focus on whatever good they saw.

I buried it with a metric ton of love for who I thought he was.

With rose-colored glasses. I always try to think that everyone has good in them. One of my downfalls, I guess. Kept giving him chances and hoping it would get better.

I wanted it to be as he portrayed it to be; it was not.

If the respondents to the Lovefraud Romantic Partner Survey had trusted their own intuitive feelings, they might have avoided the damaging interaction completely, or at least they might have bailed out much sooner than they did.

The lesson here is that it's critical to listen to ourselves.

But should we listen to others — such as our families and friends? The answer to the question is not nearly as clear-cut.

What your family and friends say

The Lovefraud Romantic Partner Survey asked, "What was the reaction of your friends and family towards this individual?" Surprisingly, it was almost evenly divided. Twenty-five percent of respondents said their families didn't like the sociopaths, were not impressed, and didn't trust them. "My dying mother hated him," wrote one woman. "She would call me every day and beg me to leave him." "None of them liked him," wrote another woman. "They all thought that he would eventually kill me."

On the other hand, 23 percent said their families liked the sociopaths. "EVERYONE thought he was amazing," one woman wrote. "Everyone who met him liked him, and thought he was this genuinely nice guy. He was that good." Another respondent marveled, "He had EVERYONE fooled, and I mean everyone. When I tell people that I am getting divorced and the reasons why, some friends do not believe me and are in shock. When I show them the proof, i.e., emails and other info, only then do they start to see my side and the truth of the matter."

Survey respondents described a few more patterns of opinions from their friends and families:

- Liked the individual, then disliked — 8 percent
- Tolerated the individual for me — 8 percent
- Mixed: some liked the individual, some didn't — 6 percent
- Thought the individual was immature, odd or creepy — 6 percent
- Said nothing until later — 5 percent
- Lukewarm, cool, neutral — 4 percent

Then there were those who had no opinion. Nine percent of respondents said that their family and friends didn't really know the sociopath because they never met. In some cases, this was intentional; the sociopath kept the survey respondent isolated. One man explained, "She was extremely rude and standoffish to my parents, and immediately drove a wedge between me and my family. I was so enamored with her, I didn't see what was happening." Another respondent said, "Some of my friends called him 'the ghost' because they never met or saw him."

Another group of respondents, 11 percent, said that family and friends were surprised, skeptical and worried about their involvement. "Jason," for example, met "Debra" while playing an online video game. Debra told Jason that she was 26, single, had no kids and worked as an accountant. "She seemed really interested in me," Jason wrote. "She called every day. She wanted to talk to my friends and family online, though most refused."

Eventually, Jason learned that Debra was 10 years older than she said, married with kids and unemployed. "She claimed her husband abused her and she wanted to leave but couldn't afford it because she didn't actually have a job like she had said," Jason wrote. "I wanted to protect her. I bought her a plane ticket, got a one-bedroom apartment and had her move in with me."

Jason's family held an intervention. Since Jason had never even met Debra, they wanted her to get her own place, so he could get to know her. "I basically dug in even more," Jason said. "I had her move in straight from the airport."

The relationship between Jason's family and Debra started off badly, and got worse. "My friends and family were very concerned about her lies and her obsession with knowing where I was, but not believing me when I told her," Jason said. "They tried to get to know her, but her constant lies made it difficult. Basically they just put up with her to keep me happy — except my sister-in-law, who said to leave because she was abusive.

"No one supported our relationship, but most did just stay out of it," he continued. "People told me about things she said or did to them, but when I confronted her, she always convinced me that they lied because they hated her and were trying to break us up."

Debra, in the meantime, kept threatening to leave Jason, move back to her home state or kill herself. "I kept going back to her, trying to keep her happy," Jason said. His family's concerns were well founded, but their intervention failed.

The bottom line, then, is that families and friends often see the sociopathic traits before you do, but not always. Some sociopaths try to dazzle you and everyone around you, and they succeed.

What the sociopath's family and friends say

The Lovefraud Romantic Partner Survey asked, "What did the individual's family and friends tell you about this person? Did they support your involvement with him or her?" Responses fell into three categories: First, the survey respondent never met family and friends of the sociopath. Second, the sociopath's family and friends didn't support the relationship, and some even tried to give warnings. Third, the sociopath's family and friends supported the relationship, often quite actively.

Eighteen percent of survey respondents reported that they never met the family and friends of the sociopath. Several survey respondents said the sociopaths had no friends, only business acquaintances.

Others reported that the sociopaths would not allow them to meet people who knew them. When they're working on a target, sociopaths spend a lot of time and effort crafting the perfect image of themselves, and they don't want their relatives and friends ruining it with the truth. "I never met any of his family or friends during our time together," one woman wrote. "He said that he didn't have any friends and that his family lived out of the province, when, of course, they lived in the same house he did."

Some sociopaths actually create imaginary friends, relatives and business associates to vouch for them and support their stories. This is really easy to do via email — all the sociopath has to do is sign up for a free email address, as several survey respondents discovered. "The only communication I had with his family was through email, as they supposedly lived in another state," one wrote. "I ended up tracing the emails once I found out the truth, and he had most likely written them all or had someone write them all from here."

If you are involved with someone who has no family or friends, or wants to keep you away from them, view this as a big warning sign. Another is if the family will have nothing to do with the individual, as was reported by 4 percent of survey respondents. These are indications that the individual cannot form normal human connections, does not bond with others, and may have harmed people.

Sociopaths may say they're alone because they're new in town, but this isn't an excuse. Everyone should have some kind of past. And be aware that sociopaths tend to move around a lot — often to escape the problems they've caused where they used to live. That may be why they're new in town.

So no matter how much he or she is proclaiming love for you, if the individual does not have a history of loving relationships, you can be sure that all the promises are empty.

Warnings from sociopath's family and friends

In the Lovefraud Romantic Partner Survey, 18 percent of respondents said that the sociopath's family and friends tried to warn them, although not always directly. There were oblique remarks, not-quite-funny jokes, negative implications and strange looks. "They jokingly told me about him and his character," one woman wrote. "But they treated it like a joke, so so did I."

On the other hand, some warnings, especially from family members, were direct and blatant. "His mother told me to run and not look back," one woman wrote. Another survey respondent wrote, "They said he was a deadbeat, was oppositionally defiant, was a liar, and were shocked he was getting married to a 'good' girl."

"Alice," for example, should have listened to the warnings. She was in her 40s and going through a divorce when "Eric" called on the phone at her job — a sales call. "This man was very interesting," Alice said. "Eric was completely obsessed with talking to me. Called me every five minutes — literally! He was extremely charming and charismatic. His voice was very appealing and he was very personable. He had an energy that I cannot describe. I was immediately attracted to him."

Eric kept calling Alice, and even though he lived in another state, he wanted to meet. They were meant to meet, he said, it was karma. So they met — the beginning of a whirlwind romance.

Alice had misgivings, but brushed them off. "I thought I was being too cautious," she said. "I actually did not want to listen to my gut, because I wanted the relationship! I did not want to think that anything was wrong with him. I was too attracted to him."

Eric eventually admitted legal problems, but said other people were trying to screw him. He also said the government wanted back taxes from him, but he had already paid them.

Alice's family did not like Eric from the start. "He was very arrogant and my father saw through him immediately," Alice said. "He put a lock on his credit the first day that he met him."

Then there was Eric's mother.

"His mother said that I was the best thing that ever happened to Eric," Alice wrote. "She wanted to make sure that he told me everything about himself and that I knew things upfront. When he started lying and manipulating and using drugs, I called her. She said, 'Take everything you own and get as far away from him as you possibly can, before he ruins your life!'"

Alice didn't leave.

She and Eric had a business together, and when he started using drugs, money started disappearing from the bank account. He stole Alice's credit card and took cash advances. He stole her driver's license and cashed a check from her account while she was sleeping.

In the end, Alice lost more than $100,000, her home and her business. She incurred debt. Eric cheated on her. Alice was physically abused and her life was threatened.

Sociopath's family encourages the relationship

Twenty-five percent of survey respondents reported that the people who knew the sociopath were in favor of their relationship.

Some of them, it turned out, were clueless about the true natures of the disordered individuals. Seven percent of respondents said the family and friends of the sociopaths apparently believed and loved them. "They were conned by him as well," one woman wrote. "I believed that they were being honest in telling me what a great guy he was, because they never knew who he truly was."

But others had their own agendas. Thirteen percent of respondents said family and friends knew what the sociopaths were all about, but covered for them, enabled their behavior or withheld information. Some family members were afraid of the sociopaths, and didn't want to do anything to cross them. Other family members were just as disordered as the sociopaths. Sociopathy is, after all, genetic, so it tends to run in families.

His friends knew everything and told me nothing. They were similar to him but not as bad. His sons and stepdad also kept quiet. I think they were scared.

I was told nothing negative about my ex, although his brothers knew he was a sex addict way before I met and married him. They, of course, kept that information to themselves, mostly because it was acceptable behavior in his family. His father and brothers all partake in sexually deviant behavior.

They all supported everything he said. Later I found out through one of his daughters that they learned early on, in order to be in their father's life, they were to say "nothing," to just "agree" and go along with anything he said. (They were grown women.) Otherwise, he stated to them, they would not be a part of his life. She told me it was the only father she had ... good or bad, he was still "her father," so they accepted his rules. Later she did tell me everything.

Becoming the "good influence"

In the Lovefraud Romantic Partner Survey, 8 percent of respondents — almost all women — reported being welcomed by the family and friends of the sociopaths as a "good influence." They were recognized as strong and caring, and the hope was that they would straighten out the sociopaths, convince them to clean up their acts and turn their lives around. In some cases, the hopes of sociopaths' families were authentic, albeit misguided.

"I was told nothing except things that seemed to support his own stories. Everyone was very accepting of me," one survey respondent wrote. "Family members later told me they had said nothing because I was 'the great white hope' — the person they thought he would change for."

Other cases, however, were much more insidious. Families of many sociopaths knew exactly what the individuals were — heartless, unreliable, sometimes unemployable, burdens. The families were tired of dealing with the leeches, and wanted to pawn them off on the new, unsuspecting partners. These families wanted the Lovefraud survey respondents to take the sociopaths off their hands.

One survey respondent wrote that the sociopath's mother didn't like her until she found out that she came from a very wealthy family. "Then she loved me," the woman wrote. "She told me on my wedding day that she was so happy that I was getting married, because now he (my husband) would be 'my problem' and not her problem anymore, and then laughed."

"Virginia" and "Walter"

In a particularly egregious case, "Virginia," knew "Walter" casually from the Internet. Then Walter began paying attention to Virginia, and was soon saying she was everything he was looking for.

Walter was a university professor from Europe, which Virginia liked — she'd lived in Europe herself. They were both in their 40s and had many common interests, such as books, travel and baroque music. He seemed serious, stable and dependable. They never quarreled; differences were resolved with short, calm discussions.

Walter introduced Virginia to his parents, and she quickly became a member of the family. She later learned why.

"The parents 'cover' for their son and are looking for a woman to 'contain' their son," Virginia wrote. "I was conned into believing that he was his mask persona — an infinitely reasonable and kind man who is a highly educated, tenured university professor."

After knowing each other for six months, Virginia and Walter married. Immediately after the marriage, Walter became abusive. Four months into it, he demanded a divorce. This set the tone for the remainder of the marriage.

"One time per month, later two times, he would go into a rage and demand a divorce," Virginia said. "Then the silent treatment for three days. Then he would come out of it. He cycled every seven to 10 days. Then there would be an episode of verbal, emotional and psychological abuse. I left when the physical abuse started."

Virginia later found out that the whole marriage was a scam. "I learned that his life history, as recounted to me, was all a 'manufactured mythology,'" she said. "He married me to get my inheritance money to buy a house above his financial means. Once he got his green card (via work), his plan was to divorce me and go to a bank and refinance the house."

Virginia said his parents lied to seduce her into taking care of their son for them. "They made his ex-wife out to be a villain," she said. "Later I would meet her, after I left him — she, too, was a victim. She told me that his parents knew all about what he did: the lies, the interest in sadomasochism (I never really knew the extent) and that he was gay (I never realized that either). His parents supported the mask of the reasonable, well educated university professor. Forgot to mention the history of psychiatric instability in his late 20s, which had lead to a diagnosis of bipolar and personality disorder. Learned that from the ex-wife."

"Lana" and "Simon"

"Lana" met "Simon" in a college class that explored the hidden barriers to social justice for minorities, including, ironically, battered women. Lana happened to grade a pop quiz that Simon failed. Lana scored 100 percent, and offered to tutor him.

"Later Simon told me that he only chooses willing victims, and that my offer placed me in that category — willingness to serve him," Lana said.

In the beginning, however, Lana didn't know that. She knew that Simon was intellectually brilliant, well read and had parents who were musicians. Being a pianist herself, she was pleased to meet someone who had an awareness of music. Lana and Simon also shared political views and ambitions for their careers and lives.

"Simon actually told me upfront that he did not believe in relationships or love, but had never met someone like me," Lana said. "It was this honesty that convinced me that there was potential that this wasn't entirely true."

Lana had even more warnings, if she had recognized them. "Simon's family and friends told me that he did not experience any feelings other than anger and hunger," Lana said. "They hoped and prayed that I was the answer to help him, which they felt for some time while he was pretending to be 'better.'"

Lana and Simon married — and the marriage quickly became a typical cycle of abuse. "He would do something truly unconscionable, would not ever apologize," Lana said, "but would wait for a while until I was utterly suffering and then tell me whatever I needed to hear in order to return."

Simon was an extremely successful software developer, so he was invested in protecting his image. Although he tried to hide his antisocial behavior, Simon was professionally diagnosed with antisocial personality disorder by his therapist. His condition was later identified as psychopathy by the PCL-R.

"He tried to peg me as mentally unstable, and avoid any financial obligations, like alimony, or negative social consequences, like the infidelities and abuse being exposed," Lana said. Eventually Simon actually attempted to murder Lana so he could move forward with his mistress.

How did Simon's family feel about that? "They supported my involvement with him while I propped him up and helped him build an incredibly successful career and life," Lana said. "Meanwhile, his bad behavior was returning and the family believed that this must be a result of me or something that I was doing. They then started actively trying to break up the relationship. When he tried to murder me and then admitted it, the family told me that it was appropriate and overdue."

Murder is appropriate and overdue? This comment shows that clan loyalty is possible among sociopaths. Sometimes the families rally around their own, no matter what the sociopaths have done. So while they may want you to take the sociopaths off their hands, when behavior becomes bad, even unconscionable, the families may also turn on you instead of offering help or support.

When they tell you what they are, believe them

Some sociopaths quite honestly reveal the unpleasant truth of who they are, but being unaware of this twisted personality disorder, their targets don't take the revelation seriously.

"Stella" was in her 40s, recently separated and enjoying a night out when she ran into "Jeff," who was in his 50s. "He told me the first night that he could be a nightmare," Stella said. "I just thought, 'Oh he has a little anger problem,' not realizing he was literally telling me the truth. I also asked him why he had split from his former wife, who was much younger, by 20 years. His response was, 'I didn't like her anymore.'

"I went to bed that very night ruminating on how he could have said that, and how he must have meant it differently," she continued. "I didn't know how he is wired completely differently. I couldn't wrap my mind around his thinking."

So Stella became involved with Jeff. He was cocky, arrogant, self-assured and had a lot of money. He acted like he wanted marriage, and Stella thought he would take care of her. Stella stayed with him for seven years. Jeff didn't take care of her at all; in fact, he was miserly and cheated on her. Because of the relationship, Stella became ill, suffered post-traumatic stress disorder and lost her job.

Stella's intuition had warned her in the very beginning. "I felt in the presence of something demonic, but couldn't put a finger on it," Stella said. "The red flags were his lying and head games."

Stella made the mistake that many of us made — she assumed that Jeff was basically the same type of person that she was, with a few differences around the edges. When we're decent and caring, we anticipate that the people we meet in our social circles are also decent and caring. So when they paint themselves as a cold, unemotional or duplicitous, well, we assume that they're joking.

It's better to assume that they're not. When someone tells you what he or she is, and it's a lot different from what you are, believe the individual and stay away.

Vetting the new romantic partner

It's always a good idea to gain perspective about anyone whom you are considering as a romantic partner. This is especially important when the individual does not live close by.

Twenty-two percent of respondents to the Lovefraud Romantic Partner Survey were involved in long-distance relationships — the people who turned out to be sociopaths lived more than two hours driving distance away from them. As this group of survey respondents discovered, geographical distance made it easy for sociopaths to lie, cheat and live double lives.

Actively vetting your romantic partner is important in all relationships, but especially the long-distance ones. Here are four ways to do it:

Vetting strategy #1 — Ask and verify.

To find out all you can about your potential Mr. or Ms. Right, start with the basics — ask him or her questions. You can do this in a conversational way, as in, "So, tell me where you went to college. When did you go? What was your major?" Then call the university to see if its records match the story. If the individual claims to be a professional, such as a lawyer, accountant or even a plumber, call state licensing agencies or professional associations to see if he or she is listed.

If your new beau — like thousands of wannabes — claims to be a Navy SEAL, here's a tip: Ask, "What was your class number?" If the guy stumbles at all in his answer, he's lying. A true SEAL never forgets his BUD/S class number.

Your new romantic interest may demur at answering your questions, with excuses like, "That's ancient history; let's talk about you." Consider such a response to be a warning. Many sociopaths are evasive about their past. Of course, as the Lovefraud Romantic Partner Survey found, many also tell elaborate stories about their past — stories that you should verify.

Vetting strategy #2 — Do an Internet search.

Anymore, this is the cultural norm — when you meet someone who may become a new romantic interest, the first thing you do is Google the person.

Almost everyone has some degree of online life, ranging from simple directory listings to massive use of Facebook. Plug the person's name and any identifying details you know into your favorite search engine to see what turns up. If the person has a common name, you may need to weed through pages of irrelevant search results. It's annoying, it's time-consuming, but do it. You never know what you'll find.

One of my goals in creating Lovefraud.com was exposing my ex-husband, James Montgomery, for the predator that he is. I didn't want anyone else to go through what I went through. I've talked to many people who felt the same way — when they realized they were involved with a predator, they wanted to warn others. They did it by posting information on the Internet. Many websites are dedicated to helping people expose their lying and cheating exes. If you have any doubts at all about your new beau, search the cheater databases. Remember, however, that if you don't find the person, it doesn't necessarily mean that he or she is not a cheater. It may just mean that no one posted the individual in the database that you searched.

Vetting strategy #3 — Meet your potential new partner's family and friends.

Insist on meeting Mr. or Ms. Right's family, friends and, if he or she has them, children. You can be nice about this, but make sure that it happens.

If the individual has no long-term friends — and I don't mean business associates — this is a very bad sign.

If the individual doesn't want you to meet family and friends, or, repeatedly makes plans to get together with them that are cancelled at the last minute, well, these are also very bad signs.

When you do meet the relatives and friends, pay close attention to jokes, innuendos or stories that someone begins to tell and then suddenly stops, especially after a dirty look from your new beau. What isn't said out loud may be more important than what is said.

Of course, as you learned from the experiences of Lovefraud survey respondents related earlier in this chapter, getting information from the families isn't foolproof. If your new romantic interest is a sociopath, his or her family and friends may be truly clueless about the disorder, believing everything the sociopath says. Or, they may be complicit in scamming you. Many families want the sociopath to be your problem, not theirs.

I actually experienced both of these situations. I travelled from the United States to Australia to meet my ex-husband's family. They were extremely nice and welcoming. They also had no idea that he was a sociopath — even though his brother and sister-in-law both held Ph.D.s in psychology.

I also spoke on the phone with, and later met, my ex-husband's long-time friend and business associate. Well, this guy was a con artist as well. He knew all about James Montgomery's history of scamming women, so he vouched for my fiancé. The friend also ended up costing me almost $5,000.

Vetting strategy #4 — Ask your own family and friends.

Introduce Mr. or Ms. Right to your family and friends, and later, ask for their opinions.

Generally, your family and friends assume that you know what you're doing, and they don't want to throw a wet blanket on your excitement and happiness. So even if they don't like the individual, they will not say anything — unless you ask for their honest opinions. If they are at all suspicious, listen to them.

Again, this is not foolproof — after all, 23 percent of survey respondents reported that their family and friends liked, even loved, the sociopaths. But their perspective may be valuable.

When sociopaths are trying to reel you in, they engage in impression management. They shower you with love and attention, mirror your interests, and seem to share your values. They are very calculating about the image of themselves that they present to you.

Often, however, they are not as careful about the image that they present to the people around you. Your family and friends are not subject to nonstop affection and communication like you are, and they may glimpse aspects of the sociopath's personality that he or she hides from you. So ask the people who care about you what they really think. If they have concerns, take their worries seriously.

Almost everyone gets some warning

If a predator has come into your life, warnings are almost always available. Let's take another look at the experiences of people who answered the Lovefraud Romantic Partner Survey:

- 71 percent of respondents agreed that they had a gut feeling or intuition that something wasn't right about the person or the relationship.
- Of those who did not feel an internal warning, 45 percent were warned by someone else not to get involved with the sociopath.
- Of those who had no internal warning and no warning from someone else, 23 percent were told of legal problems by the sociopaths themselves, and 28 percent were told of financial problems.
- In the end, only about 10 percent of Lovefraud survey respondents had no warnings at all. It seems that this group encountered the sociopaths who had

really perfected their acts, because most of these survey respondents reported that their families and friends liked the sociopaths, at least in the beginning of the relationships.

So here's my advice: Listen to yourself first. If you're feeling doubt, hesitation, reluctance or worry about your new romantic interest, pay attention. Your intuition is the strongest and most reliable defense that you have against the predators.

As a secondary measure, if anyone — including the sociopath's exes — warns you about the individual, consider the possibility that they may be telling you the truth. The sociopath, of course, will deny everything, and denigrate whoever uttered the warning. But do some research. Check out the sociopath's stories. Ask your friends and family what they think. And most importantly, if the relationship is hurtling along at warp speed, slow it down.

Heeding the exploiter's earliest warnings

The purpose of this book is to teach you the *Red Flags of Love Fraud,* so that if you see most or all of these warning signs, you recognize them as symptoms of sociopathic behavior. But recognizing the signals is futile, unless you also do something about them. And this may be the hard part.

The Lovefraud author Steve Becker, LCSW, sees this in his clinical practice all the time. He explained what happens in his blog post, *Heeding the exploiter's earliest warnings:*

> In retrospect, my clients are often surprised to admit that the exploiter in whom they chose to invest really did "tip his hand" more than they wanted, later, to admit. Not all, but many sociopaths aren't clever enough to fully disguise, even in the early stages of a relationship, their core self-centeredness and insensitivity, *if* our radar is sufficiently non-compromised.

> The key, of course, is first to recognize these signs. But interestingly this isn't the hardest challenge. The hardest challenge is then to *heed them.*

I find that many of my clients were, in fact, cognizant of odd, disconcerting behaviors/attitudes that their exploitative partners were reckless enough to reveal (or incapable of concealing). They may have even felt troubled by them. But in their intense need to want the relationship, and the partner, to be the elusive fit they so hungrily sought, they found ways to suppress their uneasiness, to ignore and/or minimize the significance of these signals, and rationalize the alarms their instincts triggered.

In other words, it's not so much that their antennae are necessarily impaired (because often they aren't); rather, it's their weak response to what their antennae properly register that is the problem.[1]

This, of course, was experienced by all of those Lovefraud survey respondents who ignored their intuition and continued the relationships, much to their later detriment.

Early in a relationship, we want it to work. Especially if we've been alone or lonely for a long time, we want to feel that we've finally found the perfect mate. We want to idealize this person and believe that our dreams have come true. So when we see signs that the person may not be Mr. or Ms. Right after all, well, we don't want to believe them, let alone do something about them. But we must.

Selecting a romantic partner is one of the most important things we do in life. Our romantic partners have the power to enrich our lives, or make us eternally miserable. Therefore, even when we're in love and in lust, this is not the time to suspend our critical thinking.

If your new romantic interest ever lies to you about who he or she is, dump the individual immediately.

If you see most of the *Red Flags of Love Fraud,* don't disregard your observation because a few of the symptoms are missing. One woman said that although her boyfriend exhibited all the other traits, he never tried to get money from her, so maybe he wasn't really a sociopath. Another wrote that her boyfriend kissed her with what seemed like such depth of emotion — how could he be lacking in empathy? They both held out hope that their romantic interests were not, in fact, sociopaths.

Maybe these two men did not meet the diagnostic criteria for a personality disorder. But if the Lovefraud readers saw most of the symptoms, you can be sure that the men were lousy relationship partners.

Remember, personality disorders are syndromes — collections of traits and behaviors. Different sociopaths have the various traits to different degrees. If you meet someone who has most of the symptoms of a sociopath, don't quibble about the one or two that may not be very pronounced. When most of the traits are present, run, don't walk, for the nearest exit.

Yes, miracles happen, and wonderful people can suddenly appear in our lives. But miracles don't scare us. Miracles don't lie to us and hurt us. Miracles don't trigger our internal sense of danger.

Knowing the *Red Flags of Love Fraud,* and more importantly, heeding them, protects us from falling into the clutches of a sociopath. When we avoid the predators, it also means that when true love comes along, we're available to welcome it into our lives.

Recap

Safeguard yourself from sociopaths
1. Know that evil exists
2. Know the signs of sociopathic behavior
3. Trust your intuition

Vetting the new romantic partner
1. Ask and verify
2. Internet search
3. Meet your potential new partner's family and friends
4. Ask your own family and friends

EPILOGUE

Letter to Lovefraud

When Lovefraud.com launched in July 2005, I invited readers to write to me about their involvements with sociopaths. In six years, more than 2,800 people, from all over the world, told me their stories.

Some are published on the Lovefraud Blog as "Letters to Love-fraud." Following is one of those stories, which was posted on March 23, 2011. As you read it, notice the *Red Flags of Lovefraud* and other symptoms of sociopathic behavior that I've described in this book. By learning the warning signs, you may protect your-self from experiences like the following.

I would rather be homeless than spend another day feeling soul-less

My story begins in August 2005 when I walked into a restau-rant and met who I thought was the most charming and compas-sionate man ever. I was with one of my best friends, and we began to chat when two fellows approached us and asked if we would like a drink. It seemed harmless to us at the time, and we accepted their offer and began chatting with them. The first man seemed intoxicated and was acting very loud and immature. He was flirting with me and I was growing impatient by his rather obnox-ious behavior. But his friend seemed to be pleasant and rather calm, so we began to chat.

He seemed so kind and was so interested in learning about me. At the time, I was going through a divorce and had just gotten full custody of my son. I spoke a little bit about my ex-husband, explaining that he had suffered from a prescription drug addiction, and unfortunately, that was what ended our marriage. He began to share his past, and how he had gone through a divorce, and he too was a single parent with one child. We shared some more about our exes and it seemed that he really showed a lot of compassion for what I was going through, and that he felt we shared a lot in common.

He knew actually what to say to make me feel I deserved a great man in my life. He complimented me a lot through the conversation. Letting me know that I was very pretty, and what a great personality I had. Finally he asked me for my number, which normally I would never give out to a total stranger, but there was something about him that made me comfortable enough to trust him.

First date

A couple days later he called me and wanted to take me out that night, but I could not go out that night so we agreed to meet the following night. We decided to meet at a restaurant in my neighborhood. When I arrived he had one long-stem rose for me and a very charming smile. He was very much a gentleman and made sure to open the door for me, as well as compliment how beautiful he thought I looked. He continued to charm me through the whole dinner. He just seemed to understand everything, and we seemed to share so many of the same things.

By the end of the night he gracefully walked me to my car and asked politely for a goodnight kiss. We shared a romantic kiss and he asked to see me again. Of course I agreed. How could I not? He charmed me all night at dinner.

By the next morning I already received a call from him, and he said he had such a wonderful time with me and he wanted to take me out the next night. He showed up at my home this time to pick me up, as he had wonderful dinner plans. He arrived again with another long-stem rose in hand and stood in front of my home like a Prince Charming. Opening the door and once again complimenting me on how beautiful he thought I was. He took me to a very expensive oceanfront restaurant and we shared another amazing night. From that night on, I was in for what was the longest roller coaster ride of my life.

Courtship begins

He called me every day, and wanted me with him all the time. He took me on expensive vacations and outings. He told me how important family and kids were, which is what I told him the first night I met him. Oh yeah, and I also told him how I was against drugs and he told me he was very much anti-drug too. Everything I wanted in life, he made sure to tell me that is exactly what he wanted in life.

He wanted to show me off to his friends almost immediately, which made me feel on top of the world. He called me all the time, all day long, just to tell me he missed me when we were not together. Within a month he told me he was in love with me and asked me to be his girlfriend. Of course I accepted; how could I not? He was such a romantic, charming man, who seemed to be everything I could ask for in a man.

When we began our official courtship, he wanted me to meet his friends and family. I was a little hesitant to introduce our kids to one another, as we had only been dating for a short time, but he insisted we needed to meet each other's children. My son was 13, and his daughter had just turned 7 years old. The day came and he surprised me and brought his daughter to meet me. She was a little timid at first, but within a short time she and I began such an amazing bond together. As for my son, he finally met him and my sociopathic ex acted like the coolest guy to my son. I thought, wow, this is going to work out great.

For the first few months together, there was nothing he would not do for me. He was always so assertive, kind, romantic and loving. Then I started to meet more of his friends and everything seemed okay, but I noticed everything we did revolved around his plans only.

The exes

I started asking more about his past relationships, and he told me he had a toxic ex-wife, and that his last girlfriend was crazy. That he had to run away from them because they were both crazy. I thought to myself, gosh, how could anyone dislike him, he is so great. He also told me how jealous his past exes were, and that had it not been for him, they would have had nothing. That he gave his home to his ex-wife so that their daughter would not have to move. That he gave everything to his ex-wife when they divorced, because that's what a real man would do for his family.

As for his ex-girlfriend just before me, he gave her money and paid for everything and she still treated him bad. That he had to change the locks on the door because she would break in and destroy stuff. That his ex-girlfriend was jealous of his daughter. I could not understand how these women could treat him this way. He also shared that his real mom was a drug addict and abandoned him when he was 5 years old. That his father raised him, and when he was 8 years old, his father remarried. He said his stepmom was mean to him and she only cared about her own kids. I felt so sorry for him. This poor guy just wanted someone to love him. So I was determined to give him all the love he deserved.

For the next five and a half years, I dedicated my entire being to this man. I realize I sold my soul to the devil.

Nothing but lies

Everything he told me was nothing but lies. Not only was he lying about his past relationships, he also was lying about being anti-drug. He claimed that he was a very dedicated Catholic, but yet he lied, cheated, used and stole from people's lives. He also had a secret relationship with his cousin for many years before I met him.

He threatened his ex-wife during their divorce that if she did not give him money, cars and half of everything, he was going to destroy her life. He had NO compassion for what their daughter had to go through, who was only 5 years old at the time. He always told me his daughter was his life, but I learned later on that before I was a part of his life, he was always dropping his daughter off with his stepmom when it was his weekend to have her. Remember this was the stepmom who he said treated him terribly as a child, but she was okay to take care of his daughter. He never paid his child support on time and owed his ex tons of back support, which he denied.

Furthermore, this was a man who became extremely jealous, controlling, obsessed, and then verbally, emotionally, mentally, and yes, physically abusive. All the qualities that he NEVER showed when we first courted. Worst of all, he has absolutely no remorse for the pain he causes. He actually turns it around and makes you believe that it was you.

Staying home

Before I met him, I had a home, a good amount of money in the bank (financial security), good credit, a nice car, lots of friends, confidence, self-esteem, a healthy and a positive outlook on life. Now, five and a half years later, I am almost homeless, jobless (because he convinced me that I needed to stay home and be a stepmom to his daughter), because his job required him to go to the night shift and then out of town, so he needed me to take care of her for him. Also my brother suffered a brain injury and my ex told me that we need to take care of family and I need to take care of my brother too. But that he would take care of the finances and make sure everything was paid for each month.

I had never been without a job, but the last year of our relationship, his ex was taking him back to court for back monies owed and custody and he needed the courts to see he could take care of his daughter. So he convinced me to quit working and take care of her and my brother, that I was a blessing to him, his daughter and my brother. That me taking care of the family, home, animals, and all other necessary things he needed was more than a job in itself.

Calling every day

He would call me every day when he was out of town, wanting to know what I was doing, who was I talking to, who was I with, and what was I doing every minute of the day. Knowing that I was at home taking care of his daughter, my disabled brother, and the home. I was never allowed to go out with friends, as he said my responsibility is in the home. But he would be out of town hanging out in the bars, then calling me hours later, drunk. He would tell me I had no right being mad, as he was working day and night to support me. That I should be kissing the ground he walked on for even taking care of the home.

When I would ask for the money to pay the bills he would tell me I had to wait, and then the bills would be behind, with shut off notices. He would verbally abuse me, and tell me if I complained he would stop paying for everything and I would be homeless with my retarded brother (he called him), and my shitty son, and the family pets. That he did not have to pay for anything, and could save his money as he lives for free out of town because the company pays all his expenses. That he did not even have to come into town at all.

Then he started disappearing at night when he was out of town, and if I questioned were he was at, he attacked me. But he had to know everything and everywhere I was. If I did not answer the phone when he called, he would verbally abuse me and accuse me of cheating on him. I had to bring the phone with me in the shower just in case he called. He would yell at his daughter and tell her she does not have a voice. When I would try and protect her, he would tell me in a loud voice, "You better shut your mouth little girl," and I am 41 years old.

I was walking on pins and needles. My health has been majorly affected by his abuse. I feel numb, empty and lost inside. I finally could not allow the threats and abuse from him anymore, so I stood up to him and he then started being physical. He had been physical in the past but said he would never do that again. But once I started standing up to him, he got worse.

Christmas

On Christmas Eve of 2010, he came home and treated me poorly and when I finally broke down in tears, he laughed at me and said, "Stop with the damn tears." Even though I worked so hard to please him, and decorated the whole house by myself for Christmas, shopped so I could cook a wonderful dinner, he did not even care. My son did not want to be around him, so he left. Then my ex told me I will regret everything I am doing and NO-BODY loves me; in fact, I would be better off dead because no one would miss me. My heart was completely shattered.

My son was resentful against me for being with my ex; my brother went to my mother's house for Christmas. I was too ashamed to tell my friends and family how bad it was, because they saw the writing on the wall a long time ago. So my ex continued to mentally and emotionally abuse me on Christmas Eve to the point that I was crying my heart out and begging him to stop. But he just kept telling me to go kill myself, as that would be a great Christmas gift to everyone. He then left and went out with his friends drinking all night.

I actually took my son's car in the driveway and considered driving off the nearest canyon. I thought, I lost my life to the devil, and maybe he is right — I wouldn't be good for anyone now. I have no money, no job, bad credit now, no medical insurance anymore (I had to give that up too because he did not pay for it like he said he would), my health was/is bad from the stress, I am now emotionally, mentally, physically, financially and spiritually bankrupted.

No more

I finally told him that I would rather be homeless than spend another day feeling soul-less because of him. He told me he would take everything from the home and not pay one dime for the rent. When he went back out of town for work — he only came home on weekends anyway — I packed up all of his belongings and put them in the garage. I placed a lock on my bedroom door and told him to come get his stuff, that he was no longer allowed to abuse me anymore.

He threatened that he would not move, that I should move out if I am unhappy. I told him no — I have already lost too much and I am not going to lose anymore. He threatened to call the property management and tell them I was unemployed and had no means to pay the rent. Oh yeah, by the way, it was my good credit at the time that got us qualified for the home. I told him to go right ahead and tell them anything he wanted, and if they don't let me stay I will have to move, but I will not let him hurt me anymore.

When he arrived the following weekend, he came into the home and saw that I was serious and had moved his stuff into the garage and then he threw me up against the wall and threatened me. I ran from him and called the police and they came out, but he left before they arrived. Sadly, they told me since I was not bleeding or didn't have any broken bones, they could not do anything. He called me later that night and left a message telling me he would be back tomorrow to take everything from our home.

Packed up

He never showed up and I had to call his parents and tell them he never showed. His stepmother told his father and his father told him to stop fighting and get his stuff out. He told his father that I was an alcoholic and abusing him. His father tries to pretend like his son does no wrong and always supports his behavior ... denial! He eventually showed up and started to pack but continued to verbally abuse me. It was hard, but I just ignored him and tried not to react to any of his abuse. He also told me that he is glad to get away from me, that I am evil and now he has a nice new younger girl who appreciates him. As hurtful as it was, I just responded with, "God bless her."

He then stopped packing and said he would be back another day to move. He went back out of town and while he was gone I opened up the POD, which is a moving box, and placed all the rest of his stuff in it. Then I had his classic car, which just sat out in our backyard, towed to his parents. When he found out, he called and left a message stating he was going to call the police on me for touching his stuff. I never responded, but I did tell his step-mother, and she said, "Good for you." She knows who he is, and she is glad he is out of my life.

Sadly, he does not like his stepmother, nor does he have much of a relationship with any of his sisters. His ex-wife said she was in therapy for nearly four years after their divorce, trying to figure out what was wrong with her that he treated her so bad. It's been seven years since their divorce and she still struggles emotionally from what he did to her.

It's been two months since he has been out of my life and I struggle every day, trying to stay above water with all my responsibilities. I don't know day to day if I will have money to support my brother, son and our dogs, but for the grace of God I have managed so far.

New girlfriend

As for my ex, he finally actually told the truth for once in his life — he does have a new girlfriend up where he works. She is 27 years old and he is 47 years old. She happens to be the bartender where he has been drinking for the past year and a half. She is going through a divorce and has two small kids. I heard he has been spending a lot of money on her. Apparently, he is a very charming man and will do anything for her and her kids. Does this sound familiar?

The only difference is, she has two kids, she likes to party, and he is in a town were no one knows his past. Sadly, she has a record of drunk driving and reckless driving, and she is a young mother. He may be able to con her a lot more, or maybe not! Scary thing is, he is extremely jealous and she works at a bar ... could this be more dangerous for her?

I felt I needed to warn her of who he is, so I contacted her at the bar and she answered. I was very polite and told her that the man she is with is not who he claims to be. She needs to be very careful. That he has damaged many lives, and this has been his pattern with relationships. That I worry for her and her kids. She obviously is lost in the honeymoon stage as her response was, "Sorry sweetie I am at work and cannot talk, but thanks for the call, sweetheart." You can't say I did not try!

Sociopaths find out any struggles you may have, and what your likes and desires are, and they build on that. Just like when I met him, I was the newly divorced single mother. What I thought was a charming man, was clearly a man searching for his new prey and I took the bait.

Notes

Introduction

1. "Silence of the Lambs script – dialog transcript." *Drew's Script-O-Rama.* n.d. Web. Accessed October 18, 2011. <http://www.script-o-rama.com/movie_scripts/s/silence-of-the-lambs-script-transcript.html>

2. Hare, Robert D. *Without Conscience.* New York: The Guilford Press, 1999. Print.

3. Maslow, A. H. "A theory of human motivation." *Psychological Review,* 50(4) (1943): 370-396. Print.

4. Saslow, Rachel. "Health benefits of falling and staying in love." *WashingtonPost.com.* February 7, 2011. Web. Accessed October 18, 2011. <http://www.washingtonpost.com/wp-dyn/content/article/2011/02/07/AR2011020703564.html>

5. Neimark, Jill. "All you need is love: here's why it's crucial to your health and how to get more in your life – Connections." *CBS Interactive Business Network Resource Library.* October, 2003. Web. Accessed October 18, 2001. <http://findarticles.com/p/articles/mi_m0NAH/is_8_33/ai_108786011/>

6. Maslow, A. H. "A theory of human motivation." *Psychological Review,* 50(4) (1943): 370-396. Print.

7. Leedom, Liane J. "Can victims become like the psychopath?" *Lovefraud Blog.* October 3, 2008. Web. Accessed October 20, 2011. <http://www.lovefraud.com/blog/2008/10/03/can-victims-become-like-the-psychopath/>

8. American Psychiatric Association. "Personality and Personality Disorders." *American Psychiatric Association DSM-5 Development.* February 10, 2010. Web. Accessed February 10, 2010. <http://www.dsm5.org/ProposedRevisions/pages/proposedrevision.aspx?rid=470#>

Chapter 1

1. Hare, Robert D. *Without Conscience.* New York: The Guilford Press, 1999. Print.

2. Han, Sang Kil, translator. "Reverend Sun Myung Moon speaks on 'We who have been called to do God's work,' July 23, 1978, London, England." *Unificaton.net.* n.d. Web. Accessed October 18, 2011. <http://www.unification.net/1978/780723.html>

3. O'Connor, Anahad. "Margaret Singer, a leading brainwashing expert, dies at 82." *NYTimes.com.* December 7, 2003. Web. Accessed October 18, 2011. <http://www.nytimes.com/2003/12/07/us/margaret-singer-a-leading-brainwashing-expert-dies-at-82.html?scp=1&sq=margaret+singer+dies&st=nyt>

4. Singer, Margaret. *Cults in Our Midst.* New Jersey: Wiley, 1996. Revised edition, 2003. Print.

5. El Paso Times. "Expert: 300 Impostors for each real SEAL." *Military.com.* February 1, 2010. Web. Accessed October 19, 2011. <http://www.military.com/news/article/expert-300-impostors-for-each-real-seal.html?ESRC=eb.nl>

6. James, Chris. "After Bin Laden raid, fake Navy SEALS are 'coming out of the woodwork,' says watchdog." *ABCNews.go.com.* May 9, 2011. Web. Accessed October 19, 2011. <http://abcnews.go.com/Blotter/navy-seals-imposters-coming-woodwork-seal/story?id=13564587>

7. Eckman, Paul. "Mistakes when deceiving." *Annals of the New York Academy of Sciences,* 364 (1981): 269-278. *PaulEckman.com.* Web. Accessed October 19, 2011. <http://www.paulekman.com/wp-content/uploads/2009/02/Mistakes-When-Deceiving.pdf>

8. Stout, Martha. *The Sociopath Next Door.* New York: Broadway Books, 2005. Print.

Chapter 2

1. Bell, Rachel. "The Ted Bundy story — attack!" *TruTV.com.* n.d. Web. Accessed October 19, 2011. <http://www.trutv.com/library/crime/serial_killers/notorious/bundy/index_1.html>

2. Montaldo, Charles. "John Wayne Gacy the 'Killer Clown.'" *About.com.* n.d. Web. Accessed January 27, 2012. <http://crime.about.com/od/serial/p/gacy.htm>

3. Leedom, Liane J. "How can you know when you've encountered a sociopath?" *Lovefraud Blog.* September 4, 2010. Web. Accessed October 19, 2011. <http://www.lovefraud.com/blog/2010/09/04/how-can-you-know-when-youve-encountered-a-sociopath/>

4. Leedom, Liane J. "The cardinal sign of sociopathy: Every sociopath ____!" *Lovefraud Blog.* July 20, 2007. Web. Accessed October 19, 2011. <http://www.lovefraud.com/blog/2007/07/20/the-cardinal-sign-of-sociopathy-every-sociopath/>

5. Adelson, Rachel. "Detecting Deception." *Monitor on Psychology.* 35 (7) (July 2004): 70. Web. Accessed October 19, 2011. <http://www.apa.org/monitor/julaug04/detecting.aspx>

6. Becker, Steve. "Getting inside the head of the abusive mentality." *Lovefraud Blog.* July 17, 2008. Web. Accessed October 19, 2011. <http://www.lovefraud.com/blog/2008/07/17/getting-inside-the-head-of-the-abusive-mentality/>

7. Hare, Robert D. "Assessing Psychopathy: clinical and forensic applications of the Hare Psychopathy Checklist measures." Montana Sex Offender Treatment Association. Hampton Inn, Great Falls, MT. October 14-15, 2004.

8. Leedom, Liane J. *Driven to Do Evil.* In press.

9. Leedom, Liane J. *Driven to Do Evil.* In press.

10. American Psychiatric Association. *Diagnostic and statistical manual of mental disorders.* (4th ed., text revision). Washington, DC: 2000. Print.

11. Straus, Murray A. "Dominance and symmetry in partner violence by male and female university students in 32 nations." *Children and Youth Services Review* 30 (2008): 252-275. Web. Accessed October 21, 2011. <http://pubpages.unh.edu/~mas2/ID41-PR41-Dominance-symmetry-In-Press-07.pdf>

12. Leedom, Liane J. "Female sociopath first described 4,000 years ago!" *Lovefraud Blog.* February 2, 2007. Web. Accessed October 21, 2011. <http://www.lovefraud.com/blog/2007/02/02/female-sociopath-first-described-4000-years-ago/>

13. Ferguson, Christopher J. "Genetic contributions to antisocial personality and behavior: A meta-analytic review from an evolutionary perspective." *The Journal of Social Psychology* 150(2) (2010): 160-180. Web. Accessed October 21, 2011. <http://www.tamiu.edu/~CFERGUSON/evmeta.pdf>

14. Leedom, Liane J. "Child victims of sociopathic parents." *Lovefraud Blog.* December 1, 2006. Web. Accessed October 21, 2011. <http://www.lovefraud.com/blog/2006/12/01/child-victims-of-sociopathic-parents/>

15. Leedom, Liane J. *Just Like His Father?* Fairfield, CT: Healing Arts Press, 2006. Print.

16. Hare, Robert D. *Without Conscience.* New York: The Guilford Press, 1999. Print.

17. Cleckley Hervey M. *The mask of sanity: an attempt to clarify some issues about the so-called psychopathic personality.* St. Louis, MO: C. V. Mosby Co., 1964. Print.

18. Hare, Robert D. "Assessing Psychopathy: clinical and forensic applications of the Hare Psychopathy Checklist measures." Montana Sex Offender Treatment Association. Hampton Inn, Great Falls, MT. October 14-15, 2004.

19. American Psychiatric Association. "Personality and Personality Disorders." *American Psychiatric Association DSM-5 Development.* February 10, 2010. Web. Accessed February 10, 2010. <http://www.dsm5.org/ProposedRevisions/pages/proposedrevision.aspx?rid =470#>

20. Oldham, John M. "Borderline Personality Disorder: An Overview." *Psychiatric Times.* July 1, 2004. Web. Accessed October 21, 2011. <http://www.psychiatrictimes.com/borderline-personality /content/ article/10168/53976?pageNumber=1>

21. American Psychiatric Association. *Diagnostic and statistical manual of mental disorders* (4th ed., text revision). Washington, DC: 2000. Print.

22. Leedom, Liane J. "Sociopaths, cluster B personality disorders and psychopathy." *Lovefraud Blog.* February 6, 2009. Web. Accessed October 21, 2011. < http://www.lovefraud.com/blog/2009/02/06/ sociopaths-cluster-b-personality-disorders-and-psychopathy/>

23. Huchzermeier C, Geiger F, Bruss E, Godt N, Kohler D, Hinrichs G, Aldenhoff JB. "The relationship between DSM-IV cluster B personality disorders and psychopathy according to Hare's criteria: clarification and resolution of previous contradictions." *Behavioral Science and the Law* 25(6) (2007): 901-11. Web. Accessed October 21, 2011. <http://www.ncbi.nlm.nih.gov/pubmed/17323344>

Chapter 3

1. Neumann, Craig S. and Hare, Robert D. "Psychopathic traits in a large community sample: links to violence, alcohol use, and intelligence." *Journal of Consulting and Clinical Psychology.* 2008. Web. *Hare.org.* Accessed August 2, 2011. <http://www.hare.org/references/NeumannandHareJCCP2008.pdf>

2. American Psychiatric Association. *Diagnostic and statistical manual of mental disorders* (4th ed., text revision). Washington, DC: 2000. Print.

3. Stout, Martha. *The Sociopath Next Door*. New York: Broadway Books, 2005. Print.

4. Yoffe, Emily. "What is narcissistic personality disorder, and why does everyone seem to have it?" *Slate.* March 18, 2009. Web. Accessed October 21, 2011. < http://www.slate.com/articles/health_and_science/science/2009/03/but_enough_about_you_.html>

5. Stinson F, Dawson D, Goldstein R, Chou S, Huang B, Smith S, Ruan W, Pulay A, Saha T, Pickering R, Grant B. "Prevalence, correlates, disability, and comorbidity of DSM-IV narcissistic personality disorder: results from the wave 2 national epidemiologic survey on alcohol and related conditions." *The Journal of Clinical Psychiatry* 69 (2008): 1033-1045. Web. Accessed October 21, 2011. < http://www.psychiatrist.com/abstracts/abstracts.asp?abstract=200807/070801.htm>

6. West, Heather C. "Prison inmates at midyear 2009 — statistical tables." *Bureau of Justice Statistics.* June 2010. PDF file. Accessed October 22, 2010. <http://bjs.ojp.usdoj.gov/content/pub/pdf/pim09st.pdf>

7. Fazel, Seena and Danesh, John. "Serious mental disorder in 23,000 prisoners: a systematic review of 62 surveys." *The Lancet* 359. February 16, 2002. PDF file. Accessed July 21, 2011. <http://download. thelancet.com/pdfs/journals/lancet/PIIS0140673602077401.pdf?id= e16241398b8eb460:-78060669:1314ea205c4:-79a1311286460951>

8. "North America > United States > People." *NationMaster.com*. NationMaster, n.d. Web. Accessed October 22, 2011. <http:// www. nationmaster.com/country/us-united-states/peo-people>

9. Babiak, Paul and Hare, Robert D. *Snakes in Suits*. New York: HarperCollins, 2006. Print.

10. "The evolution of dating: Match.com and Chadwick Martin Bailey Behavioral Studies uncover a fundamental shift." *Blog.cmbinfo.com*. Chadwick Martin Bailey. April 20, 2010. Web. Accessed October 22, 2011. <http://blog.cmbinfo.com/press-center-content/?month= 4&year=2010>

11. Albo, Bonny. "Projected U.S. online dating growth 2007-2012." *About.com*. n.d. Web. Accessed October 22, 2011. <http://dating. about.com/od/datingresearch/qt/datinggrowth.htm>

12. Madden, Mary and Lenhart, Amanda. "Online Dating." *Pew Internet and American Life Project*. March 5, 2006. Web. Accessed August 6, 2011. <http://www.pewinternet.org/Reports/2006/Online-Dating/01-Summary-of-Findings/Summary-of-Findings.aspx>

13. U.S Army Criminal Investigation Command. "CID warns of Internet romance scams." *Army.mil*. March 23, 2010. Web. Accessed July 16, 2011. <http://www.army.mil/article/36242/cid-warns-of-internet-romance-scams/>

14. Esposito A, Bratanic M, Keller E, Marinaor M. *Fundamentals of verbal and nonverbal communication and the biometric issue*. Amsterdam: IOS Press, 2007. Print.

15. Gwinnell, Esther. *Online Seductions*. New York: Kodansha America Inc., 1998. Print.

16. "World Internet usage and population statistics." *Internet World Stats*. March 31, 2011. Web. Accessed October 22, 2011. <http://www.internetworldstats.com/stats.htm>

Chapter 4

1. Wilson K, Demetrioff S, Porter S. "A pawn by any other name? Social information processing as a function of psychopathic traits." *Journal of Research in Personality* 42 (2008): 1651-1656. Web. Accessed October 24, 2011. < https://people.ok.ubc.ca/stporter/Publications_files/A%20pawn%20by%20any%20other%20name%3F.pdf>

2. Carnes, Patrick J. *The Betrayal Bond*. Deerfield Beach FL: Health Communications Inc., 1997. Print.

3. Hare, Robert D. *Without Conscience*. New York: The Guilford Press, 1999. Print.

Chapter 5

1. Cundiff, Gary. "Resource Perspectives: Everything about the sociopath invites us in." *Lovefraud Blog*. June 16, 2011. Web. Accessed October 24, 2011. <http://www.lovefraud.com/blog/2011/06/16/resource-perspectives-everything-about-the-sociopath-invites-us-in/>

2. American Psychiatric Association. "Personality and Personality Disorders." *American Psychiatric Association DSM-5 Development*. February 10, 2010. Web. Accessed February 10, 2010. <http://www.dsm5.org/ProposedRevisions/pages/proposedrevision.aspx?rid=470#>

3. Leedom, Liane J. "'How did he really feel?' and 'What did he want from me?'" *Lovefraud Blog*. January 26, 2007. Web. Accessed October 24, 2011. <http://www.lovefraud.com/blog/2007/01/26/how-did-he-really-feel-and-what-did-he-want-from-me/>

Chapter 6

1. Leedom, Liane J. "A deeper understanding of love, ourselves and the sociopath." *Lovefraud Blog*. April 20, 2007. Web. Accessed October 24, 2011. <http://www.lovefraud.com/blog/2007/04/20/a-deeper-understanding-of-love-ourselves-and-the-sociopath/>

2. Leedom, Liane J. "Sheep can teach us about love and it's pretty scary." *Lovefraud Blog*. April 4, 2008. Web. Accessed October 24, 2011. <http://www.lovefraud.com/blog/2008/04/04/sheep-can-teach-us-about-love-and-its-pretty-scary/>

3. Carroll, Linda. "Placebo's power goes beyond the mind." *MSNBC.com*. August 21, 2006. Web. Accessed October 24, 2011. <http://www.msnbc.msn.com/id/14309026/ns/health-mental_health/t/placebos-power-goes-beyond-mind/#.TlEfWs0mySg>

4. Leedom, Liane J. "Ask Dr. Leedom: 'I am really sick, aren't I?'" *Lovefraud Blog*. September 21, 2007. Web. Accessed October 24, 2011. <http://www.lovefraud.com/blog/2007/09/21/ask-dr-leedom-i-am-really-sick-arent-i/>

5. Leedom, Liane J. "Why you can be addicted to a sociopath." *Lovefraud Blog*. April 13, 2007. Web. Accessed October 24, 2011. <http://www.lovefraud.com/blog/2007/04/13/motivation-needing-wanting-and-liking/>

6. Fisher, Helen. "The Drive to Love: The neural mechanism for mate selection." *The New Psychology of Love*. Ed. Robert J. Sternberg and Karin Weis. *HelenFisher.com*. Web. Accessed October 24, 2011. <http://www.helenfisher.com/downloads/articles/15npolve.pdf>

7. Simpson, Jeffry A. and Gangestad, Steven W. "Sociosexuality and romantic partner choice." September 8, 2003. Web. Accessed October 24, 2011. < http://www.ablongman.com/partners_in_psych/PDFs/Kenrick/kenrick_CH10.pdf>

8. Leedom, Liane J. "Eliot Spitzer and unrestricted sociosexual orientation." *Lovefraud Blog*. March 14, 2008. Web. Accessed October 24, 2011. <http://www.lovefraud.com/blog/2008/03/14/eliot-spitzer-and-unrestricted-sociosexual-orientation/>

9. Leedom, Liane J. "Guys, watch out for women con artists." *Lovefraud Blog*. September 28, 2007. Web. Accessed October 24, 2011. <http://www.lovefraud.com/blog/2007/09/28/guys-watch-out-for-women-con-artists/>

10. Hare, Robert D. *Without Conscience*. New York: The Guilford Press, 1999. Print.

11. Hare, Robert D. "Psychopathy and Risk for Recidivism and Violence." Without Conscience: Understanding and treating psychopaths. J&K Seminars. Lancaster, PA. July 7-8, 2005. Conference handout.

Chapter 7

1. Raymond, Vanessa. "How to recognize signs of a cheating spouse: relationship advice." *HowTodoThings.com*. n.d. Web. Accessed October 24, 2011. < http://www.howtodothings.com/family-relationships/how-to-recognize-the-signs-of-cheating-men>

2. "Gaslight." *Dictionary.com's 21st Century Lexicon*. Dictionary.com, LLC. n.d. Web. Accessed January 17, 2012. <http://dictionary.reference.com/browse/gaslight>

Chapter 8

1. Shaver, Phillip R. and Mikulincer, Mario. "A Behavioral Systems Approach to Romantic Love Relationships: Attachment, Caregiving, and Sex." *The New Psychology of Love*. Ed. Robert J. Sternberg and Karin Weis. New Haven, CT: Yale University Press, 2006. Print.

2. Bertolote JM, Fleischmann A, De Leo D, Wasserman D. "Psychiatric diagnoses and suicide: revisiting the evidence." *Crisis* 25 (4). (2004): 147-55. Web. Accessed October 25, 2011. <http://www.ncbi.nlm.nih.gov/pubmed/15580849>

3. Becker, Steve. "Sociopaths and suicide." *Lovefraud Blog*. May 27, 2010. Web. Accessed October 25, 2011. <http://www.lovefraud.com /blog/2010/05/27/sociopaths-and-suicide/>

4. Whitaker DJ, Haileyesus T, Swahn M, Saltzman, LS. "Differences in frequency of violence and reported injury between relationships with reciprocal and non reciprocal intimate partner violence." *American Journal of Public Health* 97(5) (May 2007): 941-7. Web. Accessed October 25, 2011. <http://www.ncbi.nlm.nih.gov/pubmed /17395835>

5. Leedom, Liane J. "New hope for the children of sociopaths." *Lovefraud Blog*. May 18, 2007. Web. Accessed October 25, 2011. <http://www.lovefraud.com/blog/2007/05/18/new-hope-for-the-children-of-sociopaths/>

6. Walker, Lenore E. *The Battered Woman*. New York: Harper and Row, 1979. Print.

7. De Becker, Gavin. *The Gift of Fear*. New York: Dell Publishing, 1997. Print.

8. De Becker, Gavin. *The Gift of Fear*. New York: Dell Publishing, 1997. Print.

9. Alexander, Joyce. "Risk assessment for violence, playing the odds." *Lovefraud Blog*. December 6, 2008. Web. Accessed October 25, 2011. <http://www.lovefraud.com/blog/2008/12/06/risk-assessment-for-violence-playing-the-odds/>

Chapter 9

1. Becker, Steve. "Heeding the exploiter's earliest warnings." *Lovefraud Blog*. May 1, 2008. Web. Accessed October 25, 2011. <http://www.lovefraud.com/blog/2008/05/01/heeding-the-exploiter's-earliest-warnings/>